# Children Who Hate

FRITZ REDL and DAVID WINEMAN

# CHILDREN

# WHO HATE

The Disorganization and Breakdown
of Behavior Controls

THE FREE PRESS, *New York*

*To the children nobody wants*

*and to those members of the Junior League of Detroit*

*who wanted them*

# Preface

THE ORIGINAL INSPIRATION for the work we are reporting here comes, of course, from August Aichhorn.[1] His inimitable skill in handling wayward and aggressive youngsters remains unforgettable; his search into the motivations for their behavior and his effort to design new treatment channels for them are, by now, recognized as a classic contribution to the field. His was the first large attempt to apply what had been learned through the medium of psychoanalysis of neurotic children and adults to the youngsters with whom the usual channels and resources of treatment somehow didn't seem to work. What he has shown us about the deeper roots of their trouble is taken for granted, in this book, as a starting point from which to push further into the nature of personality disorganization and its cure.

Since his study in *Wayward Youth* numerous contributions have been made to the psychoanalytic exploration of delinquency. The list of people who have helped to pave the way to further understanding is too long for a short preface. The reader will find most of their names as contributors to one impressive volume which appeared under the title *Searchlights on Delinquency* in 1950, to celebrate Aichhorn's seventieth birthday.[2]

In the field of ego psychology, we owe a debt to Anna Freud for our growing awareness of the importance of paying increasing attention to ego aspects of the personality.[3] We were also greatly stimulated by her most lucid description of

[1] August Aichhorn, *Wayward Youth* (New York: The Viking Press, Inc., 1935).
[2] Kurt R. Eissler, *Searchlights on Delinquency* (New York: International Universities Press, Inc., 1949).
[3] Anna Freud, *The Ego and the Mechanisms of Defence* (New York: International Universities Press, Inc., 1946).

7

children who grope with the task of reacting to severe trauma in their life situations.[4]

For youngsters closer to the age range of the ones we shall describe in this book, although from different backgrounds, Bruno Bettelheim's *Love is Not Enough* contains the type of material to which we owe most.[5] His description of residential treatment and milieu therapy in action have made it possible for us to take many things for granted with the explanation of which this volume would otherwise have had to be loaded. We also owe him much in terms of specific consultation. The shaping of our theories and the interpretation of our clinical observations have been heavily influenced by the many contacts he had with our work, and in the many discussions that grew out of a long professional association and personal friendship over the years.

The experiences and observations on the basis of which this book is written, have primarily been gathered in the framework of three Projects: The *Detroit Group Project,* the *Detroit Group Project Summer Camp,* and *Pioneer House.* These projects will be described in more detail in the following chapters. To make sure that the total context within which our examples and illustrations should be viewed is clear, a few remarks are needed.

The examples used in this book usually refer to any one of the above mentioned Projects. Most of the illustrations, however, were taken from our *Pioneer House* materials. This may puzzle the reader. Why should we use for illustration this small number of children, instead of quoting more extensively from our observations of the larger child population with whom we lived over the years? The reason which led us to do this is primarily connected with the reader. We felt that it would be easier to catch all the intangibles of child life and group atmosphere as well as of styles of individual behavior if we kept at least one group more or less constantly before the reader's eye.

[4] Anna Freud and Dorothy T. Burlingham, *War and Children* (New York: International Universities Press, Inc., 1943).
[5] Bruno Bettelheim, *Love is Not Enough* (Glencoe, Illinois: The Free Press, 1950).

Many of the entries and examples quoted from our recordings for purposes of illustration are taken from the observations of our staff and our field work students. From the voluminous materials which we had, only such instances were selected as were needed to illustrate specific points we were trying to make. This invariably involves severe injustice to the talent and skill which the persons quoted displayed. For, sometimes the confusion and breakdown of a life situation with our children is more illuminative of what we are trying to convey than the incidents of most expert handling and most effective therapeutic work or control. We would like to express to our staff and students our greatest appreciation for their research courage and personal sacrifice in allowing us to print whatever is to the point. They gave us that permission even though this means that some of our illustrations will show them in moments of difficulty or even temporary failure, while their most successful and skillful handling may remain forever buried in the unprinted part of our materials. Also, the frequency with which their names appear is only a function of the chance distribution of illustrations needed and bears no relationship to volume or value of their actual recording.

Our main goal in this book is to understand why children's controls break down, how some of them defend themselves so successfully against the adult in their lives, and what can be done to prevent and treat such childhood disorganization. Through such study we hope to develop a point of view that will be applicable to both the treatment of the extremely aggressive child and the daily handling by parent, teacher, and group leader of his more normal contemporaries. The children on whose observation most of our illustrations are based, however, belong quite clearly in the category of the "children who hate." The nonpsychiatric reader who may be puzzled by this fact may remember how many of the things which we know now about health and how to maintain it have first been discovered by studying the cases where health was obviously disturbed. The pathology of the extremely sick, as well as the carefully designed observational facilities of the surgical operating room, allows us to see processes clearly at work which would otherwise escape our attention or could not be made visible at all. Since what bothers us most about normal children is the problem of behavioral control and the question of just how to help them in their ability to cope with their emotions and impulses from within in a "well-adjusted" way, we have set about to study this same problem with the severely disturbed, hyperaggressive child. The extremeness of his behavior makes some of the details look different, but the basic machinery involved in the task of self-control and the problems of influence techniques remains the same. We hope that the reader will keep this in mind and will see the impact of the picture which unfolds before him for the less disturbed youngsters he may have in mind. We shall try to help him in this task where this seems indicated, as we go along.

Since the importance of *Research* is stressed so much in this book, something should be said about this. We are using the word here in the wider meaning of the term. Since many research specialists are quite sensitive about this point, and might bear us a grudge for talking of "research" in a book which seems to have no quantitative data, no tables, no Chi-squares in it, we hasten to concede that, from their vantage point, this might better be called "exploration." This is not meant as an apology, either. For such "explorations" seem to us quite necessary before meaningful research on a quantitative basis can be undertaken. In order to make a good study, for instance, of just how frequent the incidence of "anxiety neurosis" is among certain parts of the population today, somebody had to spend many years in patient effort, trying his hand with individual neurotics on their couches, so as to isolate the basic issues well enough to be able to start more organized and more quantitative research. What we now know about childhood neurosis—and we know a good deal about this particular disease—has been gathered by painstaking work with a relatively small and badly sampled number of children. In a similar way, this book is an effort to prepare the ground for a larger and more organized research approach and is well aware of this limitation.

To those among our readers who may be disturbed by the

fact that such a small number of children are presented in this book, we would also have this to say: First, it only seems a handful. In reality, the children we chose show behavior which we have observed in equal detail in many hundreds of children with whom we have worked in our various settings. Then, our "population" does not consist of five, ten or five hundred children to begin with. Our population is literally thousands of "behavioral incidents," comparable in nature, sampled on the basis of the involvedness of certain personality-parts, with the adult's clinical attitude kept relatively constant. For we do not, as a result of our study, establish types of *children*. We try to establish types of *"disturbances of ego function,"* etc., in children's lives. Our main goal is to encourage the theoretician as well as the practitioner in all walks of life with children to take seriously the need to become more specific about the functions of ego control as well as about the techniques of handling child behavior. And, hopefully also, we want to induce communities, children's institutions, and school systems, to take new courage from an attempt to gain insights about children which have close bearing on the behavioral level and on practice in daily life. We are convinced that it is such insight that is needed to break down the barriers of cruelty, apathy, defeatism, or lack of imagination and lack of financial wisdom which still block the field of "human engineering" from making the advances and contributions which it is ready to make.

One more word about a special feature of some of our illustrations, which, unless explained, might offend a reader or two. We have tried to portray our youngsters and their behavior with as much of the original color as is possible within the framework of a book like this. To do so, we have done only a minimum of editing of our recordings. We sometimes replaced the abundant vocabulary of our youngsters by indirect allusions to what they implied. However, we felt it would be wrong to do this in all places. There is something in the direct portrayal of child behavior and child language that would be lost by circumlocution, and their vocabulary belongs as much to those children and the world that has produced them as anything else about them. Wherever we felt that transcription or elliptic allusion would be too destructive of the basic tone of behavior and life we wanted to convey, we left the wordage as it was, even though this often meant a reduction of literary finesse to words with not more letters than four.

# Acknowledgments

THE PIONEER HOUSE EXPERIENCE, from the recordings of which most of our illustrations are drawn, was made possible by the Junior League of Detroit, Inc., which adopted it as its "project" in 1946. Literally several hundreds of Junior Leaguers and their husbands and friends devoted themselves enthusiastically to the task of raising the money to get us started and to keep us alive while we lasted. The actual work, as is to be expected with as clinical a project as this one, was, of course, carried on by a small group from among the larger membership. It took people of unusual broadmindedness, social vision, tolerance, and courage to work with us and to stick with a pioneering job so far removed from the more easily interpreted and well-trodden paths of charity.

Our board was unusual, indeed. The strange behavior of our children did not frighten them, the involved ways of our therapeutic strategy did not dismay them, the difficulty of explaining to others what we were trying to do did not paralyze them. Some of them really became part of the team. Among those who were closest to the staff and shared with us the tribulations as well as the fascination of a pioneering job, special mention must go to: Mrs. John Blanchard, Mrs. Theodore R. Buttrick, Jr., Mrs. John Garlinghouse, Mrs. Daniel Goodenough, Mrs. Harry D. Hoey, Mrs. James McEvoy, Jr., Mrs. Edward C. Parker and Miss Romayne Thompson.

A project like this needs professional guidance over and beyond the staff directly involved in the job. We are most indebted to the following members of our Advisory Board: Leo Bartemeier, M.D., Miss Catherine Faville, R.N., Miss Alice B. Hanchett, Mr. Paul Voelker. We could not have stood the insecurity of some of our ups and downs without the comforting help of Dr. Editha Sterba, Child Analyst, who gave generously of her time and advice. Our diagnostic insights were immeasurably increased by the Rorschach analyses of Dr. W. Mason Mathews of the Merrill Palmer School. Dr. Paul V. Wooley, Jr., Pediatrician-in-Chief at the Children's Hospital of Michigan, kept a watchful eye over the physical welfare of our youngsters. We owe many thanks to Dr. Louis E. Heideman, our house physician, and to Miss Ruth Price, R.N., of the Children's Hospital staff, who mothered our youngsters when they had to be hospitalized.

Life in a residential home does not take place in mid-air. In a way the whole community is involved, or at least large parts of it. Our first gratitude in that direction goes to the *Detroit Public Schools* who went out of their way to provide the type of school experience that we needed for our children. Most unusual was the understanding and cooperation we found on the side of the principals, Miss Julia Wynn and Miss Rosemary Lee, and especially of Mr. Richard Kulka, the classroom teacher of our youngsters. His patience and his unusual skill in handling child behavior were as important for the job as his numerous friendly visits to the Home and his untiring willingness to share information and to be available for joint planning at any time of the day. Among the other teachers of our youngsters we are especially indebted to Miss Rosemary Collins and Mrs. Lucile Pullman. As in all schools, one of the most strategic persons in the children's lives and one not to be forgotten was the janitor. The imperturbability with which Mr. Leroy Cornell met even some of the wilder episodes in the school life of our Pioneers arouses our deep admiration. We were also helped very much by Miss Helen High, Visiting Teacher.

Not less important in the lives of our children were those whom they met as symbols of the community at large. Among them we are most grateful to the police officers of the Canfield Station, on whose "beat" we were located. Far from being hostile to a project so strange in design, they dropped in for many friendly visits and took a cordial interest in our youngsters. We wouldn't want to forget about our next-door neighbors, who suffered bravely from the discomfort that we unavoidably caused them at times without losing patience with what we were trying to do.

Pioneer House could not have existed without the extended use of larger and differently designed facilities. We owe special thanks to Mr. Alex Maleski and Mr. Don Wille of the Boys' Clubs of Detroit, whose ingenuity created recreational chances for our children even during our early tempestuous times when exposure of our youngsters to open community life was wrought with hazard.

Often we had luck and found special help far beyond what we had dared to hope for. Young students as well as experienced faculty members of many departments followed our work with sympathy and were always happy and generous when we needed their help. Dr. Jane Betsy Welling of Wayne University and two of her ablest students, Alex Zawacki and Betty Enfield, assisted us in planning and implementing some of our most successful arts and crafts programs.

We want to give our special thanks to the staff of the Wayne University School of Social Work who should really be listed as part of the Pioneer House team. Among them we think especially of Mary Lee Nicholson, whose talent for program planning was surpassed only by her skill in dealing directly with the children when we needed her help. Dr. Norman A. Polansky, then Director of the Group Contagion Research Project, not only developed special studies within Pioneer House which involved the whole staff, but became one of the most beloved friends of the children. Both really belonged to the Home.

A Treatment Home depends more than any other enterprise on the understanding and cooperation of other social agencies in the community. We were indeed fortunate to have enjoyed the closest cooperation and most unselfish devotion on the side of those agencies and their workers for whose children we cared. We owe a special note of thanks to Mr. C. F. Ramsey and to Miss Sibyl Leach of the Michigan Children's Institute and to Doris Reuel of the Lutheran Charities, Inc. Their participation in all the details of treatment policy and in the daily woes of life with disturbed children went far beyond the usual line of duty.

Another close friend of Pioneer House and an always welcome visitor to the children as well as the staff was Mr. Seymour Riklin, now of the Department of Philosophy, Wayne

University. His close acquaintance with people and life at Pioneer House turned into a special advantage when he answered our desperate plea to edit the expression of our devious theories into readable English. Only he will know how many i's we didn't dot, how many times we didn't cross t's, and we hope he keeps it a secret. We also admire the temperateness of outlook with which Mrs. Geraldine Wineman survived the ordeal of having a husband kidnaped from domestic life by the uninterrupted chain of emergencies of a treatment home.

The preparation of this book was partially aided by a research grant from the Division of Mental Hygiene, United States Public Health Service (Research Grant MH 94).

The core of work, of course, lies in the hands of the people who lived with the children. And here our greatest devotion goes to our wonderful staff. We shall give expression of our thanks to them more specifically when we get around to describing the treatment angle of our work.

# Contents

**18 / Contents**

# Introduction

## Who Mislaid Santa Claus?

OUR TROUBLE IS that we don't know enough about Hate. Consequently, we don't take it seriously enough. Just consider the Juvenile Delinquency issue in the United States at this time of writing as an example. Public opinion allows itself the most ridiculous display of cheap denial mechanisms, which surpass anything we might have been subjected to eighty years ago on issues like Tuberculosis or Venereal Disease. Remember the time when "consumption" became something akin to a fad? It made one "ethereal looking," made one "interesting," made one not exactly cute but respectable. Withering away from it became the subject of poetic compositions, and was contrasted as the nobility of the weak against the crude red-cheekedness of unthinking muscular health. There also was a time when diseases like syphilis were allowed to destroy thousands of victims unchallenged because looking at the causes might imply some kind of morbidity. And, after all, those as yet unafflicted could still enjoy, over their morning coffee, the sweet taste of triumph over the fact that the wicked got their just deserts.

We wouldn't display such an attitude today toward any disease. TB has been sobered down to the status of an unfortunate affliction which we had better fight with laborious and expensive scientific efforts instead of getting enthralled about it and romanticizing its aesthetic aspects. And VD has become just another disease. We have separated the moral disgust about the way in which some people contract it from the problem of research into its causes and into techniques for cure. We have asked the preacher, the teacher, the public health educator, to see what they can do about the moral side of the picture. The physician will approach the person afflicted with the objectivity assured all matters

21

of medical seriousness. Whatever feelings of shame, embarrassment, and guilt the public originally attached to the disease it now reserves for the fact that we still don't know all the answers to problems of prevention, that preventive and curative measures even where known and developed are still not accessible fast enough and cheaply enough in all our communities.

In our thinking about Juvenile Delinquency we have not advanced to nearly so enlightened a stage. We don't really take it seriously. Consider any one of the more shocking crimes, let's say one in which an adolescent sex delinquent murders a younger companion, not exactly in cold blood, but in an anxiety-panic and without much concern for his victim at all. What is the general reaction of the faithful reader of incomplete and usually distorted newspaper reports of a crime like that? It generally wavers between two extremes. The reader is first of all properly shocked and hopes that the criminal will be found soon, will get what he deserves, and will be put away safely so that he can do no more harm. It might be a good idea also, he thinks, to use this opportunity to cut some of the "frills" from the budget of the local reformatory, to admonish the school superintendent to see that the three R's are taught properly instead of allowing youth to be coddled by all sorts of outlandish nonsense like recreational projects and family life discussion groups and the like. It might also be deemed worth while to permit a considerable sum of money to be spent for a few additional "maximum safety rooms" for the institutions of the State. That settles the problem for a while.

The other reaction seems to move along the line of sentimental naïveté. The reader of such a news story may remember what he got out of recent fiction, or from one of those psychiatrically tinged movies, or from that speech the other day in the local PTA, and he now rallies around what he thinks is a "more advanced outlook" on such things. Consequently, he sheds hot tears on the pages of the case history of the delinquent. See, he never had a chance, poor kid. The way he was pushed around! For, after all, who is to blame but the parents and the school? He didn't read the Bible enough, or maybe he read it too much. And, of course, the movies and the comic books, you know. And, maybe we should take great pains to distribute a few more footballs in that bad housing area, and maybe we should send those new curtains to the local detention home after all. Or maybe we should suggest that the parents of delinquent children be sent to jail instead of the children, or should at least "be made" to take classes on child care. Or, perhaps, we should even offer the basement of our church for a project for teenagers, but, of course, let's be sure that only the nice ones get in, for we wouldn't want to have any bad language down there, after all, and who would suggest that the nice kids be expected to mix with the "undesirable element" of our town?

In short, the general attitude of the taxpaying public toward such issues is a pitiful sight to behold. We either "get tough" and take recourse to the most outdated and most obviously stupid defenses against shame, anxiety, and guilt, or we become sentimental and illusional, while we stare at the unfortunate chain of events that ended up in a crime such as this. On two issues, by the way, both camps are agreed. First, that somebody ought to "give us a solution soon" to these problems. Second, that such a solution has to be "simple and inexpensive." For, even though he may know better, who would dare to stand up publicly for high per capita costs for preventive or curative measures? "The taxpayer wouldn't stand for this," we say to ourselves.

Too bad that they mislaid Santa Claus and he isn't playing any more. We think that it is time for the American Community to wake up to the facts of life. We think that delinquency, and especially the phenomenon of Hatred which the more serious crimes invariably involve, is a serious thing. We think that we don't really know enough about it. We think that we ought to find out. It won't do to coddle the delinquent by finding his minor escapades "cute" until the day comes when the whole volume of his hatred bursts into unchecked destruction. And it won't do to keep him in jail, to process him through court hearings, so as to give the general public their show and assure them that "something is being done about it" and to fool them into the illusion that storage or rehabilitative care in some institution solves the problem. In the long run, it comes down to the hard fact that our civilization has grown too sophisticated and decent to resort to the crude measure of simply destroying or removing the individual who doesn't fit in. Unfortunately, it doesn't seem to be wise enough yet or able to show the necessary financial courage to take the steps which would lead to his cure.

There is no doubt in our mind about how the only answer is to be sought. The first step toward a large scale and well organized system of facilities for cure is, of course, adequate and exhaustive research into just what the disturbance is all about to begin with. No, Santa Claus isn't playing any more. There is no escape from the laborious detour by way of patient observation, experiment, and tryout of new treatment designs. And, since psychological reality is as relentless as the physical reality of our gadget world, there is no way out of the fact that the original per capita costs will be high.

## The Children Nobody Wants

Among all the troubles that are usually summarized under the term "delinquency," the most serious seem to be the ones which involve large quantities of *Hate.* Up till now, so far as the study of children is concerned, even science has literally handled the problem of hate with kid gloves. For a long time we were fooled by the old illusion that hatred is really only some sort of "lack of love" and would happily disappear on its own accord if we just could find ways of always being "nice" to people. Accordingly, even professional literature has produced many more volumes on misguided or distorted love than volumes which deal directly with the phenomenon of hate.

When Freud jolted us with his speculations on the seriousness of the "death instinct" and the genuineness of some aggression and destruction, we began to shudder enough to produce some minute and careful observations of the manifestations of aggression, at least as far as they occur along with those of disorganized love or fixated libido. We took such evidence more seriously when we caught sight of it either on the analytic couch or in the play room of our child guidance clinics, with the result that we know much more today about some of these "secondary" developments of aggression which become visible in the treatment of the psychiatrically investigated middle class child than we used to.

We know, for instance, that even the most cordial love relationships between a child and his parents, educators, brothers and sisters will be tinged by some admixture from the aggressive lineage of our impulse system, and that such "ambivalence" is to be expected and remains harmless if handled with care.[1] We also have ample materials on the various disguises which particles of aggression and hate have to assume in order to sneak close to the scene of action or find open expression in fantasy or thought. For this culture of ours frowns on the too open display of some types of aggression, which it considers in poor taste or impolite except in time of war.

We have also made considerable advances during the recent years in our ability to "handle" some of the milder and secondary forms of aggression in children with greater wisdom. The educator is busy finding new tricks by which to lure the normal child into pouring some of his aggression into "constructive channels" and finding new ways to persuade the nonprofessional adult that there is no harm in this. The therapist is eager to find ways through which the child with "bottled-up" aggression can be helped to unbottle some of it, to find substitute targets, to allow him to trim the total output of aggressive needs down to a reasonable size, or to dissolve some of his hatred altogether.

The psychologist, by the way, has added valuable information to that of the clinician. He has drawn our attention to the degree to which hatred can be produced or at least mobilized by environmental stimuli. The various studies in "Frustration and Aggression" have documented Freud's old suspicions along that line and have shown statistically that the mere frustration of basic needs or important goals in a child's life may be enough to produce unmanageable quantities of aggression and destructiveness or other disturbances even in children who otherwise wouldn't have had to hate so

[1] Karl Menninger, *Love Against Hate* (New York: Harcourt Brace & Co., Inc., 1942).

much.[2] Such data, incidentally, could have a tremendous impact on issues as practical as those of punishment in schools and reformatories, and it should be hoped that facts about which nobody has any doubt any more because they are so well documented may find their way into our practice with children during the next half of the century.

The sociologist and anthropologist have documented the hatred-producing power of poverty, social inequality, social disorganization, crowding and neighborhood tensions, and have produced ample evidence that slum areas are a luxury which no nation can afford. The anthropologists have hinted energetically at the degree to which social customs and cultural mores can increase or decrease the sum total of aggression engendered in the members of a society and have sometimes joined with the psychiatrist in their speculations about the correlation between adult aggression and the styles of early child care.

Yes, we have learned much about hatred during the last fifty years. The trouble is that we still have considered it too much as a "secondary phenomenon," or, at least, we have studied it primarily in children in whose lives it played such a secondary role. For there is still a wide gap between the hatred which a well taken care of middle class child develops as a side line to his anxiety or compulsion neurosis and that of the slum area delinquent who has to survive by aggression in a world of struggle. And there is still a great difference between the child who occasionally kicks back at frustrations or expresses the negative side of an ambivalent feeling toward brother or sister and the child who has been reeling under the impact of cruelty and neglect to such a degree that the acid of counter-aggression has eaten itself by now into the very stomach linings of his adaptational system. There is a great difference between a child whose basic personality is still in good enough shape to be approached through psychiatric treatment or through the design of a benevolent institutional program and the child in whom some of the normal behavior controls have already been destroyed by those who hated him so much when he was dependent and

[2] John C. Dollard and others, *Frustration and Aggression* (New Haven: Yale University Press, 1939).

weak and who by now is but a helpless bundle of aggressive drives. There is also a great difference between the child who breaks out into some minor aggressive rebellion from time to time in the classroom, or who betrays deep seated death wishes against us through the medium of finger paint, and the child whose aggression seems to flow uninhibited, skipping even the in-between stage of fantasy, into direct action of reckless destruction or into flare-ups of blind and murderous rage.

There is a reason, of course, why we haven't been able to learn as much about this more extreme, more primitive, more "total" type of hatred and aggression as we have been able to find out about the more neurosis-bound or more ego-controlled related but milder forms. The reason for this is quite simple: the *children who hate* very soon become the *children nobody wants.* And it is to be admitted that, even though we know that the reasons for which they got the way they are are none of their fault, by the time they are as sick as that, they are practically impossible to live with.

And, by and large, neither the homes which originally produced them, nor the schools to which they go, nor the neighborhoods in which they play, nor the communities in which they live, are willing or able to put up with what they put out.

The outward appearance and the reasons for which they become so intolerable to their communities may vary. Some of them let their hatred pour out indiscriminately in open display of an unbroken chain of aggressive acts. With others, it may be hidden behind a smooth surface of compliance, which lasts, however, only as long as they want it to last. Unrecognizable at first sight for what it is, their hatred works "behind the scenes." Still others do not look destructive at all, for a while. They seem, rather, to live in a fog of withdrawal, with hardly any relationship to what goes on around them. One of the youngsters, for instance, with whom you will get acquainted soon would spend hours just sitting by the radio, which he turned up to its loudest volume, glowering into space, or hiding his face behind a closely held comic book, seemingly disinterested in anything that went on around him. Only from time to time would he suddenly burst out, with the aggression which had kept him immobilized blasting into a full-scale temper tantrum, in order to return to the previous stage of sullen apathy after a while. Other youngsters, again, seem, for a while, to be passive and helpless and a little stupid so that you would not suspect them as belonging in the category of the children who hate. Another one of our Pioneers, for instance, would actually seem appealing and eager for a cuddling relationship to surrounding adults. One might for a long time have worried about whether he was stupid and had a low I.Q. rather than have felt tempted to classify him in this category of children who hate. Yet, after several months of treatment, the full impact of his real pathology began to reveal itself. The actual mess of fear and aggression that kept his I.Q. from working as it could suddenly became "liquid," and poured out into fits of sudden kicking and biting, of catatonic-like stiffness of body and limbs. Behind the seemingly empty and childlike stare of his detached eyes lay an ocean of unbridled aggression, destruction and counter hatred, which was the response to years of earlier cruelty and neglect, but which had been frozen into apathetic immobility at the time.

No matter how their specific pathology of "hatred" looks in the beginning, or which part of their personality has been most severely affected by it, the children who hate become an insoluble problem for the communities in which they live. The result is an enormous and unfortunate amount of human waste. In all large communities in the United States there are thousands of such children. They are literally the children nobody wants. The teachers first try their hand. They soon give up because "nothing seems to work." The adult who approaches them with firmness or even a wisely designed system of punishment will only find them stiffening their resistance and using all the ruses of their pathology in a severe battle of resistance and in a heavy guerilla warfare of daily mischief. The educator who falls for some of their cute and appealing antics or behavior or for the temporary display of dependency pleas, soon finds them exploiting him mercilessly only to discard him as a "weak sucker" when further exploitation does not seem to yield results. The group worker who tries to lure them into more organized activities or to expose them to the challenge of heavily competitive team play will observe them either retreat in defeatist disgust or get so over-excited that what was meant to be a competitive challenge becomes the source of an unbridled tantrum, a wild orgy of fighting, or the beginning of a prolonged sulk. Foster parents, of course, cannot be expected to deal with them. None of them could—and those with other children in the home shouldn't— put up, in the long run, with the disorganized and often dangerous behavior which these children are able to produce. Some of them are happy for a while until the new foster parent happens to interfere with part of their pathology. Then, under the impact of trauma or fright, the full blast of their aggression rides herd over them. Others become unmanageable or run away as soon as the foster parent begins to be really loving and accepting. For reasons to be described soon, they can take anything but affection, even though they seem to need it so much. They are, of course, impossible to treat in a children's institution or home, large or small. The peculiar perversity of their hate pathology makes them react even to a good diet of educational handling by an intensified pathology, and their presence often really makes the survival of other children in the same group a risk, or at least cuts down on the chance to develop the type of program and style of child care from which the others would benefit. When exposed to large and restrictive institutions, however, they are lost for good; the large routine structure of institutions only feeds their persecutory interpretation of life, and their inability to be grateful toward the friendly adult with the outstretched hand, or to take punishment in their stride and learn from it, soon makes them hated and isolated by everybody, other children as well as adults.

Interestingly enough, psychiatric treatment of the classical style, too, does not seem to be indicated in their case. Most of them are entirely unverbal, would balk at playing "sissy stuff" like doll house, find it face losing to ask for help from any adult, especially a kind one of the sissified middle class variety. The sociological gap between their natural life style and the atmosphere of a private psychiatrist's office is unsurmountable, and they cannot relate to an adult with whom they have relationship only in talk or play and no group contact. Worse than that, when exposed to the interview room or play room situation, they usually unpack such a volume of immediately acted-out destructiveness that the psychiatrist who hoped to be kind and understanding finds himself "forced against his will" to restrain them or even to hold them in their wild attacks. This in turn, produces tremendous anxieties in the psychiatric adult who isn't used to such things and becomes unduly frightened about the impact of all this on "transference" and on the "clinical side" of his relationship to the child. In short, even under the best of conditions, these youngsters produce so much aggression so fast that we don't even have time to unpack the medicine we brought with us for their cure. Consequently, most of these youngsters are considered untreatable by the usual channels of child analysis or child guidance work. They can't be kept in any one foster home either, and there are no institutions that can digest them for long, and there are none even planned and designed for their specific treatment and cure.

As a result of this, the children nobody wants really get in everybody's way. They clog up the channels of even good detention homes, which are not designed for their permanent care but on which they are usually dumped, after and between frantic attempts to palm them off on a farm foster home or an institution which hasn't caught on to them yet. At the moment, some communities simply get angry at these children, exclude them from all schools, public as well as private, try to ban them from most social agencies, or at least soon "close their case." Many communities draw the line with the general hostility and disgust mobilized against such children, and use them as an excuse to tighten up the punitiveness of the institutions they already have. Only gradually does it dawn upon the general public what an enormous social calamity and economic waste the fact that we leave these children untreated and unchanged imposes on our local and national life. A group of citizens in Detroit was interested enough in this problem and far-sighted enough in their vision as compared to the rest of the town to accept the financial sacrifice and the greater risk of community ridicule for "spending so much on such kids."

This is how Pioneer House came into being. Financed by

the Junior League of Detroit, it was an attempt to find out what some of those children really are like, what ails them, and what ways might be invented in order to bring their particular disease closer to the reach of our arsenal of therapeutic means.

## What to Do Until the Ego Comes[3]

Even after a very short time of trying to survive with our "children who hate" in a special residential treatment design, we were struck by an impression which shook our own clinical hypotheses to the core. This impression seems to us of far-reaching importance, not only for the treatment of the children who hate, but for the *problem of control with respect to anybody's normal child as well.*

Without going into details as yet, we can summarize this impression in the following way. The reasons why these children hate so much, the special pathology of aggression and distorted impulsivity which they display, are important enough in themselves. But the reason why we haven't been able to get anywhere with such children so far, no matter what we tried, is not their hatred. Rather, we find two other factors responsible for our educational and clinical helplessness: One is the *decomposition of behavior controls* which the piled-up aggression has wrought within the personalities of those children. The other must be seen in the *solidification of some of their hatred into an organized department of shrewdly developed defenses against moral implication with the world around them.* We think we can make those two factors heavily responsible for the fact that these children cannot make spontaneous use of even good educational conditions when they are exposed to them, and that they do not seem to be able to respond even to our best clinical methods, which seem so adequate for the treatment of children with other disturbance types. The actual output of aggression, destruction, and

[3] We owe this title to our colleague, Dr. Norman A. Polansky, whose sense of humor condensed into a short line what might take pages to describe.

hatred which these children shower upon those who try to change them is hard enough to take, but it still is only a by-product of their pathology, a smokescreen behind which their disturbed personalities hide themselves.

The full meaning of this statement constitutes the theme of this whole book. Anticipating some of our findings, we would like to emphasize here only two major points:

For the *treatment of the "children who hate"* the implications of these statements can easily be seen. They call for a shifting from the emphasis on finding out what makes them tick to the question of studying the disturbances of their behavioral control function in greater detail. It is easy to see why these children hate—enough of their histories are known to make that point. It is also easy to read the unconscious or disguised meaning of a good deal of their surface behavior. In fact, these children's behavior is not harder to read than that of the neurotic; it is only more difficult to bear. It is also clear that many of the impulses which these children gratify in a day's time are not so different from the basic need system of the normal child, or of their neurotic contemporaries, though of course they are unmatched in terms of primitivity and absurdity of degree. The real block to our treatment success with them lies in the fact that they suffer from *very specific disturbances and maldevelopments* of their "control system," or, to use the psychiatric terms, of their egos and superegos. In order to find out how to cure them, we must, therefore, first get a really thorough picture of just what those ego disturbances and superego misdevelopments are, of which ego functions are still intact and which are disturbed, and we must also know precisely *which defenses* they have developed in order to ward off the impact of the world around them. Only after such an "anatomical chart" of the seat of their ego disturbances has been made, and after the special pathology of their superego has been explored sufficiently, can we even begin to design a strategic attack on the impulsive disturbances which are also plaguing them. In short, these children need a *supportive design to strengthen their deficient ego functions,* and a *counterdelusional design to dis-*

*solve their defenses,* before any of the well known channels of therapy can be tried on them at all.

More important even than for the treatment of the children who hate is the implication of this material for the *educational handling of normal child behavior in daily life.* For, normal children are not born with a fully developed control machinery either. They develop the various ego functions gradually and over the years, and what later will be the content of their "superego" or "conscience" is again the product of many years of subterranean growth and of many factors in their lives. Thus, from the earliest years of a child's life, the educator is really saddled with the task of *substituting for ego functions* which are not yet developed and of *giving active ego support.* But, do we really know what is the full-time job that the normal ego of a healthy nine year old has to perform during a twenty-four hour day's time?

In viewing the literature in the field, it is apparent that we have allowed ourselves much too long to remain general whenever we talk about the "ego," while we have become much more specific when studying the manifestations of impulses, emotions, and drives. This will no longer do. The parent or teacher of the ordinary child is as eager to know just what constitutes adequate or disturbed ego functions, and what good ego support looks like, as he is fascinated by the question "just why does my child want to do what he did just now?" But, as yet we have not developed anything approaching a scientific instrumentology of ego support. We still leave most questions of punishment or reward, interference or permission, encouragement or criticism, approval or blame, and so forth, to trial and error, or to popularized customs of our own childhood experiences, or to stereotyped philosophical beliefs.

Many times before, psychiatry and psychology have used observations gained in the study of diseased behavior in order to discover techniques which will safeguard the wise handling of the healthy child. This book is just another addition in this line. While we concentrate most of our illustrations on the "children who hate," and while we seem to search primarily for techniques and strategies for their treatment and study their pathology, we really are after the discovery of the *specific functions of the normal ego* about which we so far have only very vague notions. It was with this emphasis in mind that we had to forego the pleasure of presenting the reader with the full details of all phases of the history and pathology of our children. We purposely sacrificed this phase of our work in favor of a more full-drawn picture of ego psychology, which we need as a prelude for a new treatment design.

# Children Who Hate

# Chapter 1

# Pioneer House: Experimentation With a New Design

WHAT WE WANT to find out about the children who hate—and through them about all children—can be summarized in a statement of three major goals. First, we certainly want to know *what they really are like and just what makes them tick*. This is especially true for the most challenging group within that category of children who hate, namely, those who live in disorganized slum areas, are very non-verbal, and have developed such skilled defenses against any and all adults that little is known about them through the usual channels of clinical work and interview therapy. Most of the stories about them are really "complaints" while most written reports on them are either full of descriptions of their behavior and its irritational impact on adults or have been shrunken to fit the clinical stereotype of a diagnostic classification. Little is known about just "what they are really like," with emphasis on the question of *how it feels to live with them*. And this is exactly what we need to know more about if our answers are to be useful to people who have to do just that. Since considerable knowledge has been gained in the psychiatric field about their basic emotional problems, our main curiosity would naturally be directed at filling the gaps of our knowledge as to how much their controls are functioning or are disturbed and as to the pathetic confusion in the effort of their egos to relate to the outside world.

Second, we want to know *how people can survive with such children*. By this we mean the question of just what needs to be done in order to tone down some of their surface behavior at times, a task which becomes important even before more deep seated therapy of their "real problem" can be attempted. In short, we want to know just what these youngsters can be expected to *do* in certain life situations, which part of their pathology will go rampant under what conditions, and how we can give them ego support or limit the volume of their behavior when that is indicated. For it is one thing to know just why they feel "that way" or which are the "basic needs or drives" which a youngster is trying to express. It is also important to know for daily survival over and beyond this when he will be able to satisfy such needs *on a fantasy level,* or when he will insist on translating them *into full blown action at anybody's expense.*

Third, we want to find out, of course, just how such youngsters may really be *"treated."* By this we have in mind a design for long range therapy. This would imply the conditions under which actual therapy can take place, as well as the wider framework of daily life within which such treatments can or cannot take a grip on them.

There are many ways by which either of these three tasks can be approached. For several reasons, we tried to weave all three of these goals into the same basic design, but we experimented with such designs on three different levels.

## Group Life as a Diagnostic and Therapeutic Tool

The surest way of finding out things about children who are hard to know is to live with them. With the children we talk about, this invariably means to live with them in a group setting. And, because of another one of their main characteristics, it also means to live with them in an "action" rather than in a mere "discussion" style of relationship. Group Therapy as a diagnostic and therapeutic medium is now widely known, and, despite its comparative unexploredness as a medium, has become considered as an important new potential among our clinical tools. This book is not, strictly speaking, a book on "group therapy." [1] Since our work has been done

[1] The merit of having developed Group Therapy with shy and withdrawn children from a vague concept into a well-designed clinical tool undoubtedly goes to S. R. Slavson, whose book *Introduction to Group Therapy* is a classic in the field. The projects referred to have made ample use of his experience and owe him much stimulation of practice and thought. The authors want to point out, though, that they are in sharp contradiction to Slavson's theory on one item mainly: they do not at all agree

in a group setting, though, we have to acquaint the reader somewhat with the framework within which the concept of Pioneer House first began to unfold.

The intensity with which the current of "group therapy" can be switched on, so to speak, seems to move on a three-notch scale. We experimented, for several years, with the first two notches, before we felt ready to try our hand at a residential design.

It would lead too far afield to list all the gains in clinical insights and the growing differentiation of technical problems which we owe to the experimentation within the framework of the Detroit Group Project and the Detroit Group Project Summer Camp, which we could, so to speak, use as a ready made tool kit at the opening of Pioneer House.[2] We can men-

---

with the demand for total noninterference, as expressed by him in many places. The reasons for this lie partly in the specific nature of the "children who hate" and partly in a theoretical and clinical disagreement about the wisdom of total permissiveness as such. Our point will be further elaborated in a later chapter.

[2] *The Detroit Group Project* was founded in 1942 by Fritz Redl, as an "agency to serve other agencies" by offering group therapy to the children they refer. It is financed by the Council of Social Agencies of Metropolitan Detroit, and is co-sponsored by the School of Social Work, Wayne University. It owes its development primarily to Mrs. Selma Fraiberg, Mrs. Marabel Beck, Miss Mary Lee Nicholson, who have assumed leadership over the project in succession, and to Mr. Paul Deutschberger, who is its present director, and of course to its staff and the wonderful cooperation of the agencies whom it serves. It is now operating with three full-time staff members, one full-time secretary, and usually a few Field Work students from Wayne University. The project also enjoys the devoted services of a most enlightened Board, consisting of prominent citizens of the community, of lay as well as professional members. It operates, at this writing, about eight clubs in various areas of Detroit, serving a total of about eighty children, of the age range between eight and thirteen. It is run, of course, on an intercultural and interracial basis. It operates both "straight" therapy groups as well as so-called "protected groups" closely tied to the group work agencies on whose premises they meet. *The Detroit Group Project Summer Camp,* developed as an extended service of the Detroit Group Project, was in operation during the summers 1944–1947. It had the use of the camp site "Chief Noonday," situated near Middleville, Michigan, and owned by the Michigan State Department of Conservation. It had to

tion but a few of them. We had learned, there, how much
respect the clinician should have for the often fateful factor
of "group composition," and we began to operate with about
fifteen or so criteria for just what makes a treatment-favorable group. It was there that we developed our concepts of the
"law of optimum distance" in terms of group psychological
affinity and that we began to be impressed with the enormous
impact of the phenomenon of "contagion" as well as with
the mysteries of "shock effect." Over a period of years we
became aware of the clinical importance of the great ego-
supportive implications of certain program styles and of
group psychological as well as individual hygiene and their

---

discontinue its existence for lack of financial support by the
Council of Social Agencies, primarily caused by the need to
develop a camp site of its own after the lease of the State site
had been terminated. Besides the Group Project budget, the camp
was supported by Charitable Relief, Inc., whose presidents, Mr.
and Mrs. Fred Johnson, deserve our great gratitude for their
enthusiastic participation. It also received help from the Mc-
Gregor Foundation, the Mendelsohn Fund, the Tribute Fund,
and other Foundations, at times. The Camp combined service to
children with an opportunity for the training of graduate students
in Social Work, Clinical Psychology, and Education from all over
the United States. A full-time Field Work Supervisor in case work
as well as in Group Work supplemented the training which the
student counselors received in classes and seminars. The Camp
was also co-sponsored by the School of Social Work of Wayne
University, which offered credit for training received there, and
furnished Fritz Redl as director and instructor at the camp. There
were many people who left their impact on the development of
these efforts in "clinical group work with disturbed children."
Our thanks go especially to: Miss Estelle Allston, Mrs. Marabel
Beck, Mrs. Selma Fraiberg, Miss Mary Lee Nicholson, Mr. Robert
Rosema, Mr. Benjamin Rubenstein and Miss Dorothea Sullivan,
and, of course, to all the members of our staff, whose names are
too numerous to list here. The Camp served about eighty children
at a time over a six- to eight-week period and had an adult staff
of a total of fifty-four. All clinics and social agencies referring
children to the camp had ample contact before and after the
camp session, and reports on individual as well as group psychological development of the children were exchanged between the
camp and the referring agencies. The children were usually between seven and fifteen years of age, the camp was co-educational
and, of course, interracial and intercultural.

detailed specifications. Our first naive expectations about the role of affection and permissiveness soon gave ground to our later more specific instrumentology of "influence and interference techniques." The similarities and differences between a once-a-week club, on the one hand, and an eight-week total-life camp experience, on the other, impressed us with the importance of gauging the structural qualities of certain group experiences. The role of routine, basic policy, and organizational detail in direct therapeutic impact was heavily underlined for us by our experiences at the camp. The chance to follow up our children in close contact with the case work agencies and clinics which sent them, and to continue work with some of them after camp through the Project Clubs, gave us a means for first comparisons of group effect on different disturbance types, and gave rise to thoughts about criteria for in-group and post-situational changes. The styles of "marginal interview work" were developed at the Camp, and our sensitivity to the great clinical importance of "group atmosphere" of varying types was sharpened there. The importance of an appraisal of the children's native "group code" and the formation of spontaneous "value incorporations" under the impact of group life showed their first tangible manifestations in some of those temporary groups.

Each year we were more fascinated by the amazing "response" of some of the children to what we were trying to do with them. For quite a while we had no way of predicting what this response really meant. Some of them simply seemed to be free of the need to act out their disturbances while they were with us because of the hygienic design and handling with which we had approached them. Others seemed equally "improved" but we could soon see that they were only hiding out skillfully by gestures of surface adjustment from our attempts to get at their real difficulties. Their good adjustment *to* the club or the camp was nothing but a defense against being changed *through* it. In other cases, we were amazed to discover that what looked like a daily frantic struggle with a child while he was with us had really left a deep imprint which became traceable only a few months after his return to the community and could be capitalized on in our follow-up work in the Clubs. The most puzzling cases were those about whom we felt that we were "getting places" while it was, at the same time, quite obvious, that their return to the heavily traumatic home or neighborhood conditions would wipe out in a short time what dents our treatment had started to make, no matter what the case worker or club leader might try to do. Among them were especially the children who hate. Many of them showed aggression and disorganization of a severity which is usually considered "untreatable" to begin with. Some of them seemed to begin to relent the intensity of their defensive warfare after a while at least enough to constitute a case of "promise," others bared so clearly to our diagnostic eye the nature of their disturbance in their frantic struggle that we felt that we were getting at the root of things even though we knew that, as far as these specific individuals were concerned, we were not learning fast enough to succeed with them.

To make a long story short, we felt we had enough clues as to the rather unexpected nature of the real disease of many of these extremely disorganized youngsters and enough clues to consolidate our findings into tentative hypotheses about treatment techniques to start experimenting, with a selected number, by switching the current of group psychology and of our other clinical equipment onto the third notch: the level of a total residential design.

Needless to add, we could try this only because through the other two projects we had attracted a wonderful, courageous, curious group of young people who, on the basis of those experiences and filled with the devotion to a tough and unsure pioneering job, were ready to venture as a team into a new task with us.

## Some Historical Aspects

This is how Pioneer House, an experimental "group therapy home" for a small group of the children, was created. The Junior League of Detroit, Inc., assumed financial sponsorship over the project, and purchased a small home in the neighborhood of the University for us so that we could start in September 1946.[3] Between then and December, when the children came, we rallied our staff, and spent all our time in organizing the home and in staff orientation to the venture on which we launched. This also involved considerable work with the various referring social agencies and institutions on the selection of our initial group of children and with the school they were to attend. The youngsters came in December.

Pioneer House was in operation over a period of nineteen months. In June 1948 we had to close the project, since it turned out to be impossible to find the guarantees of continued financial support before the summer came around. This closure coincided with our most fascinating professional development and our most visible period of consolidation of clinical gains and of progress with the children. It was a heavy blow. More about that later.

## Our Clinical Premises

It is beyond the scope of our present study to go into a detailed discussion of treatment mechanics in our Pioneer House experiment with the "children who hate." This has been reserved for separate publication since its inclusion together with the descriptive analysis of their ego disturbances *per se* would have resulted in a too lengthy and unwieldy book.[4] However, to clarify some of the clinical theory and illustrative material utilized in the later chapters of this book, it is felt that some discussion of the basic premises involved in the operations of Pioneer House will be useful.

Among the variables which affect child behavior within a treatment milieu, we would like to select three for discussion here: the impact of a hygienically prepared climate, program-

[3] Pioneer House was exclusively financed, throughout its period of operation, by the Junior League of Detroit, Inc. None of the parents of any of the children who were referred to us were able to make any appreciable contribution toward the per capita expense of keeping them in the Home.

[4] The treatment aspects referred to will be presented by Fritz Redl and David Wineman in *Strategy Against Childhood Confusion,* soon to be published by the Free Press.

ming for ego support, and the clinical exploitation of life events.

## The impact of a hygienically prepared climate

The first step toward helping children with severe ego disturbances lies in creating a climate which is psychologically sound from a mental hygiene point of view so that our direct attempts to remove their basic pathology have some appreciable chance for success. We must be as careful with respect to our psychological "atmosphere" as medical science has learned to be with the biotic atmosphere in which certain of its operations are to be carried out. No surgery can be successful if, at the same time, free passage is given to germ invasion which will then cause death from sepsis even if a diseased organ is removed successfully. Similarly, no attempts at influencing behavior pathology can be successful if, at the same time, every part of the environment is not kept scrupulously "clean" from the point of view of psychological hygiene. This, of course, covers a vast range of items involved in the clinical management of the Home. The following list is intended, therefore, as purely illustrative and does not even begin to cover what is actually involved.

§ Complete protection from traumatic handling by any personnel associated with the treatment home must be guaranteed. No one in the Home can afford to duplicate wrong handling which has occurred in previous life situations and which has been one of the responsible agents in the creation of the child's disturbance pattern.

§ Gratification grants, through activity programming, adult love, and affectional tokens, must be absolutely divorced from any consideration as to whether the child deserves them or not from the point of view of his behavior. Indeed, from the point of view of psychological hygiene, to withhold such gratifications because a child was "bad" would, in the cases of the children who hate, be as unsound as taking away cough syrup from a bronchitic child because he refused to stop coughing.

§ Symptom tolerance and leeway for regression must be an intrinsic part of the treatment environment. Yet tech-

niques have to be developed for purposes of protective interference on the part of the residential staff in moments when
the overflow of excitement and stimulation involved in some
behavior will force the child into overwhelming guilt, anxiety,
fear, or depression, unless checked.

§ The Home must not run too contrary to the sociological
taste pattern of the child. If the furnishings of the Home, its
physical appearance, even the activity programming, differ
too sharply from the neighborhood style to which the child
has been accustomed, then some adverse effect is created
which will interfere with the clinical goals. Of course, the
reader will understand that this does not mean that the deprivational elements in their former milieu will also be duplicated
just to create a total feeling of "at home-ness" but rather that
a sharp socio-economic style clash will be circumvented.

These are just some of the characteristics of any hygienic
environment. However, in summary, there are two points that
we want to make here. First, such concessions to psychological hygiene as we have illustrated must be made in order
even to consider that a valid treatment setting can be established. Secondly, the hygienic environment is more than a
mere trapping to our clinical endeavors. In and by itself it has
a definite and tangible impact on the functioning of the child
and can be credited with the removal of some of his pathology
just as much as other more direct attempts at manipulation.

*Programming for ego support*

The recreational diet and its implementation are of utmost
importance in the treatment of the ego-disturbed child. In
their various aspects, they offer the child a chance for expressional discharge within organizational, sublimational, and
frustration-acceptance levels mainly circumscribed by the
particular ego disabilities from which he suffers. The program
tools of the outer world have been too challenging and frightening to the unstructured ego of this type of child. Just to
mention a few, highly competitive games, arts and crafts situations where achievement goals cramp impulse needs, toys
and gadgets whose inner satisfaction potentials they have not
been able to visualize, all have thrown these children into a

recreational wasteland or, perhaps more appropriately, jungle, where their main adjustment has been to resort to random and destructive impulsivity. The clinician recognizes that one of the most vital and ego-nutritive experiential areas is that of gratifying play. Normal children seem to have an inner guiding hand which helps them to find these outlets so necessary to their emotional health. With the ego-disturbed child, making up for this missing mental hygiene vitamin is one of the most important functions of the residential milieu. Our assumption is that a certain amount of ego repair and change can occur in this way alone.

## Clinical exploitation of life events

Our youngsters, from the moment they enter the treatment home, overwhelm us with symptomatic behavior. This behavior spurts into the life scene with great velocity and intensity. We are glad that it does. For this gives us an opportunity to work with it in a way which would be impossible if we had to wait until the child showed up at our office at "4 P.M. on Monday," if we were seeing him under typical conditions of office psychotherapy. Because we are there, as part of the life scene in which the behavior takes place, *we can exploit it for clinical purposes* before it becomes repressed or tricky denial mechanisms and diversion tricks spring up to ward off our attempts to get at some of the subsurface motivations and attitudes that are behind it. We even try to mold some life scenes so that the disturbed behavior can be highlighted in such stark and vivid detail that the child is brought face to face with some of the implications of what he is doing, with what it means in terms of value demands and reality consequences. Eventually, after long range application of the various procedures involved in exploiting life issues, we may visualize something like trying to find out with the child why he has to behave the way that he does. In this way, running away, stealing incidents, tantrums, etc., can be selectively approached when it is felt that their handling may serve a clinically useful purpose for the child. As an integral part of the techniques of exploiting life issues, the whole interview apparatus of the treatment home shifts from "interview by appointment" to a more mobile strategy, applicable to on-going behavior at its moment of incidence. Of course, there are many times when the simple production of symptom behavior does not guarantee clinical utility, which means that attempts to cope with it for the purpose of permanently resolving it will fail. Under such conditions, the clinical milieu, through the application of hygienic procedures, as previously explained, will try to soften the behavior for purposes of temporary disappearance. The total implications of the use of milieu, all the way from softening behavior to luring it out into the open, are part and parcel of the strategy of clinical exploitation of life events.

These, then, are some of the basic clinical assumptions that were made in connection with the Pioneer House experiment. The major clinical operations briefly described, namely, the impact of the antiseptically prepared climate, programming for ego support, and clinical exploitation of life events, were expanded into a detailed scheme of strategies which together made up the total treatment design.

## Some Questions the Reader May Have

In our succeeding chapters we make frequent use of recorded material for illustrative purposes. Wrapped up together with the specific behavioral sequence we want to show are many tangential allusions to various policies and practices which the illustration itself does not explain or enlarge upon. If it did, the special accent that we want the illustration itself to show would be lost. However, because the reader may find himself understandably perplexed by the steady stream of peripheral images that we have not been able to dim out and which are still not explained, we have abstracted from all of our illustrative material some questions it would seem to hold for the uninitiated reader, and we attempt to answer them here, briefly, on a topical basis.

*Was there any limitational pattern set for the control of aggressive behavior?* The whole story of our policies with respect to "ceilings" on aggression cannot be told in a single paragraph. Suffice it to say that we used a variety of interference techniques to cope with aggressiveness. The main point we want to clarify here is that there were policies with respect to aggression and wildness. We were not categorically permissive.[5]

*What is meant when the records say a child was "bounced"?* The reader may have some understandable confusion about the use of such a term in a clinical setting for disturbed children. This, whenever it occurs, refers to the strategy of "antiseptic bouncing," which means that a child was removed from a situation where he became so aggressively wild that no other influence techniques short of such removal were adequate to cause him to tone down his aggressiveness temporarily. It does not imply the use of hurtful force or display of anger or that the child was simply "dumped" away from the troublesome situation. The adult always stayed with him to help him cope with his feelings about the removal.[6]

*Were the children permitted to smoke?* We were aware from the case histories of our children that some of them were cigarette addicts from as far back as five years of age. We also knew that, in spite of the most determined and vigilant supervision, they would manage to smoke at Pioneer House. Therefore, from the very beginning, we established a definite policy. We told them very clearly that we really did not want them to smoke and that we hoped that eventually they would outgrow this trouble as well as a number of their other difficulties. We also assured them, however, that we knew that, as with their other troubles, they might not be able to stop at once but would need to "take their time to get rid of it." For the interim the following arrangements were worked out: what smoking they did was limited to certain places in the Home and had to happen with adults around rather than in a clandestine hideout. Each boy was also interviewed as to how many cigarettes he thought he would have to smoke each day without being tempted to lie, swindle, or steal. These then were granted. This policy had the following advantages:

It removed the delinquent pleasure of "sneaking one over

[5] *Ibid.*, Chapter III, "Techniques for the Antiseptic Manipulation of Surface Behavior."
[6] *Loc. cit.*

on the adult" which they would derive if we forbade smoking and they nonetheless smoked on the sly.

Smoking, a symptom like many of their other behavioral patterns, was kept out in the open, to be dealt with clinically whenever possible.

Fire dangers from covert smoking were kept at least to a minimum.

Breaking the agreed-upon policies on the part of the child gave us a wonderful chance for marginal interviewing around issues of realism, fairness, etc. It may be interesting, by the way, to note that this was one of the policies that worked out even better than we had dared hope.

*Who are all of the adults referred to in the records?* Our professional staff, including full-time and part-time personnel, numbered at any given time approximately ten individuals. To begin with, there were the director and executive director (the co-authors). In addition, we had a housemother and, in the second year of operations, a full-time boys' worker. Also, there were usually five field work students from the Wayne University School of Public Affairs and Social Work, placed at the Home by the School as part of their training in casework, group work, and group therapy. In addition, a group work consultant, the then executive director of the Detroit Group Project, figured very prominently in consultation for and direct participation in programming with our youngsters. Finally, there were a resident cook, a housemaid, two part-time maids, and a secretary.

*With so many adults around, didn't the children get "confused"?* To begin with an obvious point, not all staff members converged on the children at any one time. There were regular duty periods of responsibility for the group assigned to a pair of counselors during any given period. As to the total number of contacts with the adults, the impact of multiplicity was reduced considerably by the distribution of roles among the adults. There were three basic adult role patterns at the Home. All students were on the counselor role level. This means that they were basically responsible for activity programming for the group, and minimally responsible for child-care functions such as feeding, clothing, waking-up, and bedtime, although in each of these they were involved to some small extent. Nor were the counselors or group leaders involved in the settlement of basic rule violations or in heavy interference tactics such as "antiseptic bouncing." Basic child-care functioning was reserved for the housemother, policy and rule issues for the two directors. This is purely a matter of clear-cut emphasis, however, and does not mean that the housemother never participated in an activity, that the counselors never had any dealings with food, rules, clothes, or bedtime, and that the directors did not participate in activities. There was some intermeshing of functions, but not to the point where there was obvious duplication or where the role image of the particular adult was blurred in the minds of the children.

*Did the children ever get tired of each other and of being in the group?* One of the advantages of our pattern of role distribution among the adults was that, when children became bored or threatened by the group, they could drift into an individual relationship situation with some of the adults around, such as the housemother or directors, who might not at that moment be saddled with group supervisory responsibilities. The housemother role, especially, was built around this anticipation of the need of the child to withdraw from group life at certain moments. Frequently a child in such a moment might drift back to her quarters to ask her to read a story to him or chat about some occurrence of the day. To protect her availability for such moments, she participated in group activities only on a "sliding scale" basis.

*Were there any rules and routines for the children to follow?* All rules and routines which were developed at Pioneer House were very carefully thought out on the basis of the particular type of ego disturbances with which we were dealing. Obviously one has to reduce rules to an absolute minimum so as not to step up too much delusional misinterpretation of adult motivation. Similarly routines were designed on a clinical basis and not from the point of view of managerial efficiency or adult comfort needs.[7]

*What were the policies with respect to destruction?* In the treatment of children whose disturbance patterns center

[7] *Ibid.*, Chapter I, "Structure and Strategy of a Treatment Home."

prominently around hate and aggression, a certain amount of destruction must be anticipated and even permitted before basic changes can take place. As in the case of aggression against persons, however, destruction has to be contained within certain limits. The range of tolerance for, and specific influence techniques pertaining to the management of, destruction are discussed elsewhere.[8]

*What school arrangements were made?* Pioneer House did not have funds to run its own school. The obvious fact that our youngsters would not fit into a standardized school program led to conferences with the Department of Special Education and the Psychological Clinic of the Detroit Public Schools. A plan was worked out to the effect that the Pioneer House youngsters would attend one of the special opportunity classes of the Detroit Public Schools. These classes are reserved for children who show excessive behavior disturbances in the regular classroom. The teaching staff is specially trained to handle problem behavior and the total teaching regime is sensitized to the clinical needs of the child. Our group attended such a class together with some ten or twelve community youngsters suffering from similar behavior disorders. There were intensive planning conferences between the School and the Home and a close and positive working relationship was established. We were especially fortunate in having a teacher whose ingenuity in handling baffling surface behavior made it possible for our children to function in a classroom setting to a degree that kept us constantly amazed and grateful.[9]

*How did the neighbors react to the Pioneer Group?* Basically we drew little hostile criticism from our neighborhood population, and from our immediate neighbors we obtained a good deal of sympathy, sometimes even support. The fact that this neighborhood was not of a typical middle-class structure was of great help in this respect. There were not large numbers of children around to begin with, since we had basically a rooming house population. This meant that no angry parents were calling us to complain that their children were either

[8] *Ibid.*, Chapter III, "Techniques for the Antiseptic Manipulation of Surface Behavior."
[9] Mr. Richard Kulka, Detroit Public Schools.

being intimidated or seduced into misbehavior. Of course, we went to great lengths to orient the immediately surrounding homes as to the nature of our experiment. The fact that we were associated with the University helped to give us some prestige and respect. The inevitable breaking of neighbors' windows and rough language in the back yard drew open criticism but not hostile complaints, since our neighbors appreciated the difficulties we were up against. Some of these reactions were even useful clinically for purposes of emphasizing for the group the social consequences of their behavior, even among people who liked them such as our next-door neighbors, who not infrequently did kind things for them such as baking pies, sending over old magazines, etc.

*What relationship existed with the Police Department?* Quite naturally, since we were dealing with children whose disturbance pattern frequently involves them in brushes with the law, there was considerable interest in our program on the part of the precinct police. Several meetings were held with them prior to the opening of the Home to orient them as to the goals of our program and some strategic ways in which they could help us, if and when our youngsters got into trouble. While in showdown issues they could, of course, not grant our children any more immunity than to any other delinquent with whom they might have to deal, they were quite interested in working within our framework of strategies whenever they could. They were helpful in a variety of preventative measures aside from open delinquency issues.

*Weren't those in charge of recreational facilities for "normal" children justifiably "leery" of letting the Pioneers onto the premises?* We are quite certain that many of the persons in charge of recreational facilities may have been understandably "leery" of our group, even if they did not show it, but they were bravely cooperative with us during our total period of operations. We devoted much time to interpretation of our program to such key persons and they built up a great deal of identification with our project. Among many community resources, the Boys Clubs of Detroit, for example, a large mass recreation setting for under-privileged boys, not only provided swimming facilities for our group, but gave us "private" times in the pool so that our children would not tangle with neighborhood youngsters and also detailed one of its most clinically skilled swimming instructors to work with them.

*What is meant by the term "program" so frequently alluded to in the records?* By "program" we usually mean the activities engaged in by the group on a given morning, afternoon or evening. We do not use this word to signify the total clinical program. Nor does it ever mean, unless specifically stated, that we planned a program of entertainment for the youngsters like a show or special musical program. It always connotes activities planned with the group in which they and the group leader mutually participated, such as athletic games, a trip, arts and crafts, etc. Details on this aspect of our program and its clinical significance are published elsewhere.[10]

*What about the parents of the children?* In most cases there was at least one surviving parent with whom the children were living at the time of referral to Pioneer House. In such cases the referring agency of the child continued to work with the parent during the period of placement of the child. This had a dual purpose:

Continuation of efforts to rehabilitate the home of the child so that he might, depending upon the outcome of such attempts, be able to return to his own home after treatment.

Keeping the referring agency, which would be in close cooperative relation with us, in the role of interpreter to the parents of the treatment process with the child.

Visits between the parents and children were arranged and some interpretation concerning our work with the child was given them but, as stated above, the brunt of this was handled by the agencies.

*Where did the children come from?* All of the children were referred from various social agencies in the Detroit area as well as from other places in the State of Michigan. Referrals were not taken from private sources.

*Was there any religious program at Pioneer House?* Children who wished to attend were taken by the counselor staff to the church of the children's denomination. Special time was set aside for this purpose every Sunday morning.

[10] Cf. *Strategy Against Childhood Confusion,* Chapter II, "Programming for Ego Support."

*What records were kept on the children?* Three types of records were kept at Pioneer House: (1) group records, maintained by the counselor staff, which preserved each day's significant events in the life of the group, (2) individual behavior logs on each child maintained both by the housemother and executive director, and (3) a special daily program analysis log which gave a detailed picture of the reactions of the children to each phase of the activity program and was also maintained by the counselors.

In the present study we have drawn very extensively on our group records for illustrative material. All such quotations are called "entries" and the date and person recording are indicated. Those illustrations not marked "entry" are also taken either from the recorded materials or from the recollection of incidents by the staff. They frequently represent excerpts from episodes, the detailed, verbatim reproduction of which would have been too clumsy for the purpose of illustrating the point for which they were used.[11]

## Criteria for Intake

Our criteria for admission to Pioneer House revolved around two basic diagnostic variables: (1) The individual pathology of the child both in terms of disturbance type and degree of personality damage, and (2) The individual picture as it became relevant to the problem of grouping, which involves the determination of just which disturbance types can be handled together in the same group. In determining the first of these variables, we leaned quite heavily on the individual case history of the child sent by the agency and on our impression in interviews with him and his parents, as well as the impression of our consultant child analyst.[12] As far as grouping was concerned, we used criteria which had been developed through several years of prior experimentation in both the Detroit Group Project and its summer camp with

[11] All names, except those of Pioneer House staff members, which appear in entries or examples are pseudonyms.
[12] Dr. Editha Sterba, Grosse Pointe, Michigan.

children of similar disturbance types. Some of the basic criteria were as follows:

### Age range

In a small group it is virtually impossible to cater to the program tastes of too different developmental phases. Feeling that our previous clinical experience promised most to them, we decided to restrict our age to youngsters who were in the pre-adolescent period represented chronologically by the ages eight through eleven. Thus, our main purpose in selection was to exclude children who were very heavily infantile as well as children who were already heavily underway in their adolescent development. If we had taken youngsters who were too heavily infantile, much of our "atmosphere" would have had to be designed along lines which would be definitely ill-advised in terms of the pre-adolescent child. If we had allowed older, definitely adolescent youngsters into our Home, the whole tenor of life, to say nothing of program details, would have had to be different from what is compatible with the pre-adolescent age range.

### I.Q.

We limited the group to youngsters of normal intelligence, since it had been our experience in the Detroit Group Project clubs and at camp that children who are too far below the normal intelligence level would need an entirely different type of program than the youngsters with average or higher I.Q. Thus, mixture of children who are of normal and subnormal I.Q. was counter-indicated and, in terms of our previous experience, we felt we had most to offer to youngsters of normal intelligence.

### Health and physique

We selected youngsters of normal health who were free of major physical handicaps. Some minor allowances, such as dietary variations, were acceptable, but anything that would prevent their full participation in most of the program of the group, we felt, would constitute too much of an impediment for our main task.

## Toughness-shyness range

We conceived of ourselves as designed primarily to take care of children with what is commonly called "pre-delinquent or delinquent" behavior patterns. This meant that, as far as surface behavior went, we expected symptoms of destructiveness, hyper-aggression, stealing, running away from home, truancy from school, temper tantrums and lying, sassiness toward adults, and most of the rough and tumble language and behavior that goes into the pattern of a "toughy" in the making. Of course, we are aware that children usually do not come in clear-cut types. So we anticipated the discovery of isolated neurotic traits mixed in with their delinquent behavior scheme, such as bed-wetting, soiling, fears and anxieties of many types. The emphasis which we placed, however, in the final selection of our group, was on the existence of a delinquent trait pattern along with the isolated neurotic traits. We did not feel that youngsters from over-protected backgrounds who suffered from a clear-cut compulsion or anxiety neurosis of the classical type would be good referrals. The more aggressive and wayward behavior of the rest of the group would frighten them, we thought, into reinforcing their neurotic problems and into further withdrawal or open anxiety attacks. Thus, when we speak of the toughness-shyness range as a factor in the selection, we mean youngsters who are operating on what one might term an "expressional" level. Such youngsters seem to externalize all of their tension into warfare with the outside world, principally with the adult as the representative of that world. They are quite different from the child who has internalized his conflict situation and who is therefore representative of endo-psychic conflicts or conflict between one part of the personality and the other which would seem true for most neurotic behavior.

## Socio-economic background

We purposefully tried to restrict our group to youngsters who came from more or less similar socio-economic backgrounds. We felt that, even with similar symptom constellations, youngsters who have widely differing experiences along socio-economic lines are probably not well grouped together. The socio-economic level that we catered to was of the lower economic group, involving a good deal of "open door neighborhood style" of life in their backgrounds.

## Known group allergies and sensitivities

We inquired carefully into the background history of children in terms of looking for any known group-related behavior which would indicate that for such children the presence of a group would bring out patterns which might be inimical to the best interests of the individual or the group. What we had in mind was something like this. Some youngsters have such severe sibling "paranoia" that the mere fact that they have to share an adult with other children produces deep regression or aggressiveness that is impossible to handle short of a psychiatric ward. Still other children, for reasons which are not well understood, simply go completely out of control when exposed to group life on a sustained basis. It is as though group experience is just poisonous to their control pattern. Thus, youngsters who had been observed at camp or who had other known group experiences from which we could approximate and in a rough sense predict possible group allergies or group sensitivities of too high an intensity were ruled out.

## Intensity of problem behavior

The fact that Pioneer House was not a closed institution or a psychiatric ward imposed a ceiling on the intensity of disturbance it could tolerate, regardless of the type of disturbance with which it was prepared to cope. Since the children were going to be exposed to a certain number of community experiences, would use recreational facilities within it, would go to school in the neighborhood, those who were so immune to reality implications and devoid of self-control that they would become reality risks in relation to physical dangers of traffic, health precautions, caution in the handling of simple tools, etc., could not be accepted. Nor could children be taken who were so sadistic and so primitive in their aggression that the welfare of the other children would be jeopardized each time an adult was not in immediate contact with the group situation, which was an expected occurrence even in an institution as highly supervised as Pioneer House. Thus, even if their type of disturbances did fit into the clinical category with which Pioneer House hoped to work, children could not be accepted if the intensity of disturbance manifested proved to be such that they could not be housed in an open institution with other youngsters.

## Final Selection and Population Shifts

In order to develop an adequate set of criteria for the selection of children for a given clinical design, it must have been in operation for many years. Experimentation with different problem intensities and types has first to be done in order to begin to perceive clearly what the particular design has to offer to the treatment of different problem patterns found in various children. We have to discover which are too severe for us to cope with or so different in structure that they had better be treated elsewhere. At Pioneer House we were just in the beginning stages of such experimentation. As it was, we used criteria for our initial selection that had been already undergoing some experimentation in the two similar but also widely differing projects with this same type of child, the Detroit Group Project and its summer camp. While we were never naive enough to believe that we could succeed in a wholesale transfer of selection criteria from these two projects to Pioneer House, they were still the best criteria we had at our disposal. Thus, we did make unavoidable errors in selection, as a normal phase of trial and error experimentation in this area of our work in the residential treatment setting.

As a matter of chronology we first selected an initial group of six children from among some thirty to thirty-five referrals to our Home from the various social agencies. Of this group of six, only three children were able to be absorbed permanently in the Home, the other three proving too advanced in their disturbance pattern to be helped in an open institution of the Pioneer House type. These latter three left Pioneer House within three months from the time the clinical work began. At about this point we added a new child who became one of the permanent members of the group and, two months later, still another who also remained with us. These five children were then our stable population during the entire period of operation. We also tried two other children after we had added our fifth permanent member but both of these were again too disturbed to remain with us for more than approximately two months. It was our experience that it took from one and a half to three months to determine if a child could be contained within our particular design. The following table shows the number of children, date of admission, date of discharge, and length of stay.

TABLE A

| Name (pseudonyms) | Age | Date of Admission | Date of Discharge | Length of Stay |
|---|---|---|---|---|
| Danny | 10 | 12/1/46 | 6/23/48 | 19 mos. |
| Larry | 8 | 12/1/46 | 6/23/48 | 19 mos. |
| Andy | 9 | 12/1/46 | 6/23/48 | 19 mos. |
| Mike | 9 | 2/1/47 | 6/23/48 | 17 mos. |
| Bill | 9 | 4/1/46 | 6/23/48 | 15 mos. |
| Henry | 10 | 12/1/46 | 12/30/46 | 1 mo. |
| Joe | 9 | 12/1/46 | 2/5/47 | 3 mos. |
| Sam | 9 | 12/1/46 | 2/5/47 | 3 mos. |
| Harry | 9 | 4/5/47 | 5/20/47 | 1½ mos. |
| Donald | 10 | 4/15/47 | 6/20/47 | 2 mos. |

In our record illustrations all of these boys appear but most frequently the first five youngsters, since they were our stable, long range population.

It is not our intent here to go into any detailed analysis of the nature of our errors in taking those children whom we had to discharge. We can, however, make this statement categorically: Our criteria seemed quite reliable in selecting problem type but not in gauging intensity of disturbance. With only one exception, Donald, we were dealing predominantly with the disturbance syndrome that we had set out to work with originally. But on the question of how advanced the children were in their symptom picture we could draw no reliable inference from prior case history materials. Of the children who left us, before the Home closed, we have some follow-up information available. Three are in detention homes or state reformatories, one has made a fairly adequate adjustment in the community, and a fifth has left town with his family, thus removing any chance for follow-up appraisal.

## The Children: This Is What Happened to Them Before They Came

We think that it is important for the reader to have some perspective into the past of the children who came to live with us. Yet we do not intend to go into such details as one would expect to find in a case history analysis since, if we attempted to do this for each Pioneer, we would require a whole new volume to present our material. What is intended is to introduce the reader to some of the important experiences with which these children came to us and which loom behind their behavioral productions as they emerge in the recorded material in succeeding chapters.

### The adults in their lives

If prevailing criteria for what constitutes an adequate child-adult relationship pattern are used as a basis for reaching conclusions, we can see very little in the case history profiles of our children that would satisfy even the most naive clinician or educator that they had had anything even approaching an "even break." In very few instances were we able to gather any evidence that there had been even continuity of relationship with original parent images. Broken homes through divorce and desertion, the chain-reaction style of foster home placements and institutional storage, were conspicuous events in their lives. Aside from continuity, the quality of the tie between child and adult world was marred by rejection ranging from open brutality, cruelty, and neglect to affect barrenness on the part of some parents and narcissistic absorption in their own interests which exiled the child emotionally from them. Certainly there were also operative heavy mixtures of both styles of rejection, overt and unconscious. One of the things that constantly amazed us when we would observe the parents and children together was how much like strangers they were to one another. In this connection, we were impressed by how little interest the parents took in what was happening to the children in treatment. Contrary to our expectations that they might become competitive with the treatment milieu on the basis of feelings of guilt for placing the child and for their own inadequacy, they never became involved on any level at all. Their main, unconcealed reaction was: "We're glad you've got them, not us. Life is so peaceful without them."

This phenomenon of casual surrender of their own children marks these parents off decisively from the parents of the typical neurotic child who has had to go into institutional placement. The parents of the neurotic child who cannot live with the child also begin to feel in his absence that they cannot live without him either. He is somehow necessary to their neurotic design. This difference in the parental style of involvement with one's own child between the two groups is of very basic etiological significance in determining their contrasting symptom structures, since it is really the difference between little or no relationship at all, as we saw in our group, and an ambivalent but strong love-hate-ridden relationship. Further, we could gather no impression, either from case histories or subsequent material productions by the children, once they were in treatment, that they had known even one adult with whom they had built up a warm relationship on an occasional friendly visit basis to which they could look back and say, "Gee, it was fun when I was with so-and-so once." There were no uncles, aunts, cousins, or friends who seemed to take any interest in them which was enough to provide significant gratifications. This whole vacuum in adult relationship potentialities cannot possibly be overestimated in terms of how impoverished these children felt or how much hatred and suspicion they had toward the adult world.

*Their siblings*

Most of our children had siblings (brothers or sisters). In many cases there was open, naked sibling rivalry and tension, quarrelsomeness and bickering between them. Usually none of the siblings was very much better adjusted than the child who came into placement. However, it was usually the case that the placed child had a scapegoat position with respect to parental attitudes in the sibling preference range. He was always the "worst" one. Upon closer scrutiny there was usually some psychological factor which predisposed the parent to hold this discriminatory position.

In the case of Danny, second oldest in a sibling group of five, there had been a long and intensive marital conflict between the parents, finally culminating in a divorce. The father had been alcoholic, abusive, promiscuous and, in drunken episodes, very brutal toward the whole family. In all of the contacts with her, the mother persistently characterized Danny as being a "chip off the old block," and in her eyes he appeared to resemble the father very minutely. Without knowing the father, it is impossible, of course, to evaluate the correctness of her comparison. However, whether he resembled the father or not, is irrelevant to the main consideration, namely, that the mother identified Danny rigidly with the father and all of her ambivalence and hostility toward the husband for this mistreatment of her became focused on the boy. Thus, we can see that Danny, brutalized by the father and hated by the mother, had very little opportunity to receive anywhere near an adequate amount of affection and positive handling from either of the parents. In addition to this, the mother is known to have frequently commented that she wished that all of her children were girls and especially is reported to have verbalized to Danny that she felt that, if he had been a girl, he would not have given her so much difficulty. Although there was another boy, he was much younger than Danny and easier for the mother to control. Thus Danny was the central target, since the remaining three children were girls. As could be expected from this, Danny's sibling hatred was immense. He not only wanted to be the only one around the adult but he also had fantasies of being a girl so as to pave the way to his mother's affection. The other siblings all disliked Danny because he had been so brutal to them.

In addition, such careless, neglectful, overtly rejective behavior by the parents not only victimized any individual child but predisposed the siblings to open hostility toward each other on the basis of general insecurity. In some cases severe sibling tension was related to the presence of a step-parent in the home when such a parent rejected the child in favor of his own children—just as the typical story-book stepmothers do.

Andy, whose mother separated from his father when he was still an infant, was immediately placed by her after the separation. He lived in various boarding homes, having little or no contact with his own mother for long intervals of time. When he was six, his mother was killed in an auto accident and his father, who had in the interim married again, took him to live with him. The stepmother was a cold, unfeeling woman, overprotective of three half-siblings while confronting Andy with obvious rejection. She loaded him with household chores, criticized and nagged him. He in turn released all of his hostility against his siblings. At times he was sadistic and tried to burn them with a wood-burning set. His jealousy was chronic and on every possible occasion he tried to inflict injury upon them in whatever way was possible.

Generally, we felt that little or no incentive had been given the children who came to our attention for adequate sibling adjustments in their own homes. In each family, on one psychological basis or another, the placed child was the most severely mistreated and unwanted of the total sibling group.

*Life in the school and community*

Invariably the children who came to our attention had extremely poor adjustments to the communities and schools from which they came. In the school, both on a behavioral and scholastic basis, they showed severe disabilities to the extent of having to be in special classes or of being excluded from school altogether. Truancy, bullying, lying, stealing, swearing—all of these were familiar complaints. In their communities, they either ran with the other delinquent children or engaged in "lone wolf" activities of a delinquent or impulsive nature. In both school and community areas, they suffered from the same loss of continuity and stability that occurred in their adult relationship patterns. Because many of them were shifted about so much they never became acquainted with or rooted in any one community milieu.

Sam, who had been in several different foster home placements for four years prior to Pioneer House admission, had run away fourteen times during the second year. He was an accomplished "escape artist" from detention homes. Once he tied up his case worker in a chair as part of a game and ran away following this piece of trickery, making his way to Chicago. He had been in many schools, both suburban and in the city of Detroit. He chronically tried to avoid school through pretending illness and, when forced to go, almost always ran away. Thus, from the point of view of his many shifts in placement as well as his truancy pattern *per se,* he practically had no community life during this period.

In the rare cases where there had been more continuity and children had been in one neighborhood for several years the disturbances had become part of community legend.

Bill, a youngster whose family structure had been one of the more stable of the Pioneer House group, was in severe rivalry with a slightly older brother. The mother was unable to manage situations where the three of them would be in the house together (i.e., she and the two boys). This tension was not confined to the home itself. In school and at the YMCA where both boys had memberships they were so abusive toward each other that they had to be given definite hours in which they could attend the Y so as not to conflict with each other; different schools had to be used to avoid severe bickering and quarreling to the point of upsetting the routines.

In some cases the degree of disturbance in the school situation made it necessary for the authorities to exclude the child from school altogether.

Joe was tried in every public school in the small community in which he lived. He was either consistently truant, or, when in school, so aggressive and defiant toward his teachers that class room morale was disrupted to the point where the rest of the group could not function. He was continually on the move, bullied other children, and was unable to accept any rules or routines whatsoever. In addition he engaged in chronic stealing.

Some children who were not severe behavior problems in the school situation still had built up intense fear and anxiety about school because of emotional barriers to learning which involved them in continual failure. While this was not so typical as overt aggression and defiance against rules and routines, it existed sometimes as an isolated symptom, frequently in combination with other school-related disturbances.

Larry had such an intense fear of school that it practically amounted to a phobia. In his own community, teachers had found that he could be managed only if they catered to his frank infantile demand pattern. Otherwise, he remained completely detached and daydreamed all day long.

## Traumatic life events

All children encounter experiences which have some degree of traumatic impact. Ordinary experience cannot be so protected that the human organism is spared, in its development from infancy, from encounters with various circumstances that have some shock effect. The child who is severely hurt in an automobile accident and has to spend long weeks or perhaps months in a hospital away from parents has been traumatized. Similarly, children who lose a parent through death are certainly exposed to trauma, even if their future experience is most carefully protected through the most loving adult handling from parent surrogates. Even these, however, are traumata whose basic impact can somehow be coped with by the child if his total environment is friendly and devoted to his needs. Seldom do we see children who have been so grossly and continuously exposed to traumatization on so many different levels as the "children who hate." With them benign experience is the exception, trauma the rule. From the things we know about them, it is this that emerges as the most powerful theme in their prior experience.

Andy, who had spent most of his first years in a chain of foster homes, was episodically taken in by his grandmother, a professional prostitute. Here he visualized open sexual relations between adults, including various perversions. The grandmother, perhaps in keeping with her own instinct-dominated pattern and also as a means of avoiding any responsibility for real ego training, was extremely permissive with him, granting him many exorbitant gratifications unless he displeased her, at which times he was severely beaten. When he was six, he was taken to live with his father and stepmother. Here there was as little basic acceptance as had existed in his former life but in addition an increased quality of rejection in that the stepmother was completely ungratifying and critical. His father, a passive, insecure man, completely dominated by the stepmother, added to this chain of trauma through his inability to protect Andy against the stepmother, thus completing the sense of disillusion and feeling of unwantedness that Andy may have hoped to overcome when he came to his own home with his "very own" father.

The injuriousness to ego growth of such casual, inconsistent, and emotionally cold contact with adults can be readily assumed. For psychological trauma is not only a function of destructive things that are done to the child. It is, just as eloquently, a product of what is not done for the child and, in the case of Andy, we can see an obvious mixture of both.

In other instances, the degree to which the child had been severely brutalized, in addition to having been exposed to inadequate, libidinally barren adult handling, was quite impressive.

Larry, born out of wedlock in a charitable institution, remained here for the first two years of his life. His mother visited him only occasionally. Between the ages of two to five he was shuttled about from foster home to foster home. Occasionally he lived with his mother in the home of maternal grandparents. When Larry was six, his mother came to Detroit and married a man much older than she. Shortly thereafter Larry came to live with them. He was six and one-half at this time. The mother was weak, passive, detached. Her tie to Larry appeared to be on a very tenuous level. The stepfather was a short, squat, powerfully built man. He was severely alcoholic, profane, brutal. From the very beginning of Larry's entrance into the home, he became the butt for the stepfather's primitive bullying. The degree of sadism that the stepfather expressed toward Larry is almost unbelievable. He was beaten severely, threatened with a shotgun, booted, thrown into a drainage ditch in front of their home, and locked in a woodshed for long hours without food. Many times the stepfather threatened, shotgun in hand, to kill him. The stepfather's motivation for this treatment of Larry, aside from an apparently frank and obvious sadistic temperament, was accentuated by the fact that Larry was slow, forgetful, clumsy in performance of heavy chores, and extremely infantile. In addition the stepfather, who had a thirty-eight year old son from a previous marriage from whom he was estranged, expressed an open hatred for all boys, saying they were "no good, dumb, can't be trusted, etc."

In the case of a child who has had such predisposing factors toward emotional disturbance as five and a half years of foster home and institutional care, to "come home" finally to such a pair of parents is the final blow to an already traumatic life situation. It was small wonder to us that, when we first met Larry at Camp Chief Noonday, prior to Pioneer House, he seemed to be in a state of shock, wild-eyed, disorganized, extremely infantile and primitive. It was only after the most careful demonstration to him that we really liked him and wanted to give him gratifications, that he could afford to come out of his shell of apathy, detachment and anxiety, at least enough so that we could eliminate a diagnosis of psychosis.

Events of this type were quite common to many of the children who were referred to Pioneer House. Their basic significance is the degree to which they display the extent and intensity of trauma which the children encountered. While the etiological relation of these factors to the disturbance we dealt with and which we describe in other chapters of this book is still not too well understood, it can be inferred. Clinically, there is no reason for doubting that these events were destructive to ego development in themselves, although the exact dimensions of the effects they exerted and how they are blended with other factors not in the traumatic area must be left to later research.[13]

*Did anything "good" ever happen to them?:*
*the missing links in their lives.*

From the short description we have already presented of the children, it seems apparent that, as we look into their past, we observe very few of the things that we might call "good" or "lucky" or "happy." Like the children themselves, who, as we shall later show, had such a pessimistic view of what the world might hold for them, we come away from this peek into the past with something like horror that a child should live through things like these and with a sense of amazement that even more destruction than we observed had not taken place. If we were to make a list of some of the "missing links in their lives," it would look something like this:

1. Factors leading to identification with adult, feelings of

[13] A significant beginning in this direction is already under way. See Ben Karpman (chairman), Louis A. Lurie, Hyman S. Lippmann, Reginald S. Lourie, Ralph D. Rabinovitch, Frederick H. Allen, Rene A. Spitz, and V. V. Anderson, "The Psychopathic Delinquent Child." Round Table, *American Journal of Orthopsychiatry,* 20, (1950) 223–265. Also illuminating on this question is some of the pioneer work of Bender and Schilder. See L. Bender and P. Schilder, "Aggressiveness in Children," *Genetic Psychology Monographs,* 18, (1935).

being loved and wanted, and encouragement to accept values and standards of the adult world.

2. Opportunities for and help in achieving a gratifying recreational pattern.

3. Opportunities for adequate peer relationship.

4. Opportunities for making community ties, establishing a feeling of being rooted somewhere where one belongs, where other people besides your parents know you and like you.

5. Ongoing family structures which were not in some phase of basic disintegration at almost any given time in their lives.

6. Adequate economic security for some of the basic needs and necessities of life.

It is important to emphasize that these items were missing from their environment—not that their disturbance patterns themselves prevented them from absorbing and utilizing them. This overview of the past lives of our children may provide a perspective with which to approach some of the more specific details about their pathology once they were in the treatment home.

# Chapter 2

## Disorganization and Breakdown Of Controls

### The "Control System"—suggestions for a purposely one-sided view

IF WE READ in the papers that the dam and locks on one of the wonderful reservoirs which our engineers have erected all over the country broke down and the whole force of the stored-up water flooded the valley below and caused unchecked destruction, we might have many theories as to "just what must have gone wrong." They would all boil down, though, to two basic "variables" which we might hold accountable for the event. We might assume that the dam and locks were perfectly all right, were in wonderful working order, and had been well built for the job that could be foreseen for them to perform, but that something went wrong on the "water force" side of the picture. For a variety of reasons, such an enormous and unexpected onrush of hydraulic intensity may have occurred that even the best equipped dam and waterworks arrangement could not be expected to cope with it. On the other hand, the "variable" to blame might not be the waterpower at all, and we could assume that something had gone wrong with the construction or the working order of the machinery or building material. In that case, it would not have taken an unusual and unprecedented act of nature. In fact, the water pressure might have been exactly what a normal dam of that size is supposed to cope with, but something gave way and couldn't check the force it was supposed to control. From just hearing about the flood, by the way, we could not know just which of the two situations we should hold accountable, and presumably in most cases there might be a combination of both involved.

No technological analogy should be stretched too far, for we know, of course, that human behavior is much more com-

70

plex than that, but the similarity in the situation does carry us to the one point we want to make: In spite of the known complexity and multiplicity of causes in human motivation, the question as to why a particular piece of behavior occurs in a particular individual can be viewed in terms of two larger sets of "variables." One may be summarized under the term *"impulsive system."* By this is meant the sum total of all urges, impulses, strivings, desires, needs which seem to push in the direction of gratification, goal attainment, or expression at any one time. It is somehow held in check by what might crudely be referred to as the *"control system"*—by which is meant those parts of the personality which have the function and the power to decide just which of a given number of desires or strivings will or will not be permitted to reach the level of behavioral action, and in which form. Whether one child hits another over the head may be viewed with profit in a manner which bears considerable similarity to our illustration of the water reservoir, if we can force ourselves to forget for a moment the obvious dissimilarities in the picture. His hitting the child may mean that the trouble lies with his impulsivity. His reality perception, his feelings for what is fair and decent, may be as well developed in him as in the next child, and his behavior may have been due to an onrush of sudden impulsivity which "overran" his controls. On the other hand, it may be an entirely different case. He may not suffer from any such present or case history conditioned upsurge of aggression at all. He may just feel a mild urge to hit somebody, an urge no more intensive than that of another child at any one time. Only, it so happens that this youngster has no "controls" at all. The part of his personality which is supposed to screen and check his impulses before they are allowed into open action may be deficient, not functioning, or closed for the week-end.

It would not be clear which was the case if we knew only that he hit him. The direction of the "repair job," however, would be decisively influenced by finding out whether this is primarily a situation of the one or the other, or a mixture of both.

There is just one more lesson we want to squeeze out of our technological simile before we leave it alone. The engineers who are responsible for the adequate functioning of our dam and lock works would, of course, be equally interested in both of the variables we have singled out before. They would want to know exactly where the water comes from and how much of it there will be, they would want to know the "Case History" of all the tributary rivulets, and they would certainly want to estimate the potentially "traumatic" experiences which might happen on any part of the stretch and raise havoc at the control end of the line. While they make this analysis of the "water force" side of the picture, they may temporarily forget about the details of the dam and locks themselves, even though they will never forget that eventually both pictures have to be brought together. Similarly, our engineers might, at some phase of their concern, concentrate entirely on a very specific analysis of just what job the dam has to perform, which part of it has to do what, and what might go wrong with it. If we asked them to demonstrate to us, they might invite us to go with them on an inspection tour. It would not be necessary to drain the dam of water for some of this. They could show us just how the various parts of the "control system" work. They could just ask us to "ignore temporarily" the question of where the water comes from and concentrate on the control works themselves for a while. And here is where we leave our simile in a hurry. It doesn't help any more from here on. For it so happens that, in the science of human engineering, we have much more specific knowledge of the "water force" side of the picture and its case history than of the "control system" and the way it works.

And this is where this chapter comes in; we are not going to attempt to write the whole story about the "children who hate." This would be a task for many volumes, even if we used only what we have accumulated about the children with whom we worked directly. We plan to concentrate entirely on trying to describe more specifically just what functions the control system of a child has to perform in daily life, at which points it breaks down most easily, and what such breakdowns look like when they happen. We know that this is an artificial isolation of factors, which can only be justified on heuristic and didactic grounds.

## The Concept of "Ego" and Our Clinical Task

Psychoanalytic theory has different names for what is in this book called, with intended colloquial looseness, the "control system." The psychoanalysts would relegate the "control" of impulsivity to two separate "systems," which constitute special "parts of our personality," the superego and the ego. Sometimes there is a third one described in psychiatric literature, the "ego ideal," but we think we can safely adopt a widespread custom of considering it as a special part of the ego and reduce the basic issue to just the two. For the non-psychiatric reader it may be explained that the "superego" is more or less the same as the "conscience." It is that part of the personality whose job it is to remind us of value issues that arise in daily living. The "ego" is supposed to "keep us in touch with reality," a statement whose specific meaning will soon be amplified. The distinction between "ego" and "superego" is not as difficult as it is made out to be. If a youngster doesn't take a dollar which just fell out of his mother's purse because he is afraid of being caught and getting thrashed, then we would say that it was his "ego" which limited his possessive urge along the line of "reality consequences." If a youngster doesn't take that dollar, even though he is certain nobody would ever find out, because he would feel bad to do anything which he considers to be a sin, such as stealing, then we would credit his "superego" with the success in impulse control. The concept of superego will be discussed more fully later. First, that peculiar agent within us which was given the name "ego" long ago by Sigmund Freud will be examined.

The history of this concept of "ego" itself would be a fascinating chapter to write.[1] Suffice it to say that, from some

[1] A most comprehensive discussion of the psychoanalytic theory of ego will be found in Heinz Hartmann's paper, "Comments on the Psychoanalytic Theory of Ego," *The Psychoanalytic Study of the Child,* V. (New York: International Universities Press, 1950). In it there is also reference to other important contributions by Paul Federn, Thomas French, Anna and Sigmund Freud, Edward Glover, Ernst Kris, Hermann Nunberg, Robert Waelder and

vaguely conceived agent within our personality which desperately tries to stem the flood of the "id" impulses, as a loyal servant of the "reality principle," it has gradually developed into a much more structured "department" within our personality, whose job description can be given with relative precision. Freud himself developed this concept of the ego only late and gradually and subjected its conception to many changes and improvements. As we have pointed out earlier, it was primarily his daughter, Anna Freud, who elevated the ego and its mechanisms of defense to a respected place in therapy, especially in work with children. Since then, speculations about the intimate and not always peaceful interrelationship between the "ego" and the superego and many other details have taken increasing space in psychoanalytic literature. The growing interest of psychoanalysts in work with schizophrenics has given "ego" psychology another boost, and the need to bring psychoanalytic conceptualization closer to the action scene, which was especially increased through the development of all sorts of "group therapy," has added its push. Foregoing the fascination of portraying those details and what they mean for the therapist, we shall be satisfied with attempting to sketch what, today, are usually conceived as the "tasks of the ego."

From what Freud and his followers said, and from what can be inferred from the way they use the term in context when applying it to clinical observations, the "ego" actually is expected to fulfill at one time or another, the following functions:

## 1. Cognitive Function

A. COGNITIVE FUNCTION, EXTERNALIZED. It has always been conceived as one of the main tasks of the ego to establish contact with the "outside world." In this respect, it seems to be the job of the ego to size up just what the "world around us" is like, and to give adequate signals about its imminent

---

others. See also Richard Sterba, "The Fate of the Ego in Psychoanalytic Therapy," *International Journal of Psychoanalysis, XV,* (1934).

promises or dangers to our well-being. This vague notion of "sizing up outside reality" must, of course, today be replaced by a much more specific breakdown into at least two sides of this "outside world." One is what we may call the "Physical Reality." That means, it is the job of the ego to estimate actual dangers or advantages inherent in physical situations. "I don't want to go to that dentist today," says my anxiety-ridden and comfort-greedy id. "You had better get there fast. Remember what they found out about tooth decay and dentist bills if you wait too long?" my ego is supposed to chime in. The other side of "reality demands" to which we are subject in this world might be shortly and rather crudely summarized as "Social Reality." By this is meant that the behavior of other people, individually or in groups, directly or through their institutionalized laws, customs, pressures, etc., is also a factor to be reckoned with. It is obviously also the function of the ego to become aware of existing reality limitations from that source and to give appropriate warning signals, should our behavioral urges threaten to run into conflict with them. Even a child who is clearly delinquent in his value identification, that means, one with little "superego" at all, would be expected to have his ego make a careful assessment of just in which case stealing is "safe," in which other case the very openly enjoyed and guilt-free act of stealing had better be omitted because of "reality risks" involved in discovery, capture, too threatening legal consequences, or difficulty in getting rid of the loot. In short, it is the ego's job to size up the world around us, in its physical or social aspects, and to give danger signals if any one of our desires is too seriously in conflict with the "reality outside." The term "cognitive" is taken from psychology, and it simply refers to the function of "assessing, discovering, sizing up, finding out." Our use of this term in no way implies whether the ego "finds out" consciously, or whether some of this reality appraisal remains unconscious while it takes place. We would assume both possibilities, depending on the specific situation, but the question is irrelevant for the establishment of the function itself.

B. COGNITIVE FUNCTION, INTERNALIZED. In the earlier definitions of the ego, its function of "establishing contact with the world around us," was usually emphasized. From the way the concept is now being used, though, it is obvious that an emphasis on a "cognitive appraisal of what is going on inside us" is an equally important job. In fact, some of the basic definitions of the role of psychoanalytic therapy are based on that very issue, namely, on the assumption that some id-contents cannot be got hold of by the ego, because they are repressed, that means, not even accessible to the conscious perception by the ego. If the ego doesn't even know what is going on, how can it get hold of it? This was the underlying tenor of the thinking even in the early stages of theory development leading to the demand that the repressed be made conscious. We can portray the situation implied in the following way:

COGNITIVE APPRAISAL OF ITS OWN ID. By this we mean the awareness by the ego of the most important impulses, urges, desires, strivings, fears, etc., that obviously motivate our behavior, but are not necessarily always known to us. To know as much as possible about what is really going on "in the cellar of our unconscious" always has been a primary job of the ego, if it wants to retain or regain its health. In other words, it seems that all insights, including those into ourselves, are a function of the "ego."

COGNITIVE APPRAISAL OF ITS OWN SUPEREGO. It is also one of the tasks of the ego to register "value demands" coming from within, not only to register "reality threats" coming from without. It is the job of the ego to know which behavior would run counter to what the specific personality "believes in," what its own superego considers fair or decent, or which behavior would, if allowed to go through, produce the horror of deep shame and nagging guilt. Ample evidence was produced in later psychoanalytic work to show that superego particles, too, can be unconscious and repressed. In those cases, it is the ego's job to become aware of the voice of its own conscience, and the therapist's task to help the ego onto that road. In short, "know thyself" does not only mean "know what your most secret strivings would make you do if they had a chance," but also "know what price you would have to pay in guilt feelings, should you give in to them."

## II. The Power Function of the Ego

Though not always implied in the definitions, it has always been assumed that the task of an ego that is in good working order is not only to "know" what reality demands are, but also to exert some force, so as to influence behavioral strivings in line with that knowledge. Or, in other words, if my ego is smart enough to tell me I "ought" to go to the dentist today, but not "strong" enough to get me there, it does only half its job and is not much help to me really. This "Power Function" of the ego is a most fascinating metapsychological problem, because we have so far wondered and speculated a good deal as to just where the ego is supposed to get the "power" to suppress impulses and drives. This problem was a difficult one in the early phases of theory, when the ego was supposed to be little more than a "voice" telling us about the world outside. We have come a long way since then. We have to assume, for any usable conception of the ego, that it somewhere has access to a power system and then can use whatever energies it has at its disposal to enforce the dictates of its insights upon our pleasure-greedy impulse system. By the way, this is what we should mean when we say an ego is "weak." Unfortunately, the term "weak" is also used freely to indicate simply that an ego doesn't function well. We shall limit our use of the term "ego weakness" only to those situations where a disturbance of its power function is clearly meant.

## III. The Selective Function of the Ego

When confronted with an outside danger or an inner conflict, it is not enough to know what the situation is and to be ready to block inadmissible impulses—the ego has a few other decisions to make. For there is usually more than one way to react. The old idea that all the ego has to do is to decide whether an impulse can be afforded or not is an oversimplification which needed debunking long ago. Even in the most flash-like and simple situation, where the ego resorts to ready-made, stereotyped, reflex-like "defense mechanisms," it still has to select one from quite a number. Let's assume that a child suddenly becomes aware that the rest of his pals are engaged in some "dirty talk" which seems highly status-loaded in their gang but of which he doesn't understand a word because of parental overprotection and lack of sophistication. He has a variety of ways in which to react to the emerging conflict. He can deny his desire to be in on the talk. He can add "reaction formation" to this trick to make it more foolproof. Then he will get very indignant at the very insinuation that he might want to know about things like this and will even ward off his friendly therapist's help along the line of sex information. He may, on the other hand, simply withdraw, and this he may do on different levels and with varying scope. He may, for instance, simply avoid being near those bad boys; he may try not to have to play with them. On the other hand, he may ask to be transferred to a different group. Or he may have to cement his withdrawal with wild accusations and gossip propaganda against these youngsters. Finally, he may not do any of these things. He may successfully repress during daytime what is going on inside him, only to be flooded with bad dreams or night terrors, or plagued by insomnia or anxiety attacks.

Of course, our youngster doesn't have to resort to these automatic defense mechanisms at all. In that case he has to meet the problem on a reality level. Then, his ego has to make even more far-reaching decisions. Maybe he simply can tell his father and have a man-to-man talk and ask him what all those things the kids are talking about mean. Maybe he can ask another boy or his counselor. Or maybe his group skills are so well developed that he simply forces or inveigles the others into "cutting him in on it," swallowing the unavoidable transitional razzing he will get in order to solve the problem once and for all. In these cases, too, his ego will have quite a job to do. It will not only have to appraise just which of these paths are open to it but it will have to "inspect the tool by which reality is being met" as to its potential ability to solve the problem. It will have something like a "tool selection job in terms of efficiency appraisal" to perform.

This "selective function" of the ego has not been sufficiently dealt with in psychiatric literature. It is usually thrown into the general chapter on "reality testing." We think that it is important to differentiate between the testing of the reality to which the child has to adjust and the testing of the techniques and their reality-relatedness by which the child tries to bring about this adjustment. In the study of the "children who hate," the disturbance of this function becomes painfully obvious. We would like to see it established as an ego function in its own right.

## IV. The Synthetic Function of the Ego

The concept of a synthetic function, a much later addition to ego psychology, has led into fascinating but also specifically metapsychological speculations. One of the latest studies around this issue is that of Nunberg.[3] Here, we do not want to enter into such metapsychological speculations. We are using the term "synthetic function" in a somewhat simplified way. This is what we have in mind: if we assume that there are a number of "parts of the personality" at work, each one apparently equipped with some "influence" in the internal household affairs, then the job of putting them all together and keeping them in some sort of balance with each other must somewhere be ascribed to "somebody" in the picture. We suggest that the ego be given this task. In other words, it is also the ego's job to decide just how much a personality shall be predominantly influenced by the demands of the impulse system, the demands of outside reality, the dictates of its own conscience. It seems that "personality disbalance" can result from any one of a number of "wrong" assortments of power distribution. For instance, if the superego is allowed to dominate far beyond what an individual can sacrifice and still remain healthy and happy, you get a virtuous person, who will finally break down under his own frustrations or have to become hostile and nasty for the same reason. On the other hand, if impulsivity is entirely rampant, the present state of happiness will soon be destroyed by the conflict with the "outside world" which may result in lifelong incarceration, or by the "nagging guilt" from within, if too strongly estab-

[3] Hermann Nunberg, "The Synthetic Function of the Ego," *International Journal of Psychoanalysis*, XII, (1931).

lished value issues are allowed to be violated by a too little vigilant ego. In brief, it is the job of the ego to balance the various demand systems and to keep this balance "reasonable" on all sides. We think, by the way, that the term "balanced personality" should be reserved for this issue rather than be used as widely as is currently the custom. The most glaring illustration of a one-sided handling of the synthetic function by the ego is the one which will engage us soon, namely, the case where the ego throws its weight entirely on the side of impulsivity or of a delinquency-identified superego —a situational distortion for which we plan to use the term "delinquent ego."

It seems, from all this, that the "ego" has to cover quite a wide variety of functions. We think that a rebuilding of the whole personality "model" is long overdue.[4] For the duration of this book, however, we prefer to stick with this somewhat widened but basically unchanged conceptual system, for reasons of traditional convenience.

## Ego Psychology and the Practitioner

The therapist dealing primarily with adult cases belonging in the realm of classical anxiety and compulsion neuroses, hysterias, and their close relatives, and operating within the framework of the interview technique on the couch, has been late in developing his interest in ego psychology. Not that the basic concept of the ego as developed by Freud had not always been taken for granted. But there was little need for him to elaborate much further on it. Indeed, most of those people whose disturbance falls into the description above have their egos pretty well intact, with the exception, of course, that it is over-ridden by their libidinous pathology in the special area of their disease. The therapist is interested, therefore, in the shenanigans of the ego only in so far as it hits his treatment scene along the line of resistance and defense, and he has learned how to deal with it there. Only in recent

[4] Interesting steps in the direction of a new design seem to be taken in Erik H. Erikson's *Childhood and Society* (New York: W. W. Norton and Company, Inc., 1950).

years has there been a sudden upsurge of interest in "ego psychology" and the need for it is especially felt by those who are trying their hand with more mixed disturbance types, or with character disturbances and psychoses, or who deal with patients over whose life they assume partial responsibility by being attached to organizations like hospitals or the armed forces.

The therapist dealing with children has had his fascination for ego psychology stirred up long ago. Since Anna Freud's classic books, the respect for ego psychology can be said to be an earmark of the psychoanalytic school, as contrasted with those watered-down psychotherapies which still indulge in the old pre-Anna Freudian delusions of "therapy through total permissiveness of libidinous discharge." [5] It is interesting, by the way, that the public at large is not aware of this at all and, contrariwise, is inclined to assume the total permissiveness idea to be more typical of the orthodox Freudian child analysis. As long as the child analyst confines his work to selected classical cases of anxiety neurosis, compulsion neurosis and the like, and some character disturbances produced on the upper middle-class market, the interest in the "ego" is still relatively limited. The emphasis on ego psychology is primarily important in order to protect the integrity of ego needs on the natural life scene of the child. It is also a warning to the therapist not to forget that children's egos, like their superegos, are still growing and being shaped, and a reminder that even in the pure job of treatment, so far as children are concerned, "ego support" may be an important task, not of the educator only, but of the therapist himself. Valuable additions to our knowledge of "ego development" are due to this emphasis on ego psychology in the classical child analysis. The trouble here is not the emphasis but the total shrinkage of the field itself. With the narrowing down of trained child analysts in the United States numerically to a negligible handful, and with the reduction of even their practice to only a small children's load, this source of additional material for ego psychology has practically been drained off.

The situation is nearly reversed as soon as we leave the therapist who functions in a protectively designed office,

[5] Anna Freud, *op. cit.*

couch or play therapy framework, and talk about the "practitioner" in terms of the people who somewhere have to survive with the surface behavior of children in the raw. In this category fall all the parents, the teachers, group workers, recreation leaders, workers in children's institutions, and also all those workers on the margin or in the midst of the clinical scene, who are more heavily loaded with direct responsibility for child behavior than the therapist in his classical role. This includes, then, police officers, probation workers, social case workers, clinical psychologists and psychiatrists affiliated with schools and institutions where children live. Workers and psychiatrists in social agencies and child guidance clinics and the like also partly belong in this category because of their wide-open case load. Even where their task may be limited to special therapy like that of the child analyst, they are not able to select the cases with classical problem syndromes for which psychoanalytic therapy was originally designed. They are flooded with cases which they feel don't really quite "belong" to them, such as open delinquents, pre-psychotics, schizophrenic children, or the secondary emotional and behavioral implications rising on the grounds of physical handicaps, epilepsy, etc. They are, of course, also flooded by the deluge of behavior syndromes which somewhere are classified as "character neuroses," "primary behavior disorders," "psychopathic states," or just "personality disturbances," for lack of an open admission that we don't know what's wrong with them.

The moment workers are saddled with such cases, their proximity to the behavioral scene comes close to that of the parent or teacher. In direct proportion to this proximity their interest in what we called the "control system" goes way up. For there is, indeed, little material available on this question. We know more about just why children want to do what they do, and what caused them to get that way, so far as the specific content of their urges, impulses, and emotions are concerned. We have few publications that give us concrete information about just what it looks like when a youngster's control system is out of joint, or what techniques on our side would be directly supportive of the ego over and beyond what we can do in a straight therapy situation in terms of verbal ego support.

It is because of this helplessness which the total field is in, the moment it comes to a specific knowledge of the functioning, the pathology, and the instrumentology of ego disturbances, that we have decided to give this book such a heavy slant in that direction.

The reasons that the "practitioner" who also works in the fox holes of child behavior in the raw is so concerned with more data on ego psychology and the functioning of controls seem to flow out of three facts:

*Symptom Survival*

Even in cases which are being treated in classical psychoanalytic detachment from the scenes of daily life, somebody in the framework of their natural habitat has to survive with the symptoms as long as they last. This somebody may be the child's parent or foster parent. It may be his group leader, teacher, housemother. It may also be the other child in his group, in his block, in his dormitory. Now, survival with a child's symptoms is strongly dependent on just how much of the child's ego is still intact. And, where it is not, we have to plan just how his life frame must be manipulated, how his behavior must be handled, so that the child and others around him can still exist. Somebody will have to react to the child's behavior. Even though this reaction is not meant to be part of the "real therapy," it has to be efficient at the same time that it remains "hygienic." Those who live with the child, therefore, will have to know, and those who do their special tricks in their own interview work will usually have to tell them, not only why the child got that way and why he feels he wants to "set the joint afire," but also, just what you do when he tries. They will have to help them to find out how to stop him without injuring their relationship to him, just what life situations his ego might manage without losing control, which other life constellations would throw it into confusion. They will want to know under what conditions his pathology can be expected to remain safely dormant, which others lure it into uncheckable acting-out.

Wherever the therapist enters an "action frame of life," as in a clinical camp, a therapy club, a treatment home, the issue of "symptom survival," of course, becomes even more directly his concern. The very process of therapy may have to be modified because of this. It is one thing to encourage a child to claw out the doll-sibling's eyes. They can easily be replaced. But none of us would advise this as clinical strategy where a live prop is involved, like another child in a therapy group. Yet, the therapist obviously could not forbid the youngster to have such desires, or to express them. He would be eager, however, to give the youngster enough "ego support" so that he can keep them on a "fantasy level."

In short, without knowing more than we do know about just how the "control machinery" works, our advice to parents and child practitioners in the field of daily life would be bound to remain general, vague, and not very helpful. And our own ability to handle more children in life-involved therapy situations would be in desperate straits.

## Developmental and Educational Support

All children, even children in treatment, go through certain clearly marked "developmental phases" with their own tasks and their own problem. In this process, especially in highly "transitional moments" from one phase to the other, the "control" system also undergoes changes and finds itself suddenly confronted with an enormous task. We know this especially well from the study of the transition from later childhood to early pre-adolescence, and again at the onset of sexual maturation around puberty. Just what happens to the ego at that time, which of its functions will have to be supported or even substituted for, and what internal changes can be expected to occur? Current publications have a tendency to focus more on a description of the transition through the oral, anal, and genital phases of libido development than on the question of just what happens to the ego at the time. The very phrase "latency period," by the way, which has been so frequently picked up even by non-psychoanalytic literature, betrays the lopsidedness of this approach. For "latency" simply refers to the fact that open sex exploration is temporarily less active than it has been in the preceding stages. What an odd way of naming a phase after what is *not* happening in it! We would be as interested in the question of just what else is going on, and what happens to the ego of the child at the same time, as in the fact that libido development seems "latent." And a good deal happens to it, indeed, and ego support is one of the primary tasks of the educator, especially during transitional phases. How can we know how to support something the specific nature of which we haven't adequately explored?

Beyond this, all children, whether in treatment or not, require "educational support." They have a learning task to fulfill, in order to become normal members of the adult group in a specific culture. Not all this learning is directly related to the oral, anal, genital phase issues and the very agent which controls most of the "reality contact," the ego, is of course heavily involved. Especially the acquisition of sensitivity toward and of skills in dealing with what we called the "social reality" requires an enrichment and growth of the ego far beyond its earlier childhood stage. What can be done to support the ego, even that of a child with some pathology along other lines, to do its educational, acculturational job efficiently? How can an ego be helped to remain in good touch with reality and in good condition in the area of learning which it would have to undergo anyway even though and even while some other part of its pathology is being worked on? Or where are social protective measures needed, and just what is the "post surgical job" to be done to a youngster whose childhood neurosis has kept him from adequate social contacts, who is now free to start them, but who has missed the necessary ego development in that area in the meantime? The therapists will have to be interested in that, even where they direct other people to do that job. The "practitioner in the fox hole" can hardly live a day without hoping for more knowledge of the "control system" all along the way.

## Milieu Therapy

Bruno Bettelheim's term is originally meant to imply the exposure of a child to total environmental design for treatment.[6] It may also be conceived on a partial basis, in so far as we think a child's problem requires his placement in a foster home, the exposure to a therapy group every Wednesday afternoon, or the summer experience of a specially designed camp. In all cases we expect "environmental stimuli" to do the treatment job with us or for us. Whether partial or total, whether supportive or direct, in all those cases we want to design at least a piece of the child's environment so as to fit the whole child in a treatment-favorable way. We deal with the whole child in a total life situation even if only for a short time span, and with children this invariably means acting, not talking or fantasying only. In short, the problem of reality-contact and the question of control functions are immediately involved. How can we gauge, for instance, just how much encouragement a child should have to "admit his hostility against his brother" to himself, before we know whether his ego is in good enough shape to keep such hostility within limits, or whether it is disturbed enough so that he may have to try to choke that child to death? How do we know just how much of the need for aggressive expression should be allowed into the open, before we know which game structure will help the child's partially disabled ego to keep impulses on a halfway bearable sublimation level? How can we tell when to confront a child with the awareness of his "fault" before we know how his ego will react to shame and guilt and how much of these it can bear without breaking down entirely?

In short, the very attempt to treat children in and through environmental settings opens up a wide avenue of therapeutic enrichment, undreamt of before. At the same time, it also requires as an important condition more knowledge of the

---

[6] Bruno Bettelheim and Emmy Sylvester, "The Therapeutic Milieu," *American Journal of Orthopsychiatry*, XVIII, (1948), 191–206. See also, by the same authors, "Milieu Therapy," *Psychoanalytic Review*, XXXVI, (1949), 54–68.

"control machinery" and its areas of disturbance and of techniques of supporting and repairing it.

The most vital urgency for more data on ego psychology, however, is presented by the "children who hate." It seems to us that some of their basic pathology is intimately tied up with direct disturbances of the ego functions to begin with and, where their disturbances are limited to the impulse system itself, the problem of supporting their ego so as to survive "treatment shock" becomes a new issue in its own right. It seems to us that any of these children can be approached successfully only with a total treatment design available. In order to attack some of their direct ego disturbances, more knowledge about just what is disturbed to begin with is mandatory. It is for this reason that we want to focus now primarily on the description of some of the disturbances of ego function which we could observe in the Pioneers and in hundreds of other children, while we had the chance to live with them.

# Chapter 3

## The Ego That Cannot Perform

IT IS A WONDERFUL spectacle to watch a normal child at work or at play. And even a youngster who suffers from some minor neurotic disturbance or other but whose ego is basically in good shape takes most of the usual irritations of daily living in his stride. Take a ten year old, for instance, who just came home from a strenuous and not quite conflict-free day at school and, just to make the situation sound less idyllic, has had his plans for outdoor games thwarted by a sudden downpour of rain. True, he may be a little irritable at first, or hang around his parents or the kitchen and make a nuisance of himself for a while. Soon, though, he is likely to wander up to his room. The first irritation at the frustration of his plans mastered, he will survey his books and toys. Images of previous happy times spent with them will emerge in his mind. He will select the one or other that promises most pleasure gain at the time. He may even voluntarily add some more delay-frustration to his chore by thinking of friends he could call up or making plans for something special to do. In any case, he will know that it was only the rain that spoilt his fun, and he will not blame his parents for it. He will be more entranced by the potential pleasure from his toys than by the temptation to vent his ire on them for having to stay indoors. He will hardly stay for long in a sulk over his misfortune; you will find him engaged in something else, with the absorption normal and happy children are able to display in any task they engage in. If parents and educators only knew what a complex process is really taking place in order to make such a seemingly simple situation possible! If they only knew how many things could have gone wrong along that path, they would be grateful and confident rather than anxious and irritated by some minor discomfort which child behavior so often implies. Of course, not all situational challenges can be met, even by normal children, so easily in their stride as the above one. From time to time, their ego needs outside support. If this comes through, all is well. Therefore, parents and educators may be eager to know just how to support an ego in a moment when it meets a task somewhat beyond what it can cope with.

There is no better way of finding out than watching closely what happens if an ego *cannot perform*. The children who hate furnish us with a wide range of illustrations for that, and from them we may get ideas and suggestions of how we might meet the challenge of ego support for those whose problems are less severe. It is with this in mind that the following description of disturbances of ego function should be of interest to all, even those whose children's troubles differ sharply from the problems that beset those youngsters whose behavior we are about to put before them.

We think that all practitioners and all the teachers and parents of normal children, as well as those who survive in treatment or group care situations with disturbed ones, would benefit from knowing just what the job of a normal ego is, during a day's living. Since the complexity of the well-functioning ego is usually hidden behind the smooth performance of its job, the specific observation of the ego whose function is disturbed might give us the clues as to what really is going on, even where things go well.

In the following pages, then, we are making a purposeful detour, are committing an equally purposeful one-sidedness. To avoid all major misunderstandings, the following facts should be kept in mind while reading about the "ego that cannot perform": The fact that we concentrate on the issue of "disturbances" of the ego function does not imply that we want to explain them. This chapter is meant entirely to be on a descriptive level. All questions of just what may cause a specific disturbance are purposely excluded here.

This chapter tries to describe the job the ego is supposed to perform in specific life situations. The illustrations used cannot, of course, show the ego isolated by itself, but are forced to describe whole life situations, including the emotions and impulses in the handling of which the ego of our children fails. This may give, to the cursory reader, the appearance that our illustrations try to imply that the disturbedness of the ego function is considered by us to be the "real cause" for things going wrong to begin with. No such implication is meant. All we try to show is what it looks like when an ego fails in a specific life task in a specific situation. The illustrations must be read with this very clearly in mind.

The headings we give the various ego tasks, unfortunately, could not be kept on the same level, for linguistic reasons. We would have liked to name all of them either after the disturbance implied, or the function to be disturbed, or the situation in which ego failure takes place. To remain so consistent in nomenclature would have raised great language problems. We sacrificed, therefore, logical consistency in favor of readability. In each item, however, no matter what the title we gave it may sound like, we want to describe what task a normal ego really would have to perform in certain specific life situations. No more is implied.

The listing of our twenty-two points is, of course, somewhat arbitrary. Some of them are more complex than others. There is a good deal of subtle overlapping among them. Besides, each one of them can be disturbed in one and perfectly intact in another child. In short, the question of which of those disturbances appear in what syndrome formation is a problem not touched here as yet. It constitutes, though, an important issue for further research.

## 1. Frustration Tolerance

If we say that children have an unusually low "frustration threshold," we really refer to two entirely different situations. The first one is more or less a case of "impulse breakthrough." This means that a particular child, when exposed to a situation that might be frustrating, does not allow himself to be frustrated, but insists upon a total gratification of the full impact of impulses waiting to be released. For the practitioner this constitutes a great problem and is one of the reasons why such children seem so intolerable and unmanageable when placed with more "normal ones" in the same program or the same home. Unable to take even mild frustrations, they insist on pouring the whole power of impulsivity into the open no matter how disastrous the result.

The second situation referred to by the term "a low frustration threshold" is equally exasperating for the educator, but involves a rather different psychological problem. In this case, the children allow themselves to be exposed to some minor doses of frustration, but are totally unable to handle the feelings which are produced by that frustration. The irritation these soon cause is not so much a breakthrough of their original impulsivity, but is the result of the aggression, anxiety, or panic produced by the situation itself. While able to enter, for a short while, a potentially frustrating situation, they seem to be hopelessly disorganized as soon as the first frustration effects set in. They develop frustration panic, aggression, and destructive outbursts in situations the more normal child would easily "take in his stride."

In both situations, it is obvious that the ego doesn't do its job. In the first case, it seems helpless in view of an onrush of impulse intensity or some "impulse pile-up" and cannot block the breakthrough of impulsivity no matter what the price. In the second case, the ego seems helpless when confronted with the quantities of aggression, fear, discomfort produced by even mildly "frustrating" situations, and the child breaks into disorganized confusion in the face of even low frustration doses.

Both situations reveal by indirection what a complex job the healthy ego really has to perform and how what is really the result of quite specific ego functions is frequently taken for granted and hardly noticed until something goes wrong.

Our Pioneers certainly provided us with ample evidence about the mechanics of "frustration tolerance," by the obvious breakdown of ego control in a wide variety of situations. They were especially low in their ability to block any ongoing impulse push for even short periods of time, and the helplessness of their ego in view of even mild doses of frustration-produced aggression or fear was pathetic to watch. Even in the midst of a happily enjoyed game the slightest additional hurdle to be met or mild frustration to be added would throw the whole group into wild outbursts of unstructured bickering, fighting, disorganization, and griping. Even small quantities of limitation, no matter how wisely imposed, and how realistically designed, would bring forth temper outbursts which, in other children, would only happen as a result of exposure to extreme threat or mishandling.

The kids burst out of the station wagon in their usual exuberant mood and barged madly up the steps into the house. Luckily, this time the door was open so the usual pounding, kicking of door, etc., wasn't necessary. I was in my office tied up in a phone call and the door was closed. Mike yelled for me, shouting something about his jack knife which I was keeping in the drawer for him. I put my hand over the receiver and said "O.K., come on in." But the lock had slipped on the door and he could not open it. Before I even had a chance to excuse myself from my phone conversation, and say "Just a minute, I'll be back" he was pounding on the door, kicking it, calling me a "sonofabitch" repetitively. I opened the door and gave him his knife. Even this failed to quiet his furor and, when I commented on the obvious fact that I hadn't even meant to make him wait, that the lock had slipped, all I got was a snarling, contemptuous "Shit." (Entry: 4/7/47, David Wineman)

One of the most regularly occurring frustration reactions, during the early phase of treatment, would be produced when, on our numerous station wagon trips, we had to stop and wait for traffic signal lights. This was intolerable to the children. Even though they knew that this delay would be automatically terminated in thirty to forty-five seconds, though they could so to speak *see* it right out there in front of their noses, still they were unable to handle their tension. Aggressive behavior would break out: throwing things at the counselor who was driving, cursing and hitting each other, etc. Shouts of "Goddamit, let's go, hit the bastard up there, what the hell are we waitin' for," would fill the air.

## 2. Coping with Insecurity, Anxiety and Fear

The description, diagnosis and explanation of the high number of anxiety stages and fears our children displayed over the years, would be an interesting task in itself. The attempt to get at the roots of some of these anxiety stages constituted an important part of our total therapeutic job.

All this, however, is an entirely different story from the one we want to get into here. We are not interested, at this moment, in the description and evaluation of the anxieties and fears children have, but in the problem of just what their ego does with them. It is true that in cases of a classical anxiety neurosis the role of the ego in the production of the final symptom is so submerged that it becomes hardly visible without painstaking reconstruction. Yet, the task of coping with anxieties and fears is not limited to the egos of anxiety neurotics—it is part and parcel of the daily job to be fulfilled by any ego, even that of the most healthy child. It seems to us that this factor is worthy of special emphasis. Most children have a wide array of techniques available with which they cope with minor or medium-sized quantities of anxieties and fears. Without stretching terminological distinctions too far, for the purpose of this study we might want to differentiate roughly between such stages of anxiety which are very reality-related—where there is at least a large factor of real reason for "danger" inherent in the situation which produces the fear—and more "neurotic" types of anxieties—where the emotional state thus named seems to have little relevance to actual outside stimuli. It seems, in the main, to come as an "onrush from within." It would be convenient to call the first type of experiences "fear," the second "anxieties," but we know that common language usage cannot be pinned down to such willful distinction.

Most youngsters have a wide variety of ways in which to cope with situations of reality-determined "fears": their ego gives a clearcut danger signal, and then proceeds to utilize any one of the techniques so amply described in psychiatric literature. A child may simply decide to sharpen his reality testing, so as to be more vigilant in the future. He may gain security from practicing realistic skills of danger avoidance or danger-victory, as the child does who happily learns how to box and wrestle, when he suddenly finds himself confronted with survival in a neighborhood group tougher than the one he was used to before. Others may simply put much effort into learning to avoid the danger, without having to leave the danger-involving activity itself—as, for example, the child who learns to master the cautious use of ax or firearm instead of having to develop anxious avoidances of such preoccupations altogether. The most reasonable way out, for others, is simply a readiness to ask for help around the danger area, as any happy child in a cheerful learning situation at school would do when confronted with a sudden hurdle in his pursuit of problem-solving. When confronted with unavoidable areas of danger that cannot be met, a child may decide to surrender the dangerous occupation area but may search for substitute gratifications in similar, more sublimated, or otherwise safer areas, thus balancing the partial loss an avoidance withdrawal would imply.

For another child, the emotional tie to a beloved person present at the time of danger, or the exposure to a "secure" and acceptant group atmosphere, may suffice to cope with fears which might have kept him from entering an activity.

The techniques used by children to cope with anxiety stages from within have been equally well described, and most lists of so-called "mechanisms of defense" could easily serve as a rather complete inventory. Some children simply hang on to an activity structure, so that minor doses of inner anxieties and fears can be taken in the stride of a well-planned activity program. Others develop supplementary daydreams to outbalance the otherwise dangerous loss of security that might come with an anxiety attack or withdrawal necessitated on the basis of neurotic fear or compulsive restriction of the life space. Others, again, manage to stretch their skill of gaining security through emotional ties to people they love from a technique to meet outside danger into an effective weapon against anxiety from within; with the friendly teacher around, the anxiety attack remains tolerable, while it would lead to panic or total withdrawal if it had to be suffered in "emotional mid-air." Some children, again, manage to build partial avoidance techniques around their symptom area quite skillfully into their total life space, so they can remain protected from too serious anxiety attacks without being considered more than "somewhat fussy or peculiar." They often even get understanding adults in their surroundings at least to tolerate if not respect their special "ritualistic avoidance machinery" and thus live with their anxieties without too much loss in their total life diet.

For both fear with real danger elements and anxieties from within most children manage to use displacement and acting out in daydreams as a rich resource. Clinging to fantasies of power, force, indestructibility or omniscience, or acting out terrifying play behavior or bravado gestures, they cope happily with what otherwise might become a state of panic or an anxiety attack.

Only in extreme cases, where the outside danger is too serious and too hopelessly unpredictable to cope with, and where the inside danger is based on too unbearable conflicts of guilt, do ordinary children resort to extreme reality denial on the one hand, or total repression on the other hand. Where the size of the outer or inner problem to be avoided justifies it, even the use of such extreme techniques is not considered as pathological as the techniques themselves might imply. We expect the child that would suffer total loss of love from the most important adults in his life for even a minor sex thought to have to repress sex curiosity far beyond what other children would have to do. It is not surprising that the imminent danger of total destruction through warfare leads even adults into stages of unrealistic but very comprehensive denials of all outside reality pointing to such dangers. Only in extreme situations would the more or less normal person resort to techniques otherwise reserved for more elaborate degrees of pathology, and the very existence of the "extreme situation" takes away the clinical stigma from such behavior.

The children we deal with here cope with anxieties and fears of all sorts in much the same way. There seems to be little doubt, however, that the following statements would characterize them and set them somewhat apart from their less or differently disturbed age mates.

The ego is *pauperized* in terms of specific attempts to deal with specific anxiety, fear, or insecurity feelings. It seems to be especially poorly equipped with those techniques which might reduce the fear or anxiety reaction to a minimum and keep other ego functions and activities intact. Even milder feelings of fear or anxiety may lead to total control breakdown, while other children would become anxious, but would still be able to carry on, especially if help were given.

Their ego seems to have to reach to rather extreme and drastic measures, which mainly lie along two lines. One can be described as *total flight and avoidance,* in which an otherwise pleasure-promising activity is abandoned in panic and avoided in the future, if even mild anxiety or fear elements are involved. The other is *ferocious attack and diffuse destruction,* where whatever is within reach, or whoever is near, becomes the immediate object of attack, or where the children "tear off on a binge of general wild behavior and destruction" in a more diffuse way.

They have a tendency to react so fast by these extreme techniques that self-awareness of the very experience of insecurity, anxiety, or fear, has no time to develop, or, if it does, is totally repressed. From their point of view, their panic flight and anxiety-based destructiveness are undifferentiated from a case of real disgusted withdrawal from an unpleasant situation, or triumphant display of aggression and courage. It is a problem for the clinician as well to learn how to differentiate flight and destruction which are based on such anxiety attacks from their genuine counterparts.

Where their ego chooses less extreme measures but tries to cope with fear and anxiety on a displaced-fantasy level, it is still incapable of enough organized and simple fantasy structures to do the job. It has to resort, even then, to heavily prop-loaded fantasies, and nearly always involves extreme acting out. Thus, where a less disturbed child would gain comfort in an anxiety state from a daydream of fairy-tale power, our children would have to try to act like wild beasts, biting, threatening, tearing around, so that what their ego had obviously designed as a fear-coping mechanism created an additional source of conflict and problem with the world around them. In short, their ego, even where it tries to cope with anxiety stages, seems to be under such time pressure that it does not act reality-wise. For, even where Joe bites Larry out of *fear*, Larry is liable to react to the biting rather than to its original intent, and additional complications on the scene of actual life are the price the ego pays for such clumsy attempts at anxiety-coping.

> Practically the whole first year he was with us at Pioneer House, Mike had almost nightly attacks of excitement and aggressiveness at bedtime which would reach a climax when the counselor would leave the sleeping room after the story reading. His antics were very disturbing to the rest of the group. He would make high banshee wails, striking out at his pillow like an imaginary attacker, muttering fierce counterthreats against it (I'll kill you, bastard, bitch, mother fucker). Or he might branch out into vicious aggression against one of the other children mixed with teasing erotic seduction of the other into his wild mood pattern, with occasional sex play thrown in. Inevitably, every evening, we would have to take him out and sit with him for sometimes thirty to forty-five minutes. He would usually start out on a high plane of hysteric euphorics with whoever was holding him, again repeating with the adult some of the erotic aggressiveness he had displayed toward the children, wriggling and wanting to dart through the house so that he would have to be physically restrained by light holding until he reinstituted some controls. All along the only verbalization that was possible at all was gently soothing reassurance like "O.K., Mike, let's quiet down, everything's going to be O.K., you know it's like this every night. When you quiet down a little, you can go back to bed." Should we make any attempt to probe, to ask him what was bothering him, we got absolutely nowhere; as a matter of fact, it only increased his upset. Gradually, after about a year at the Home, Mike began to show definite indications of some new abilities to conceptualize some of his fantasies through words as well as through acting them out and thus, in connection with bedtime behavior, we

were slowly able to get him to talk. Finally, he was able to actually say that every night he was "real scared" that someone was going to "get him" and that this was worse after the counselor left and he was alone with the "guys." In this way, we were able to make the connection clear to him: "When you're scared, you get wild." It took a year before this point was reached with Mike.

The afternoon activity consisted of making very simple leather belts. The boys responded quite well, with the exception of some open gripes about how "hard" this stuff was to make. Most of them were quite interested and things weren't going too badly. Joe, one of the very last to get into the crafts room, happened to come in just at the precise moment when Larry was squawking about how hard the "darn things were to do." This apparently disturbed him, for he looked questioningly at me and Larry (I was helping Larry at this moment), grabbed his belt materials, ran out of the room into the toilet and flushed his materials down, shouting out to the others that he wasn't going to monkey with this "goddam junk that nobody couldn't do." The aftermath was even more ironic. He came back and began to snipe at me because now he "didn't have nothin to do . . ." (Entry, 1/1/47, Barbara Smith)

## 3. Temptation Resistance

An organized ego can give clear-cut "danger signals" if situations arise which "appeal" to impulses the gratification of which would lead to danger or guilt. An organized ego should also have a certain amount of "emergency energy" available, to throw into the fight whenever impulses are especially "tempted" by a situation in which the child may find himself. It is true that no ego is entirely foolproof along this line, and the idea that even the best of us may fall has become proverbial. But it seems that a certain amount of "special temptation resistance" is one of the normal tasks any ego has to live up to, and its inability to do so would be a disturbance of a special kind. With our youngsters, of course, temptation resistance is low. This means it doesn't even take a very heavy impulse, or the onrush of severe pathology, in order to produce a piece of unacceptable behavior. Often enough, these children are acting so much worse than they really are—by which we mean to indicate that even mild action potentials along the line of mischief or delinquency are easily mobilized in them, provided something in their life situation "brings out the worst in them." It is interesting to state, however, that often enough that "worst" has to be "brought out." Just what is it that "brings out the worst in children" anyway? For the practitioner's sake, we would like to arrange the most frequent "tempting" elements in children's lives around three categories:

*Situational Lure*

It seems that the mere presence and existence of certain gratification potentials is often enough to bring out impulses along that line into open action, even where such impulses were momentarily dormant or at least not very intensive at all. Few children, for instance, will withstand the sight of an accessible jungle gym, even though a need for climbing has hardly been among their priorities a few minutes ago. The presence of a large space to run in, a tunnel with certain echo chances, columns or trees around which to chase and hide, will immediately produce running, yelling, chasing, hiding behavior even though there is no special need for such activity.

Similarly, it doesn't take the full mobilization of the dormant urge of one of our youngsters for stealing for him to take some money that is left lying around, or the presence of which in the pocket of an abandoned coat is an irksome challenge to resist. It is better not to leave a football, hockey stick, or capgun lying on the chairs when we bring a group in for a discussion, ready though they may be to have a serious talk. The very sight of such mobility-gratification opportunities would "tempt" even a well-behaved child.

In short, even where specific impulsivity in a certain direction is not high at the moment, the mere accessibility and visualized usability of gratifying activities constitutes, in itself, a heavy pull toward acting out.

This afternoon, Shirley D. and I took the group to the zoo. It was a lovely spring day, temperature just right, gay Saturday throngs but not too crowded; the youngsters had a really marvelous time, with the exception of a neurotic sulk by Donald when we simply had to move on from one of the monkey cages to which he had formed a mysterious but strong attachment and where he was feeding one of the monkeys with his peanuts. This insistence on moving on was necessary out of group reasons since the others were getting quite restless and beginning to climb up on the outer rail, etc. All of the exhibits fascinated them, although they were always much more on the verge of climbing across guard rails than many of the other spectators. In some respects their behavior was quite typical for fairly active children until we got to the natural fish exhibit. This proved to be a veritable booby trap for youngsters with the disturbance patterns of our kids. For the natural fish exhibit was exactly as its name implies. While everything else in the zoo is caged in and protected from its human relatives, the fish in this particular part of the zoo are swimming comfortably within reach in a swiftly running but very narrow artificial stream. You see them just as in real life. Although there are signs in bold print reading "Do Not Disturb" "Trespassing is Punishable by Fine," the children were unable to resist. Harry suddenly announced "Those pike—jeez!" Off came his shoes and socks and with the same swift, flowing movement he was scurrying in the stream like a frenetic water bug and the others, with the exception of Larry, who immediately showed his characteristic anxiety and withdrawal at such taboo behavior, swarmed in after him. Other children, standing around and equally fascinated by the sight of those catfish and pike so temptingly close, were quite shocked by this display. (Entry: 5/4/47, David Wineman)

I took the group for a walk around the neighborhood at their request. It was a balmy, spring night and as we got near the School of Social Work, Bill and Mike announced they wanted to go up to see "Fritzie Witzie." I said "O.K." and that the other guys and I would go up, too. The place was half deserted; Fritz was in his office and not with anyone and it looked like a nice opportunity for a friendly visit. Somehow, in the melee, Bill and Mike were gone for a while and then showed up again, saying they had been to the lavatory just around the corner from Fritz' office. Then we went home and had an uneventful bedtime. Fritz reports, however, that the next morning the Dean of the School, who occupies the office across from his, was missing some money from his desk—about $2.00 in nickels that he had in the top drawer. When the group came home from school today, we talked with them about it and finally it narrowed down to Bill and Mike. After some considerable alibiing and stalling around, they finally admitted it. This is what happened: while they were milling around in Fritz' office, they noticed the Dean's door open. Naturally, they were curious and peeked in, and then saw a jar filled with sharpened pencils which he always keeps on his desk. They went over to look at the pencils, and, once so close to the desk itself, began to rifle it. When Fritz talked with them about it, they were not defiant and surly as they usually are after a confession of theft. They seemed abashed and embarrassed, especially Bill, who said, "Gee, Fritz, we really only wanted to come up and see you . . . Do you think we can come again . . . Will this get you in trouble in school?" (Entry: 4/20/48, Joel Vernick)

## "Gadgetorial" Seduction

It would appear that things actually talk to children, and suggest that they want to be used, somewhat in the way the fairy stories imply that children would "understand the language of flowers and birds." It seems that they have an inordinate need to enter the various activities a specific gadget appears to suggest. Thus a gun suggests manipulation, trigger-pulling, pointing, with certain throat noises accompanying the act. A piece of clay "suggests" the possibility of molding, manipulating, or maybe throwing it. A tree suggests climbing, a fence triumphant hurdling—whatever the specific gadget may be, it really seems to "invite" children to its use.

This fact has not been given the weight it deserves. For a long time suspicious of such argument because it sounds too much like an easy alibi for the mischievous exploit of harmless equipment, or a somewhat overanimistic interpretation of the lifeless things of this universe, we finally come back to it as a rather puzzling fact. Without at all being able to explain why this is so, we feel that the practitioner will agree with us that the inability to explain should not blind us any longer to taking this fact seriously, as it deserves. In short, even the ego of a normal child has a specific function to fulfill, whenever visualizing gratification-promising gadgets whose specific use is not appropriate at the moment. Without having had any impulse toward destruction on its hand, a child's ego may suddenly have quite a job to do along that very line, just because of the darned gun lying around . . .

> This being Easter vacation, the group was taken for a two-day overnight to the E. hostel where they had been once before during the summer of '47. They were really quite positive toward the place and especially toward Mr. E., a jovial, placid man, quite in sympathy with our program. He was, however, quite put out with them because of some rather reckless behavior in one of the lodges, in which they really messed up some spring beds by jumping on them just after Mr. E. had finished showing us through the building. As soon as he got out of sight they began to war whoop around and do acrobatics on the springs which were exposed, the mattresses being stored away until summer. In so doing, they did some damage to the springs. This was all the more striking because they were not in a wild mood, they like the place and Mr. E., want to come back. But the sight of those naked spring mattresses in that big empty room was too much for them. (Entry: 4/8/48, David Wineman)

> I took Mike downtown today for his shopping trip. In addition to regular shopping, he also had a gift coming—a rabbit's foot—which I had promised him, and we went upstairs to the toy department where, unfortunately, they

had some bowie knives on display. Mike was fascinated and, although I tried to divert him, he swiftly picked up the plastic bowie knife, hefted it and, although I made an interference gesture and said "Put it down, Mike; maybe another time we can buy one," it was too late for he already had sailed it down the aisle. As it was, no one was in the path of the knife, but the floor manager was quite indignant as he huffily put it back on the counter . . . (Entry: 2/5/48, Emily Kener)

## Contagibility

More "tempting" even than accessibility of space or seductiveness of gadgets as such is the visualization of enjoyment processes in action, the perception of ongoing activities enjoyed and indulged in by people. The mere fact that a youngster sees one of his less relaxed contemporaries throwing things around, banging his fork against the plate ferociously, jumping up and crawling under bed and table, may in itself suddenly set loose behavior in him of which he really hadn't thought until that very minute. In short, it seems as though sometimes behavior will "spread" and become "infectious" by the very lure its visualization implies.

We have named this phenomenon "contagion," and have been puzzled by its mysteries for many years. Some of it is very complex indeed, and has led us to such elaborate assumptions as the "exculpation magics of the initiatory act." [1] Other such instances seem heavily tied up with social relationships and prestige patterns. In a special research project we have had a chance to explore some of the peculiar laws it follows when viewed with such complexity in mind.[2] Sometimes the phenomenon seems to involve subtle issues, as, for instance, the problem of "impulse-control balance" and the machinery of anxiety assuagement and guilt. But the most basic effect within the whole complex of phenomena is this:

[1] Fritz Redl, "Group Emotion and Leadership," *Psychiatry* II, No. 4, (Nov., 1942).
[2] Norman Polansky, Ronald Lippitt, and Fritz Redl, "An Investigation of Behavioral Contagion in Groups," *Human Relations,* III, No. 4, (1950).

sometimes the mere visualization of acted-out behavior itself becomes the stimulus that gives intensity to a previously dormant urge, or throws the ego's watchfulness overboard, or does both.

Needless to add, individuals differ widely as to the conditions under which they would "contage," the impulse areas in their lives which would be open to such type of suggestibility, the people and status roles which could initiate contagion for them, what the counterforces might be, and how high their "contagibility" is altogether. Suffice it to say here, for our children contagibility was extremely high, and their ego was more than usually helpless confronted with contagion challenges. Even in areas and at times where their ego was capable of considerable amounts of impulse control, or had just made a serious resolve to be more vigilant, it found itself helpless in view of contagion effects.

> Before dinner tonight, the group was scattered around the living room floor playing with various quiet games—checkers, parchesi, cards. All was quiet and peaceful until Mike, who was playing cards with Andy, picked up one of the cards and idly sailed it across the room. Then he sailed another one, this time calling attention to it. Andy then whooped gaily and heaved several cards around. Danny, clear on the other side of the room, began to throw checkers. When Dave (executive director) started to interfere, it had no effect on the situation whatever, and Bill picked up the checker board, saying, "Watch this one," and heaved it. Larry elatedly grabbed a small wooden bowling pin and raucously threw it in the fireplace. The others were also throwing whatever was around and within reach—the air was thick with checkers, cards, pieces of candy, all in motion. Andy especially was exploiting the whole episode and Dave finally removed him from the room, taking him into the office where he had, to finish the whole show, a screaming tantrum which lasted about twenty minutes. (Entry: 9/7/47, Barbara Smith)

All in all, these three phenomena, situational lure, gadgetorial seduction, and contagibility, are of great importance for the adequate evaluation of what our children did, as well as, of course, for the problem of behavioral management itself. We shall meet all these phenomena again in other contexts. At this point, what interests us most is the inference that a person's ego, no matter how well or badly it functions in its overall tasks, may sometimes vary widely in the efficiency with which it fulfills its "temptation resistance" job. Our children had obviously disturbed "ego functioning" along this line, a fact which constituted a problem the seriousness of which we shall be able to appreciate when we arrive at our discussion of treatment techniques. The problem of just how to strengthen this specific ability of an ego to deal adequately with temptation situations, however, is not interesting only from the angle of dealing with the children who hate. It seems to us to be of primary importance for all educators and parents along the most normal line of educational tasks.

## 4. Excitement and Group Psychological Intoxication

We don't really know what the peculiar phenomenon called "excitement" is. The conditions which bring it about, the degree to which individuals are "caught" by it, vary widely and could stand more specific exploration. In general, it might be correct to say that two things happen more or less simultaneously—intensity, urgency, and vehemence of "impulses" goes way up, while the controlling forces of the personality seem to be reduced, either in power or in the quality of their functioning.

With children, we find two situations around which such states primarily seem to develop. (1) They often show a sudden increase of impulsivity on an individual basis—either for no apparent reason "from within" or in response to an especially stimulating activity their "excitement" reaches stages far beyond what we usually see them display. Any normal child impresses us as being much more "wild" at some times than at others, or works himself into a stage of "overstimulation" in the process of a game or while playing with an especially seductive toy. (2) More interesting for our study is the type of "excitement" which seems to be generated under certain group psychological conditions. Beginning with some minor free-floating contagion of the one or the other more excited youngster, the whole group sometimes may break out into stages of impulsive wildness which surpass anything that we usually would expect of it. Such a "group mood" seems to be especially catching, and under its impact even otherwise controlled individuals are liable to get "higher than a kite." We call this phenomenon "group psychological intoxication," because it really approximates most closely the well-known state of toxic inebriation, with all its concomitants differing only in that there is no alcoholic stimulant needed at all. What gets groups into such a state is in itself a most fascinating question worth a study of its own. At this point, we are not interested in the causation of such states, but in the specific predicament in which the child's ego finds itself when in its grip. Basically, there is a tendency for a considerable "loss of control" by the ego, and the more complex ego functions, even where otherwise intact, seem to go out the window first. Reality testing may become so blocked that recklessness of behavior may become seriously dangerous. Even otherwise existing value signals are not heard any more, or receive no ego response. The "here and now" of gratification greed seems to be unobstructed. The sublimation level of gratification channels goes way down, until the individual acts like a "primitive" or a person who is obviously drunk.

It seems to us, however, that this is not only a matter of degree, but that the ability of an ego to stand up under the impact of excitement and group psychological intoxication constitutes an item in its own right. It seems to us that, more or less independent from the question of just how much and what type of ego control a person has developed, the ability of the ego to stand up under those situations is a variable to be added to our psychological calculations. Even with normal children and adults, for instance, we can observe that some people of a high degree of control are apt to lose their heads entirely, even in a relatively minor excitement stage, while others, though impulsive and less controlled on the whole, seem to keep whatever ego controls they do have, even in the face of intensive excitational conditions. In short, it nearly looks as if it would be worth while to develop the concept of a "excitational and group psychological melting point of ego controls." It is this phenomenon that bothers us so much when even "nice" teenagers sometimes go hog wild under the impact of a group psychological orgy, and they themselves seem as unable as we to explain or understand what happens to them. The fact that generally low ego functioning or control power need not go parallel with a low melting point under the impact of excitation and group psychological intoxication is best documented by the amazing fact that some youngsters seem to be able to remain unaffected and "cool as cucumbers" where others, usually more controlled ones, "lose their heads."

From the observations of our children, we think we can make the following generalizations which may be of interest to the parent and practitioner:

With the exception of some specific cases where some of our youngsters would remain cool and calculating while others would lose their heads, most of the time the melting point of ego control under the impact of excitement and group psychological intoxication is *extremely low*. It does not take much to throw these youngsters "for a loop," and exposure to even relatively mildly excited group moods is liable to cut the youngster off from whatever control patterns he would have available otherwise.

The factor of high contagibility mentioned before increases the number of life situations which lead to total mayhem, while less contagible youngsters will be able to stay "out of them," limiting the problem area to fewer members of the group.

The rapidity with which our youngsters are sucked into the whirlpool of excitement is great, so that counteractions by the supervising adult have to be very fast indeed, and the diagnosis and anticipation of such states becomes a problem in itself.[2a]

With normal children there needs to be a certain "affinity" between the activity to be intoxicated by and the natural

[2a] For an interesting and acute description of some examples of such phenomena see Selma H. Fraiberg, "Studies in Group Symptom Formation," *Am. J. Orthopsychiatry*, 17, No. 2, (1947), 278–289.

mood trend within the child at the time. There also seems to be a considerable limit in "distance," by which we mean the range within which the laws of contagion still hold. Thus, for instance, a better organized youngster exposed to a rather extreme scene of wildness into which he hasn't been worked up gradually will be slow to respond. If the wildness goes beyond what he himself would consider fear- and guilt-exempt, he will not only fail to respond, but will develop a "shock reaction." He will be frightened and indignant; he will withdraw or seek protection from his own temptations.[2b]

With our youngsters, the law seems to be that exposure to almost any type of excitement, no matter how similar or strange to their previous mood, is "catching," and that even extreme behavior forces imitation, leaving little leeway for individual freedom from the phenomenon.

Dinner tonight was marked by an overflow of excitement which boded ill for our after-dinner program. Andy was a veritable "high voltage center" of contagion, having infected Mike and Bill with his obscenity half way through the meal to such a point that we set up their remaining food for them in the adjoining living room. While those of us who were left (counselor Bette, Danny and Larry, and our housemother, Emily Kener) were on dessert, we heard a hilarious screaming and shouting in front of the house with a furious blowing of horns. I rushed out to find Andy and the other two inching the wagon out into traffic, whizzing by at rush hour speed, by pushing on the starter. Seeing this, Danny, too, became immediately excited and tore out to join them and climbed up on the roof of the wagon. With considerable difficulty, I got them out of the wagon, whereupon the four of them rushed into the back-yard and from here into the alley behind the Home. Holding a brief "council of war," they proceeded to climb up on the roof of the garage and pepper me with debris. I knew that the only way I could get them off was to climb up after them, which I did. I expected them to continue

[2b] Fritz Redl, "The Phenomenon of Contagion and 'Shock Effect' on Group Therapy," in Kurt R. Eissler, *Searchlights in Delinquency* (New York: International Universities Press, Inc., 1949).

some place else which might be less dangerous. Screaming and whooping, they ran into the house and Andy, ringleading with virtuosity, egged the others on to throw rocks at me and also at the lights. On the way, incidentally, Andy slapped Emily viciously when she tried to stop him and also smashed a flower pot. By this time, they literally were so delirious that they didn't even know at whom they were throwing things—me, Bette, Emily, or each other. In this overflow of confusion, Mike and Bill picked up some pepper shakers, still on the table from our ill-fated supper, and began to heave pepper around wildly, in this way throwing it at each other as well as all over. The first time Bill was hit by pepper, he howled with rage and went after Mike, sprinkling it so badly into his eyes that he went into a fit of pain and rage. When Andy and Danny saw this, they got scared for the first time (thank goodness) and calmed down a little, and Emily and I ministered to Bill and Mike while Bette involved Andy and Danny in listening to the radio and a comic book story. (Entry: 9/4/47, Henry Maier, counselor)

## 5. Sublimation Deafness

The undisturbed ego, when visualizing a situation, activity structure, or a gadget which is potentially usable to obtain certain satisfactions, will be able to differentiate the usage which the situation or the gadget "inherently" suggests and the use it might be put to, in violence of its inherent potentials, as a tool for some other momentary need. A happy and well-organized child, for instance, seeing clay or finger paint material in a moment of relaxation, will have a quick grasp of what gratification such material is "meant" to offer. He will begin to mold it, use it in a variety of ways which arts and crafts experiences might suggest; occasionally, and in moments of comparative disorganization or excitement, the same child may pick up such a piece of material to use it as a weapon of defense or attack rather than as a means for the expression of an artistic urge. Or, to change the context, chairs are usually suggestive of a chance to sit down in them. This seems to be their inherent, their "built-in" function. In a moment of total disruption in a riotous political meeting, the same chairs may suggest themselves rather as weapons for a good fight, in obvious contrast to their "inherent" meaning.

With our children, it was easy to see how often the "natural voice" of situations and things would be out-yelled by the screams of their inside urges and impulses. It seems that they were "deaf" to the natural challenge of life around them, while sensitively geared to the push of their impulsivity from within. This ability to listen to the built-in, sublimational challenge of situations and things is a special function of the ego, the disturbance of which certainly poses a problem for the practitioner. The neglect of this type of ego disturbance has held up the educator and clinician considerably, and in a way has helped to cement a rather naive and unrealistic outlook on therapy, still to be found, from time to time, in recreation projects or even among clincally trained professionals. The general theory which still prevails and holds that disturbed children will become well if only they are surrounded by worthwhile recreational tools and opportunities, and that their impulsivity will easily yield to sublimated order, if only such a pattern is put within their reach, is invalid. We would agree with the importance of having sublimation challenges available at all times. We would differ in the degree of optimism with which we would expect the mere exposure to sublimation challenges a sufficient force to move the child into accepting them. Where this works, the problem is one of neglect rather than ego disturbance to begin with. With the children we describe, "sublimation deafness" is not cured that easily. Needless to add, this very fact of "sublimation deafness" does, of course, constitute one of the greatest challenges and problems for the group leader and for the construction of a clinically wise program. Having to learn by trial and error methods, we were faced with prematurely destroyed materials, with game chances ending up in general mayhem and destruction, before we could diagnose the existent "sublimation deafness" range of the individual children and the group.

A typical scene in the upstairs playroom during the first month . . . Joe would be darting around the room in his usual erratic fashion. Part of the time he would badger Larry, flicking out at him for pure enjoyment. Then he and Sam would chase each other, wrestle a little bit, separate and maybe pick up one of the already smashed toys and carry the destruction one step further. In this way, he would brush up near the old typewriter we had sitting in the playroom. It was old but it still worked after a fashion. Joe would smash at it, full fist style, and then, when the keys got all gnarled up, in frustration begin to curse at it, "Y'old bitch"—smash—"yah"—smash. Counselor might call over, "Want to type something Joe? I'll get you some paper." Joe's answer would be finally to knock the typewriter off the table and then kick at the keys before he dashed off in pursuit of Sam.

Andy sauntered into the upstairs playroom, picked up the box of erector set material and, after studying it for a moment, began idly to pitch the pieces into the fireplace —no fire—and then switched from this to throwing them at Larry, who is being severely scapegoated. (Entry: 12/15/47, Barbara Smith)

It was quite fascinating to see how the children used an old mahogany wind-up phonograph during the early stages in treatment. Tiring within minutes of its entertainment value as a record player, they would climb up and perch on its top and then jump off onto an adjoining piece of furniture. Or they would sail records at each other or against the wall. In view of the fact that, later on, record playing became one of their most popular activities, this initial unsublimated handling of the phonograph is especially impressive.

We took the group to the Sportsmans Show at Convention Hall, a large public, indoor arena, for which the sponsors of the Home had provided tickets. There was a profusion of guns and outdoor equipment and some natural born Indians at some of the exhibits. Although there was an initial flurry of interest, only Larry and Danny remained involved to any degree. We had to keep retrieving Mike, Bill, and Andy from the lavatory where they repeatedly escaped to smoke cigarets. Once back out with the rest of the group, they would run around looking bored or nervously flicking through comic books, impervious, seemingly, to the allure and excitement of many of the items on display and small sideshow activities that were going on in some places.

This contrast, by the way, becomes especially noticeable if we change from gadgets to live toys, especially animals like cats and dogs. The idea that the exposure to a dog would immediately make our youngsters respond to the challenge inherent in the culturally defined role dogs are supposed to play for children, or to the actual advance a specific dog might make to them, would be illusional indeed. His desire to be loved, his proverbial readiness to be loyal and companionable, his challenge for happy "have fun and play together" experiences so touchingly portrayed on calendars and posters, would be lost on our youngsters for a long time. Their reaction to the animals would depend less on the "inherent readiness" of a particularly well-chosen pet, and more on the level of ego disorganization at the moment at which they were confronted with him. Thus, for instance, exposure of our Pioneer House children to even the most cuddly dogs or cats in the early beginnings would have been disastrous. After a few moments of traditional cuddling and petting behavior, they would have reacted to the animal in terms of the impulse pile-up dominant at the moment, or in terms of the tempting willingness of the animal to be friendly, which, in their case, only meant temptation toward the display of wild quantities of sadism, power, and cruelty. Even at a later time, when we felt we could safely rely on the somewhat improved ego control and sensitivity to new gratification potentials in various walks of life, we had to remain watchful lest at any moment the original sublimational structure might collapse and the animals be mistreated. It takes an ego intact and sufficiently in control to perceive and exploit the natural, inherent, and culturally expected gratification potentials in the usual household pets. Their introduction into therapeutic life might be recommended as a test for achieved treatment rather than as an original therapeutic tool.

Bob Case, head counselor, reported to me that there was some sex play with the dog, Shep, over the weekend, the trio—Bill, Andy and Mike—being principally involved. They appeared to be using the dog as a new object for their sex crudities—wiggling hips and pushing out penis area of body in provocative way. I observed the same thing on Monday evening and on one or two other occasions. The pattern seems to be as follows: One or the other of them yells "Yeah, Mike" (or Andy or Bill, whichever the case may be) just as they do when they are obscene with each other, but they complete the gesture with the dog instead of each other. The dog gets excited (but not sexually) and runs over, sniffs and jumps around, whereby they start teasing him by running and then starting all over again. Danny has evolved a system of quite sadistic teasing, just as one would expect. He gets down on the floor with Shep, holds his legs and cuffs him, at first lightly and then harder and harder until the dog gets mad and starts to snarl and bite, which Danny lets him do and even encourages by putting his hand in his mouth, etc. Larry has developed a protector-pal relationship with the dog in which he lies on the floor, making fantasies of being attacked with Shep standing over him to protect him against his enemies. The fascinating thing about the dog, and it is already beginning to come out clearly, is that each child duplicates in his relationship to him some of the essential symptomatic patterns that occur in the relationships to humans:

Andy:   Disdainfulness and fastidious aloofness plus some sex activity.
Mike:   Sex excitement.
Bill:   Sex excitement.
Danny:   Sadistic-masochistic play.
Larry:   Reaction-formation against powerful insecurity feelings by protector-pal fantasies. He, incidentally, has the strongest reaction of all to Shep's being isolated during meals. He originally prom-

ised Shep on his first day at Pioneer House that this was one place where "nobody ever gets locked up." (Entry: 2/1/48, David Wineman)

## 6. Taking Care of Possessions: Guaranteed Later Use

The relationship of people to things owned can, of course, have the most complex implications. Such relationships may be highly dependent on attitudes to people of whom those things remind the owner; they may be filled with the ambivalences as well as all the other variabilities of interpersonal relationships. Besides, a lot of narcissistic investment may go into them, and occasionally the relationship to possessions—both inanimate and alive—may suffer all the distortions and deviations of the whole gamut of human emotions, through the range from healthy realism to pathological confusion.

All this is well known, and we would, of course, expect the relationship of our youngsters to gifts, toys, money, clothes, property, and whatever pets they have to fall into the same category at any time.

There was one thing that amazed us, though. At times, the relationship of a child to a possession as such was reasonably clear and simple, and even then he seemed to lack an ability which seems to be something rather special in the list of ego attainments. Even where the children openly coveted a possession and prized it, and even where their emotional relationship to it was relatively untinged by the complexity of the rest of their life, they didn't seem to know what to do with it. We mean—they didn't seem to have any capacity for what would constitute "responsible care" of the possession in question. For, no doubt, there is a certain minimum of respect and protection and care any possession does demand, if future use is to be guaranteed. It is this realistic minimum of "guarantee for the future" care which we have in mind, and which seems to be lacking at times, even where there is no special emotional complication in a child's relationship to an animal or toy. In short, we would expect our youngsters to lose, destroy, mislay, break possessions in the usual process of emotional ambivalence and confusion. We found, however, that even without that they simply seemed to be lacking in what is required to take care of or keep anything. This is why toys, fountain pens, watches, were used up so fast, why the turnover of wallets, flashlights, tools, was so great, even where we had not made mistakes in the choice of such items to begin with. With more complex mechanical possessions, by the way, there seems to be a recognition of the separateness of this ability to care for possessions even in normal adults. We might be sure of a friend's lack of ambivalence, but would still hesitate to lend him a typewriter, gun, or car, simply because some people without other emotional complications in their relation to the owner have no sense about the type of care possessions need, and cannot be trusted to treat them accordingly.

This disturbance around the task of "responsible care" constituted quite a handicap, since gifts and possessions of somewhat more complex structure were often needed for other clinical considerations and since the low frustration tolerance and the confused paranoid thinking of the youngsters often made emotional catastrophies out of even minor losses. It was fascinating to notice how our youngsters, when their ego was enough improved to desire and accept without conflict certain possessions and gifts of a more sublimation-demanding nature, would ask the adult to take care of them temporarily. This was especially true as a temporary and rather realistic anticipation of their own confusion and forgetfulness under moments of excitement: before a game or a fight, or on a trip, or for overnight care, the adult would frequently be made the guardian of possessions, even though the same adult had just before that been the focus of some entanglement or conflict. They had, by that time, a sharp enough perception of "responsible care" as a separate life task, of which basically friendly adults are capable even while you are mad at them, so that they simply loaded us with this special task as an intermediary step.

I took the group on a special tour to various gas stations and out of the way restaurants for the purpose of collecting Pepsi-Cola tops, which they need for a huge prize contest which is now sweeping the country. They were delighted with their yield and there was much fantasy about all they would win, bickering about who had collected most tops, who was "in," who was "out," etc. They finally made a combine out of it and all was peaceful. The tops were kept in an old oatmeal box. When we pulled up in front of the house, they sailed out of the wagon in their usual pent-up style and in so doing whoever was carrying the box dropped it in the flurry. I called after them to bring it to their attention and not one of them would even turn around to pick up any of them—their precious tops which they had spent two hours collecting. Mindful that this could be the fuel for a later group blow-up, I went in and more vehemently called it to their attention and said I would be glad to help but didn't they think they could help me pick some up? Danny didn't even look up from his comic book, and Mike and Bill, giggling and running around the room, apparently didn't hear. Finally, Larry, the most anally penurious one of the lot, came out with me and helped me pick them up. (Entry: 3/15/48, David Wineman)

This behavior was especially impressive because for once the group was really interested in collecting these items. How differently the normal child would have acted in guarding a collected treasure!

## 7. Newness Panic

For a while we missed this entirely. We were so fascinated by the spectacle described in "treatment shock," that we were liable to interpret any one of the behavior messes we got into when our children were confronted with any challenge whatsoever as another instance of their special "resistance" against change.[3] We saw in almost any confusion of that type either

---

[3] The term "treatment shock" refers to the intense reaction to the total impact of the clinical milieu which we observed in our children during the first three months at the Home. Their whole adaptation system, geared as it was to cruelty, deprivation, and neglect could not cope with an adult world that was benign and gratifying. The disturbed behavior that resulted is discussed in detail in Chapter VI, "The Phenomenon of Treatment Shock."

their "sublimation deafness" or their rather well-demonstrated attempt to ward off all implications of love, permissiveness, and kindness, so dangerous to their old pattern of "life against adults."

After things settled down a little, it became evident, however, that we had an additional deficiency of their ego to deal with, which is of a different sort and constitutes one of the greatest challenges to the program planner imaginable. The phenomenon referred to can be best described as a sort of "panic" which would hit those children whenever they were exposed to situations which are "new."

Of course, the question of what constitutes "newness" is a fascinating topic in itself. For the purpose of conciseness, let us be arbitrary and state that we shall refer to two different factors here, when using this term. Sometimes we mean by "newness" the fact that similar situations have not been experienced before (experientially new), while at other times we think more in terms of the youngsters' customary taste pattern and neighborhood style of life, compared with which the situations to which we expose them may have to be experienced as "strange" (sociologically strange). Under the first item falls the case where a child experiences something for the first time, and where this non-experiencedness in itself makes it impossible for him to perceive at all gratification potentials which this new experience might hold for him. Only after repeated and gradual exposure to such new experiences does the newness wear off, so that whatever perceptive acuities he might otherwise possess can help him size up the situation for what it really contains. The second phenomenon (strangeness) is especially noticeable in those instances where we deal with children whose taste patterns and behavioral styles are not identical with those of the book-reading and group-leading middle class. That means that such situations or such adult behavior is not only new to them, but seems "strange," which may have an undertone of being funny, ridiculous, frightening, despicable, as the case may be. This very "out of focusness" of the general atmosphere compared with what these children are used to may be sufficient to throw their cognitive apperception possibilities entirely out of gear. Needless to say, such inability to function in the face of new or strange life situations in itself constitutes one of the major hazards of an environmental total treatment design, and the assessment of just which life experiences or which adult behavior will throw the children into confusion on just that ground of newness and strangeness will constitute one of the major skills in program planning and treatment style for a long time to come.

Equally interesting is the type of behavior which these children most usually show when flooded with "newness panic" of either type. Three styles of reacting to it seemed prevalent among our Pioneers.

### Delusion of familiarity

We first misinterpreted some of the statements they would make when we got to a new place, a part of town unfamiliar to them, as an attempt to "brag." However, the phenomenon became so clear that we soon noticed that no such implications were involved most of the time. It seemed to us then that they were merely reacting to the implication of newness by denying it and superimposing on this denial delusions of familiarity.

> Enroute to Pioneer House, Larry kept bringing up at different points on the highway far from his parents' home that he knew this field and that farm house and this gas station. There were so many points mentioned that it is not conceivable that he could possibly have known all of them, especially in his diffused and detached state . . . (Entry: 11/31/46, Fritz Redl)

> Sam: Hey, Joel, did you ever live up in Alpena?
> Joel: No, Sam, I never did. I'm from New York.
> Sam: Hey, you musta! Are you sure? I knew a guy that looked just like you. He had curly hair and everything just like you. He was a nice guy. Maybe if he wasn't you, he was your brother or cousin or something . . . (Entry: 12/4/46, David Wineman)

> During the first month at Pioneer House every time we went out for a station wagon ride of any length at all

Danny "saw" one of his uncles, who was a truck driver. He had a simply unbelievable number of uncles and they all, according to him, drove trucks. Each time that we would run across a big truck, he would egg us on to overtake it so he could say hello to his uncle. The group, by the end of the second week, poked fun at him, but he remained quite serious in his insistence that he was right and that he really was sure that the trucks we saw were driven by his uncles.

## Assaultive mastery

Another reaction to "newness panic" especially where straight newness was mixed with "strangeness" in sociological style, seemed to consist of diffuse aggression, an intensive need to touch, manipulate, handle roughly, penetrate into, and explore everything within reach. Such "exploration," however, was quite different from the planned "casing" of a new place by an organized delinquent child. It had all the elements of panicky haste, nervous incompleteness, and flustering jumpiness, which marked it as a panic reaction rather than as goal-directed behavior from the start.

At the home of a friendly Board member who had invited us out to the country there was a kind of minor bedlam. Joe insisted on scurrying around poking through a secretary style desk they had in a den off the living room. There was no question of "casing" or "swiping' anything since our hosts, myself, and the counselors were in plain sight and a seasoned delinquent like Joe would never expect to get away with anything under conditions like that. It was rather a restless, aggressive coping with the unaccustomed novelty of a house like this with its luxury and many strange new items. The others too were seized by this frenzy of aggressive handling and poking around. Larry knocked over all of the fireplace implements—whisk broom for ashes, shovel, coal tongs—in a frantic movement to use some of them, and for good measure knocked the screen into the smoldering fireplace. Danny, of course, invaded the children's toy room and was shifting his clumsy bulk over tiny little fire engines and trucks. Andy insisted on doing acrobatic tricks from the furniture and was most difficult to calm down (Entry: 1/18/47, Fritz Redl)

### Buffoonery and ridicule

One of the most primitive ways of reacting to what is new or strange is, of course, ridicule (the new and strange thing or person is simply silly, funny, ridiculous beyond words). Even more primitive is a type of behavior for which the word "buffoonery" is only a feeble metaphor. It consists of behavior commonly called "goofing off" among the children themselves, and can be described as "clowning" only if all coherent structure or really witty comment is taken out of that term's meaning. It consists of a combination of grimaces and jerky and disjointed movements which are meant to be funny even though they do not contain any clue as to just what they are supposed to ridicule. All that, together with an astounding rate of turnover of gestures, postures, and mobility combines to form something like "diffuse clowning."

During a lull in the conversation which had been pretty positive after the very happy special treat of horseback riding, Joe suddenly said to Vera (counselor) very softly and gently, slightly mimicking her soft Canadian accent, "Vera . . . ?" and then paused. Vera answered, "Yes, Joe," to which he replied just as softly, "Are you gonna take a shit when we get home?" The group responded by cackles and snorts of derision, delighted by his coarseness. It seems as if being nicely treated by friendly adults who are interested in them is a little hard to get used to. The way Joe led her on with his soft intonation was just classical. We both thought he was going to make a very friendly, related comment. (Entry: 12/4/46, David Wineman)

I took a group over to the Arena Gardens for their first visit to an indoor skating rink this afternoon. They had all been clamoring for it, except the blasé Henry who chose to go to a movie instead. We had to stand in line for about 10 minutes before the rink opened. There was a huge crowd of all shapes and varieties of pre-adolescents and adolescents around. Mike started to clown around, acting like a drunk or "goofy" man, crossing his eyes and staggering around. Andy followed suit and added the innovation of throwing his hat up in the air, catching it on one of the fixtures and making me retrieve it. Joe was swooping around pretending he was skating already and Larry was making disjointed clown-like movements. Here again the difference between our group and most of the huge throng of kids around struck me forcibly, for none of them were acting anywhere near as exaggeratedly giddy as our kids and they couldn't all have been old timers. (Entry: 1/13/47, David Wineman)

By the way, we are aware that normal children occasionally show similar behavior. However, the smallness of the "newness item" which sets such behavior off in our children and the distortional degree to which they will go under slight provocation confirm the fact that the functions supposed to help persons to cope with newness realistically are seriously disturbed. For, coupled with this display of panic behavior, there is also a nearly total *absence* of the type of behavior with which an intact ego would try to reduce newness anxiety realistically; our children were little interested in really exploring or understanding those new situations, did not ask questions where other children would have expressed curiosity, and were inaccessible to the offerings of adults to show them things, to explain and interpret. They obviously did not want to cope with the newness item. If anything, they wanted to deny it and ward it off. Therefore, any attempt on our side to help them "cope with it," increased their panic and with it the irrationality of their antics.

## 8. Controlling the Floodgates of the Past

The amazing degree to which "fantastic and irrational behavior" may interfere in the lives of even otherwise "well-adjusted and normal" people has become nearly proverbial for "the culture of our time." We know that even people with good reality testing otherwise will often allow their case history to interfere when it comes to handling their own children or to assessing the feelings of people around them realistically.

The modern neurotic has been credited, by the very definition of his problem, with the right to have his case history creep up on him in such life areas as are directly related to his special symptomology. A person suffering from agoraphobia, for instance, may have all his ego functions intact, and may possess what is proudly referred to as a very "strong ego." Even he, however, will be expected to be unable to control his life reactions if something in the scenery comes too close to reminding him of a previous symptom-related trauma. Then, all of a sudden, his anxiety may flood his whole system, in spite of the fact that his reality testing is still intact. He knows there is no real danger from crossing a certain space, yet he will break out into cold sweat at the mere thought of having to do so. This means, actually, that only part of his ego function is well intact, that of reality testing. Another ego job is obviously not fulfilled—for he loses, against his own insight, all controls over the traumatic onrush from the past.

Demanding, on this basis, the concept of "control over the floodgates of the past" as a special function of the ego, which may be disturbed while other functions continue to work efficiently, it becomes obvious that in the lives of our children this special ego disturbance constitutes an enormously complicating factor. The difference of our Pioneers from the ordinary neurotic adult or the normal child lies primarily in two directions. The areas of life situations which may bring on such a sudden onrush of past case history beyond the ego's capacity to deal with it are not confined to special well-describable neurotic symptoms but seem to encompass a much wider range of things, and the totality with which a loss of ego control takes place once the floodgates of the past are opened is not comparable with anything the normal adult or child or the neurotic would do in a similar case.

This is, of course, a technical challenge for therapy—and for anybody who is interested in custodial care of such children. For program, as well as adult handling, has to be planned constantly with this concept in mind, and any experience, well designed for all but this one point, may turn from a therapeutic blessing into behavioral chaos at the drop of a trauma. This is one of the reasons, by the way, why such children need the total environmental approach, why the person around the child when he "acts-up" is more important in the total therapy than the strategy planner of the psychiatric map, and why the practitioner of the past has felt he has been helped so little in his task if only given basic insight into the disease's main design without practical hints for the manipulation of surface behavior. Needless to add, this very phenomenon is of great diagnostic value in work with children whose ability for verbal recollection or artistic expression of previous life traumas is as limited as that of the Pioneers. The following illustrations are meant to render the flavor of such incidents rather than to take the place of a laborious interpretation of the process as such, which has been well described by other authors before.

Mike began singing "Here Comes the Bride" in dirty words when Betty (co-counselor) came into the room. Since there was already considerable group psychological excitement and this was just a final stir-up which would have precipitated a riot of obscenity and aggression, when Mike refused to stop immediately, he was removed. Larry then picked it up and again refused to stop upon request so that the head counselor, obliged again by reasons of group hygiene, had to remove him from the room, too. This was too much for Larry. Although usually docile and clinging to the adult and well aware that he is loved and well-treated, this spectacle of the head counselor actually removing him bodily played back into memories of brutality-loaded moments with his murderous stepfather. As if by a pre-arranged signal, the moment the head counselor began to move him, he unleashed a torrent of counter aggression, and hooked his legs in a steely scissors grip on a nearby table. I helped the head counselor take him to the office and finally it was necessary for me, too, to begin to help in the holding. His usual stuttering disappears in the rage states, his voice is actually projected at you, and the content of his verbalization is of the most aggressive sort, a wild and primitive torrent. In the giving up of partial reality testing, he began to revile the head counselor paranoiacally with accusations such as "You want to twist my arm off, you want to kill me, you want to hurt my muscles, you want to choke me" all of which things, as we know from his case history, his stepfather actually did threaten to do. Along with this phase of the attack came his most serious dropping of reality thinking with remarks like "I'll kill you, yes, I will (all with most primitive lunging, biting movements of his head), I'll throw something right through you." (Entry: 11/22/47, Paul Deutschberger)

After a visit from his mother, Bill suddenly and spontaneously, in a semi-detached way, went upstairs, announcing to no one in particular that he was going to take a shower. I went up after him because this was a notably queer impulse, he wasn't dirty, it was not shower time, he was not interested obviously in wild shower room play since there was no invitation in his attitude toward the rest of the group. Abstractedly he undressed himself and began to soap and wash himself, still retaining that kind of somnambulistic facial expression that had first attracted my attention. Suddenly, in a savage outpouring of verbalization, he began to curse with the most primitive swear words at nothing at all. When I asked what was wrong, he shifted to his mother, saying she was a no good bitch, a fucker, was never any good, he hated her, his goddam brother was mean and wouldn't help his father who was going to die and he, Bill, had to go home and help out. (Entry: 4/13/48, Paul Deutschberger)

In this sequence of behavior, we can see Bill between two stages of ego development: The earlier Bill, during the first stages of treatment, might have burst out in this way in the middle of a game that he joined after his mother left. Or, maybe at dinner or snack time that evening. By this time, however, his ego shows improvement in his assessment of social reality. He removes himself from the group situation to the privacy of the shower. While this is undoubtedly a gain, his ego is still quite helpless to cope with the impact of suddenly unleashed case history material *per se*—the outburst has to erupt even though in the safety of the shower room.

## 9. Disorganization in the Face of Guilt

Guilt feelings are the signals by which a normal conscience makes itself felt when values for which it stands have been infringed upon. Thus, far from being something "pathological" in themselves, normal guilt feelings are one of the most essential constituents of a healthy personality.

The main trouble here with the children we talk about is not that they have too many guilt feelings, but that they have too few. Just why that is so and what is wrong with the superegos of our Pioneers will be described in a later chapter. At this point, we have something else in mind, which remains an important task for the ego of any child. For, let us forget for a moment just how many justified guilt feelings a child may develop. The question still remains, what does he do with a guilt feeling when he has one? So, while the problem of guilt and conscience as such belongs to a chapter on superego functioning, the manipulation of guilt feelings once they are there belongs to the task assignment of the ego. In short, besides the problems our children show in terms of value identification and superego control to begin with, they even have trouble if they finally have a guilt feeling where it belongs. The normal reaction to guilt would be along the lines of insight into the nature of the offense, self-recrimination to the point of stir-up into change of self, gestures of appeasement toward victims of the guilty action, attempts at restitution of damage, some marginal defensive actions like avoidance of guilt-raising persons or places, and, most of all, if intimate ties are in the picture, a need to confess and "settle" bad feelings with people who count in one's life or their substitute. All this and more is well known. What we are less aware of is how serious things get if the ability to react normally toward guilt feelings is disturbed. For then, even if we have repaired a child's conscience so that it functions appropriately in giving the right kind of guilt productions, the child still remains a mess, because he doesn't know what to do with guilt feelings when he has them.

Our Pioneers were characterized by the following: when

producing guilt feelings as they should—which happened rarely enough in itself—they were unable to take the steps indicated above which might lead to their constructive extinction. Instead they showed all the chaotic reaction described in "coping with insecurity, anxiety, and fear." The therapeutic dilemma this throws us into, however, is much greater than in the anxiety case. For while we want to help children cope with anxieties, realistically, we do not want to produce them through our treatment if we can help it. With superego-deficient children, however, the very production of guilt feelings where they belong becomes a therapeutic task, and we then face the dilemma of having to produce an emotion within them before they are ready to handle it. In fact, in our previous experimentation at Camp with a much larger number of children, this very dilemma began to bother us so much that we realized how important it would be to solve the ego problem first, before we built up superego functions for which the ego wasn't ready yet. This is another reason, by the way, why "value conversions" or "miraculous identifications with friendly adults or values" never last long, unless ego repair is attempted simultaneously. For such a prematurely virtuous child will show guilt, and then will break down under the pathology of his ego, which does not know what to do with it.

As far as our children go, unable to travel the channels for realistic guilt-assuagement mentioned above, they would most frequently show behavior of the following type: unwillingness to talk about anything at all, aggression and sulk-hatred against the person to whom they had enough of a tie to make him a value-symbol for them, increase in the production of general irritability, aggression and destructiveness all over the place, final scapegoat focussing of the main bulk of irritation against an adult or another child usable for that purpose, increase of general resistance against any and all routine conformism and against even otherwise accepted adult demands. Since the illustration of these processes is too space-consuming, one illustration may serve for many.

Bill, who ordinarily is quite positive toward me, was quite rebellious when I reminded him that he wasn't supposed

to hit golf balls over into the next door neighbor's yard. Instead of replying with his usual "O.K. Yo-Yo," (his and the group's pet name for me) and coming along with the suggestion, he snarled back at me, "Yer mammy" and knocked one over the fence deliberately. When I insisted that this was not acceptable and reminded Bill that I would now have to confiscate the club, he ran away, throwing the club at me. Five minutes later I found Bill trying to break down the office door with a two-by-four because he thought I had put the club in there. I relieved him of the two-by-four and asked him what was bothering him that he should act so "mean" this morning. Bill said that he was going "to take that club to school" or he wasn't going and I said "Now come, you guys never get to take your golf clubs to school anyway" but he was adamant and refused to go along so the group was taken without him. When I returned, Bill was even more upset and was angrily packing his clothes, saying that he wasn't going to stay at this "goddam dump no more" etc. I said nothing but just stayed with him, finally bringing out that something must be bothering him and that I was sure it wasn't just the golf club—what was it? First, Bill said that nothing was wrong and then angrily threw out, "That goddam Danny, he thinks he can shove everybody around." I replied that I hadn't seen Danny do anything special this morning to Bill or anyone else. Was Bill sure that was it. He didn't answer and I said, "O.K., if you don't want to talk about whatever it is, I guess we'll have to skip it but I think it would be better if you came out in the open . . ." Finally Bill, in a gust of feeling, said, "I didn't keep none of it and I ain't going to get blamed for it . . . Last night Mike went over to that old lady that lives next door and gave her some flowers. I was with him and we saw she had a roll of bills this big (rolls up his fist). Mike said for me to watch out in the yard this morning and he would go over and swipe it and I did but I ain't got any of it and I won't get blamed for what he did. The wallet is hidden in the garage . . ."
(Entry: 5/13/48, Joel Vernick)

## 10. The Evaporation of Self-contributed Links in the Causal Chain

When children are accused of being poor in reality test-ing, we usually don't bother to specify just which phase of the total reality they are liable to ignore or misinterpret. For practical purposes, however, it seems to us that just what they leave out makes quite a difference. The young child, for in-stance, who hits his head against the corner of a table because of a jerky uncoordinated movement, and subsequently be-comes angry at the table that hurt him, does make the mistake of animistic projection. However, was his reality perception entirely wrong? There is no doubt about the involvedness of that table corner with the pain perceived. His mistake, be-sides animism, seems to be that he ignores the contribution his own behavior made to the total end result rather than that he misses the reality factors outside him entirely.

We think that this is a story quite different from the usually described inability of children to size up reality at all, and therefore try to give it a name and place of its own. For in the lives of our children, this inability of the ego to remember and single out their *own contribution to a total causal chain* seems to be at least as tragic as the much-mentioned reality blindness and projection of the fully psychotic state. For a while we confused this item with the well-known purposeful denial which such children are capable of, when trying to ward off punishment or guilt. Such clear-cut defenses are strong, and shall be described at a later point. We are con-vinced, however, that even long before actual organized reality distortion sets in, there is, in many of them, a real "simple forgetting" or non-perception of their own share in life events.

We have innumerable illustrations in mind of how children would really not remember, even after a short time, what share they had in the production of a fight or an aggressive or destructive scene, and how it usually took hard work and fast interview pick-up to bring such items back to mind. Since a challenge to a child to change is meaningless if the very reality situation is only partly perceived, and especially as long as that part which is most obviously the challenging one is missing, namely, the one related to the child's own behavior, this "fast evaporation rate" for his own contributions to the causal chain becomes a most serious item in all therapeutic plans.

The things they forget so fast usually lie on either of two different levels. The first is their own feelings and motivation and the intent and intensity of what they did. Thus, a youngster may furiously accuse his pal of hitting him for no reason, may quickly admit, on being reminded, that he did call the other one a son-of-a-bitch first, is unable, however, to remember how furious and aggressive he himself was when doing so and that it was this fury and threatening aggression rather than the simple words to which his partner really reacted. The other level, even more disturbing, occurs when the youngster even forgets surface behavior which was obviously involved. In spite of the barrage of lies and alibi defenses our children had available, we think we may safely state that sometimes they were not lying. Unless reminded immediately afterwards, the recollection of what they had done a short time ago was actually totally obliterated in the deluge of the incident that followed. A child involved in an exciting free-for-all with sticks and stones, may really not know any more that he was the one who threw the first one to begin with. The child who is unconsolable about a toy that broke is often really unable to recall the greedy fury with which he mishandled the toy to begin with but perceives the event as "just an accident."

On many occasions Mike would taunt and torment Larry into a wild attack upon him. We early began to interfere in this pattern by calling to Mike's attention each time he would start out on such a spree that sooner or later Larry would counterattack and there would "be trouble." Yet, each time after the inevitable happened, he would accuse us of not protecting him, even forgetting that we had warned him of what was to happen and insisting that he hadn't done anything to provoke Larry. Everything in his tone, facial expression, and other manifestations differed sharply from his really deceitful moments which we had come to know so well in other situations. There was no doubt that so far as his own difficulties with Larry were concerned, he actually would forget what his own contribution was and that we had tried to interfere.

In fact, it is the existence of this very ego disturbance, it is this unusually fast evaporation rate of self-contributed behavior, which makes the usual "Monday afternoon" or "twice a week" style of interview technique unusable with these children. The proximity of the therapist to the daily behavioral scene is essential so that he may catch up with the speed of events and counteract the fast evaporation rate of such incidents through special strategy. More about that later.

## 11. Spontaneous Establishment of Substitute Controls

Even in normal children, the control system of the ego does not always have to stay switched on to its full volume just to keep things from getting disorganized. Much of the time, ego vigilance and ego control can be switched back to low, just because there are adequate outside control forces at work. In those cases, the ego gets its flow of support from the presence of authority figures, the soothing awareness of a relaxed and friendly atmosphere, the perception of existing routines or well-oiled rules and regulations, the actual inaccessibility of otherwise tempting toys, gadgets, and tools, or the fascination of ongoing game and activity structures which "bind" loose energies of the children as efficiently as any supervising adult might, or any and all those factors together.

Sometimes, especially when impulsivity runs high, even well-adjusted children have trouble keeping to the level on which they were performing when such "outside controls" suddenly drop out. Thus, the end of a game and transition to the next one may produce more confusion and horseplay than expected, the teacher leaving the room may find noise rising in the classroom in spite of the warnings or pleas she left behind, the change over from a more highly pressured classroom to one with a wider range of permissiveness may cost ten minutes of temporary disorganization.

The normal child is supposed to have some reserves to institute inside controls quickly after the outside ones have petered out. He has something like an emergency reservoir which he can draw upon, when greater inside ego vigilance against onrushing impulses is made necessary in transitional moments.

The problem becomes severe when this special job of the ego, to substitute inside controls for outside ones in a hurry, isn't working as it should. We know that what we might call the "organizational maturity" of a group depends on this function, and it seems now that the same is true for the individual child. In fact, we could think of no better test for the emergency vigilance of ego functions than just such moments of withdrawal or breakdown of outside structures or controls. The children we speak about seem to have special trouble along that line. Even after some amount of ego control had been established with the direct support to the ego along the lines described above, the temporary dropping out of whatever outside control support had been instituted would throw them all out of gear and quickly lead to total disorganization. It also seems that this special capacity of the ego spontaneously to produce substitute controls from within when needed is one of the last ego gains to be made in treatment. Even after we had the children so far advanced that only mild structural supports were needed some of the time to keep them well functioning in a game, the end of that game or any interruption of structure would usually find them incapable of dealing with whatever submerged impulsivity had been kept in check. This means that an unusual amount of planning for adequate program structure was needed, that, even when things were going well, the presence and relatedness to adult figures directly on the scene was indispensable. For a long time careful arrangements for other substitute controls had to be mapped out strategically to avoid total ego breakdown in transitional moments of their lives.

On the way home from school, in the station wagon there was some incipient scapegoating of Larry and also a good deal of aggressive throwing. This forced us to stop the wagon several times. After treats, following our arrival home, the counselors suggested a game of dodge ball in the backyard. The group is quite keen about this game, only they call it "murder ball." The game went well. Larry was forgotten and they did not select him unnecessarily as a target. The few rules which this game has—such as waiting until the "target" knows you are going to throw and admitting when you are hit, etc.—were well kept. There was obvious keen enjoyment of all the throwing. Their ability to stick to rules was especially amazing in view of the ugly mood they were in before the game. Just before dinner we stopped, and, as though by magic, the offensive pre-game disposition returned and Larry again became a target for group attack. He was accused of doing things wrong in the game which while it was going on were completely ignored—if they were not even being manufactured now. Even his "baby" behavior at school was hauled out as an issue; they started calling him "piss-willie" though he is one of the few who do not wet. Mike climbed up on the garage roof and started heaving debris at him and then fanned out to a more generalized "bombing," and Danny began lumberingly to chase Larry around, calling him "Larry, the berry," a phrase which for some reason infuriates him and by this token is relished by the group as an insult. (Entry: 2/13/47, David Wineman)

## 12. Remaining "Reasonable" under the Impact of Unexpected Gratification Offerings

The European saying that, if you offer the devil your little finger, he will soon want the whole hand, didn't impress us too much at the beginning. We felt we rather noticed plenty of evidence that they didn't even want our outstretched finger. We were clearly reaching out toward these children with signs of acceptance and love only to harvest hatred, insult, and attack. We inserted many, for other children most desirable, offerings of activity, gifts, toys into their life, only to have them thrown at us in disgust, wrecked, destroyed. In the beginning, certainly, the adage didn't seem to hold much truth. Rather than becoming too demanding, except when it served the purpose of proving us wrong, most of the time our Pioneers wouldn't have any of it, and refused the little finger, or even the readily outstretched whole hand.

We soon learned better, though. For not long after the impact of the "treatment shock" period petered out somewhat, the problem to which this point is dedicated began to show itself in many moments of their lives with us. It became obvious what was going on some of the time. When they finally were at a point where they would admit the granting nature of our attitude toward them, and trust the forthcoming gestures of acceptance for what they were, a host of earlier desires, frustrated over the years or partially denied and repressed, suddenly welled up behind the immediate gratification front. The onrush of such demand-intensity, released by us all of a sudden, made the really offered grant seem insignificant, which ended up in a most bizarre and seemingly contradictory situation. At the very moment when we were offering affection and gratification of one kind, we would often be attacked and accused of being hostile and cruel withholders of fun, much more so than when we actually had to limit and interfere. This phenomenon seemed to go in either of two directions, depending on the child or momentary mood involved. Sometimes they would become afraid of their own onrush of frustrated desires, and out of this fear refuse the acceptance of the granting gesture altogether, at other times they would increase their demands to such absurdity that no one could or should live up to them, and then, asking for the impossible and unreasonable, would fall back upon their usual hostility and displayed disappointment.

The implications of this for treatment practice are immense and are to be discussed in detail at other points. It certainly taught us to realize that the dosage of love, permission, and gratification offerings has to be clinically weighed as carefully, and measured out as thoughtfully, in relationship to their ego-intactness along that line as anything else is. It is this item which makes the average child-loving but professionally naive volunteer entirely ineligible for this type of work. Later on we felt that the ability to remain reasonable even under the impact of love and gratification offerings could be considered one of our most evident progress criteria for total ego recovery.

Over the period of the first month, Larry lost some of the shyness and detachedness that he showed initially. Along with this, he switched from his cringing fear of the adult, inspired by the vicissitudes of his cruel life experience prior to placement with us, especially the sadism of the step-father. This converted to a rather claiming attitude which at points revealed a real form of infantile demandingness. He would say, rising grandiosely at his chair at the table, "I command that somebody bring me the salt," or "I command that we have pumpkin pie." In these moods, fired by his narcissistic zeal, he was difficult to manage. He actually tried to back up his "commands" by having a type of temper reaction if one did not cooperate with him. The tantrum was marked not so much by open show of violence as by a sudden mulishness. Thus, he wouldn't sit down again, or he might not eat because the "pumpkin pie" was not magically materialized. All along he would maintain a hilarious insistence on getting his own way.

During the first week of the Home's existence, we attempted a group interview in which some of the policies of the Home were reviewed with the boys. Each of these policies had previously received some individual handling with each boy. Thus, the various points raised were not entirely new to them. Still, it was felt there might be some value in having a group interview around these policies. In this way, the smoking policies of the Home, the money arrangements, etc., were discussed. Joe, especially, was the picture of snarling defiance all the way through. When the director indicated that the allowance would be fifty-five cents per week, Joe bargained for one dollar, saying, "Fritz, you bastard, it's a buck or nothing." Sam, sitting there quite meek and sanctimonious, shushed Joe, saying that he ought to be glad to be in a place like this where they treated you so "good" and even let you smoke. Where he came from (a Detention Home), he said, they never let you do anything. We were not so surprised at Joe's attempts at exploitation since he knew us all from camp and had some preview of the design offered by the Home. Thus he started off by being more initially unreasonable than Sam. However, a swift metamorphosis took place in Sam within the next ten days. Inch by inch, his "gratitude" began to wear out. Within two weeks, he was openly imperious in his demands and expected to be exempt from all limiting rules. In connection with smoking alone he openly broke all of the rules in rotation. At the same time he bargained with us fiercely for full franchisement as far as keeping privileges were concerned. For example, after being caught by the director in possession of stolen cigarettes, he was asked to give them up. Knowing full well that he had broken our original "deal" in which he was guaranteed cigarettes if he stuck to the rules, one of which was "no swiping cigarettes," he accused the director of being cruel, called him filthy names, vowed vengeance, etc. On another occasion, after being taken by the director for a ride together with Joe, as a special Christmas gesture, and after having received a box of candy, he and Joe both insisted on smoking in the car. When the director insisted on waiting until they got home, both boys exploded against him, calling him a "filthy mother fucker" and again accusing him of numerous cruelties.

I had some candy ready for treats when the boys came home from school. It so happened that they were nut bars which most of the boys enjoyed on a previous occasion. Unpredictably, however, they were not receptive toward nut bars today and there was intense and vehement griping, especially from Andy, who literally went into a rage and smashed his on the floor. "Yeah, yeah, we never git what kind we want" he yelled. I reminded him that, aside from my treat, they were given candy every day by Dave (Exec. Dir.) and there was certainly plenty of variety. This infuriated Andy even further and he picked up the pieces and threw them at me, calling me "a dirty whore," asking "what did I know?" Interference from the executive ended the scene, with Andy continuing his hysterical harangue in his office. (Entry: 2/18/47, Emily Kener, Housemother)

## 13.  Using Previous Satisfaction Images as Resource

It seems that normal children have a variety of possibilities to fall back upon spontaneously when confronted with moments of boredom, confusion, excitement, unhappiness, moodiness, or whenever the outside world fails to come through with adequate equipment or structural aid. If left to their own devices, most of them will simply "remember" something that had been fun before, or else a word, a piece of rope, an item of toy equipment, will remind them of something that could be done in a new combination right now. They may remember, when a rainy day spoils their plans, that a book may offer the fun it had granted once before, they may dream up fantasy games out of pictures or stories they used to like, they may pull out an old abandoned toy and keep happy, varying old pleasurable themes with a new twist.

Our children seemed to be utterly destitute in situations like this. And it soon dawned on us that not all the chaos and destruction we saw around us was simply their real pathology of impulses coming to the fore. Much of it was rather "incidental" in content, arising simply on the basis that they could not think of anything to do when left helpless for even a short time. We first thought that maybe these children had never been exposed to toys, games, activities, and so forth, a hypothesis which was good enough in some of the cases. But the pauperization of their lives was not that great, not that uninterrupted, to account for all we saw. It finally became clear that, besides everything else, these children lacked the ability to make use even of experiences they had enjoyed before in moments in which their ego was in difficulty.

This fact became especially clear after we had had them with us for a while. For we knew what games they had played, what toys they had had, what activities they could enjoy. For a while it was as though everything we had exposed them to before had been thrown into an empty hole in which it had simply disappeared. They couldn't even remember. After a while they began to remember all right, but it took a lot of prodding, a lot of arguing, before we could assure them that this game would be fun. Didn't they remember when we played it last week, how much fun it was? "We never done anything like that, fuck you" would be the invariable retort, until in the middle of the game recollection would return, often with a flash. Still later, they were able to remember previous gratification situations—but that was all. An admission these had happened, a grin about how much fun it was—they still could not remember spontaneously and make use of such memory as a resource in a moment of anxiety, boredom, or loneliness. We felt like marking in red ink the day in our life with them when, for the first time, they would exclaim, "Say, let's play that game again, what's its name? Remember, that was fun . . ."

Resourcefulness in terms of the ability to revive and utilize previous satisfaction images when needed does not loom large on the agenda of clinical conferences or in the lists of case history outlines. It certainly seems to us, however, to be one of the most vital tasks for survival an ego can count on, and one of the most important ones to repair when damaged.

The chapters on programming and our records quoted there will contain numerous bits of evidence for the phenomenon described here. We don't want to repeat. May one specific incident serve instead of many to illustrate what had been disturbed, even though this became evident only just about when this disturbance began to clear up:

After dinner, there was a considerable degree of disorganized boredom with no one quite able to find a place for himself. This fanned out quickly into a mild, diffused aggressiveness against the adults as well as each other. Bill and Danny began to bicker over a yo-yo, while Mike and Andy used the occasion to tease Larry about something that happened in school. Andy then began to throw some checkers at Larry and this was quickly picked up by both Bill and Danny, diverting them from their own quarrel with each other. The general excitement was added to when they began throwing around an indoor ball at each other. Joel, counselor on duty, diverted them into a regular style baseball game in the backyard which seemed to work like magic once he made the suggestion. He galvanized

them into action by picking up the ball and tearing upstairs to get a bat, saying he'd meet them outside in a
minute. Although they have played baseball so many times,
here again we see their inability to divert themselves on
their own through an activity structure which, once the
group-identified adult offers it, they are able to use. Earlier
in our experience with them, however, they would have
been unable to move this quickly into an activity pattern,
even with an adult. (Entry: 5/17/47, David Wineman)

A short while before the above incident the counselor's game
suggestion would have fallen on infertile ground, and their
ability to make use of an image of a game to promise such
fun couldn't have been counted on. Yet, they still had a far
way to go after May 17, 1947, for it still took the counselor's
action to give the signal and "rub the image." For later life,
they will need to be able to make use spontaneously of such
resources of past experiences.

## 14. Realism about Rules and Routines

All children can be expected to develop a somewhat persecutional attitude toward rules and routines, from time to time,
considering them as an especially vicious invention by nasty
adults, primarily designed to make life miserable for them,
rather than as unavoidable parts of the relentless reality of
life. Normal children will show such persecutional interpretation of rules and routines especially under four conditions:
One, if this is actually true. In that case, no comment is
needed. They simply are right, are too smart for us, and have
"caught on" to what is really wrong in the picture to begin
with. And it does happen at times that adults design rules
and routines out of their own needs rather than in line with
reality demands and in awareness of the children's age, needs,
rights, etc. The second case is the one where rules are basically justified but their design is developmentally out of focus.
This may be the fault of the rules, as in the too strict demands
for keeping certain hours made upon a really very reliable
young adolescent boy, who needs some rule defiance for

reasons of pride of emancipation, or it may be simply the case that developmental need and reality limitation are in a hopeless conflict which at the time is not interpretable to the child. This would be the case where a somewhat impulsive and incautious but status-eager twelve year old may have to be told he cannot use his rifle unless an adult is around. The third case where even ego-intact children develop acutely persecutional misinterpretations of regulations and rules is the one where the way the adult reacts in the handling of such rules is psychologically confusing to the child. Thus, a normally mobility-hungry adolescent boy may accept curfew limitations by a father who grants him budding emancipation in all other areas and shares his pride in his new status as a young adult. He would rebel by distortional misinterpretation of such rules, however, were they imposed by a stern autocrat with all the accompanying display of obedience demanded of an infantile inferior. The fourth case where rule misinterpretation by any child would be considered normal would be the one where the reality because of which the rule has to be developed is too complex for the child to comprehend, or where adequate attempts to solicit cooperative understanding of a rule or routine have not been made. This is often the case in institutions, where certain routines like waiting in line and sharing equipment and other materials are unavoidable because of the size of the group or limitation in space, but where such reality-demanded routines are never worked over with the children, so that they must seem to them as though they were simply devilish inventions of the adult world.

Needless to say, we are aware of all that, and have none of these situations in mind when we complain that our Pioneers lacked in "realism about rules and routines." We would expect them to show all the troubles mentioned above in connection with normal children to the nth degree, of course. What we have in mind here, however, is this: Even in such areas where their ego was cognitively clear enough to understand and accept the issue as such, even then rules or routines, because limiting, would be interpreted in a persecutional way, no matter how skillfully such rule situations had been handled by the staff. The ability of the ego to separate unavoidable, reality-conditioned displeasure from personal attack seemed to be especially underdeveloped in our children. In consequence, we would also claim that the ability to show more realism about rules and routines is one of the measuring sticks for ego recovery that are tangible enough.

Clothing administration was one of the most irksome and chronic problems that plagued us with our group. Everybody had at least one or two items that were his favorite things to wear from among all the things he owned. When he could have them, well and good. But on those days that these items might be in the laundry we literally had "hell to pay." Very carefully and patiently and with great detail, we tried to show them that no matter what any of us wanted, our laundry simply couldn't be moved any faster. Also we stressed that no laundry in the city would deliver clothes any faster than ours which took them on Monday and would bring all the things back on Wednesday. It made no difference at all. We were still "mean bastards" because we didn't "have my pants whenever I want them." Many of Danny's morning blow-ups, for example, involved this inability to see the reality basis for this routine.

Bill persisted in throwing things at me while I was driving and also opening the rear window to heave things at passing cars. When I asked him to stop, it was as though I were doing something to him, not he to me and to other people. He was furious and rebellious and kept threatening me that he would run away. He didn't have to ride in this "son-of-a-bitch" wagon where they never let you do "anything." I said, "What do you mean 'anything' . . . Do you call what you are doing 'just anything'? This could end in a serious accident or get the police after us . . ." His reply, "Sure, doncha like it?" (Entry: 10/5/47, Bob Case)

## 15. Warfare with Time

We know that the concept and the experience of "time" is one of the most complex and subtle problems of psychology, that much has been written on it, and that more is yet to be learned. We are also impressed with the fact that whole nations, and maybe the whole human race, seem to have problems of weighing past, present, and future against each other realistically, and so maybe we shouldn't be too hard on our Pioneers for being not less mixed up about the phenomenon of "time" than everybody else. We also know that some specific disturbances in the sense of time belong to the chapter on neuroses, others some place else, and that this is the last place to deal with them or their causation. But one thing we would like to make clear is that there are certain partial ego functions related to the phenomenon of time which, if disturbed, have a disastrous effect on a child's life and on the chances for education and therapy to take hold of him. This is what we have in mind when we say that our children were constantly "at war" with time, and that much of our clinical work with them was complicated by that very time element.

Most distinctly, we could point to two major disturbances of their ego functioning as far as time elements are concerned: One is their great difficulty in making any distinction between what we might crudely term the "subjective experience" and the "objective measurement" of time. Some of the reasons for this are simple: Several of our children never acquired any concept of objective time, couldn't read a watch, confused yesterday with tomorrow, allowed weeks, days, months, years to slide into one another with the abandon usually limited to the very little child. We are not concerned with the reasons for this. We are concerned with what it did to our attempt to help them get de-confused. We would be tempted to rate this seeming "little" disturbance as one of the most plaguing blocks in our treatment plans. For this very reliance—even of those youngsters who could, theoretically, tell time and had their calendar concepts of time straight—on subjective time as the only "real" thing caused innumerable confusions and fights and much unhappiness, and seemed to feed straight into their pathology of a "paranoid interpretation of life." For of course, they experienced, as everybody does, that the time one is happily busy with what one enjoys seems short, the time we watch others enjoy it while waiting our turn seems unduly long, etc. The result was that even mild irregularities in time distribution would cause endless squabbling and would always tend to put us in the wrong. Consequently, even a normal game would breed the germ of sibling rivalry, because it seemed to them that A was allowed to have the ball so much longer or so much more often than B, that everybody else was getting what he wanted right away, while "only I always have to wait so long," etc. The details of this daily warfare with time need not be described: some of them will emerge more clearly later when we describe our countertechniques.

The other basic problem revolving around time was the severe disturbance of these children's relation to the future, including their own. Now, this again is an item in connection with which perhaps no adult living today ought to throw too many stones first. However, our Pioneers were even more deficient in this respect than the average member of the population seems to be. This came out in two ways primarily. One, that all reference to the future of any request was, for a long time, simply identical with outright refusal. When one of them got something, like a haircut, today, the suggestion that the other one would get his tomorrow was met in the same way as though we had refused him that privilege for the rest of his life. Or, if we tried to point out "future consequences" of anything they were about to do, we might as well have saved our breath. For what is trouble that may be brewing for tomorrow, no matter how fatal, compared with even mild fun right now?

The other trouble related to the concept of the future was, of course, that these children had not developed much of a realistic concept of "themselves in the future" so that there was little to appeal to, one way or another. What "ego ideals" they were swaggering around with, if existent at all, were totally delusionary and mostly borrowed from radio, movie, or comic book, and even then only on a flighty "enjoyment of present illusions" basis. They didn't even have a good delinquent ego ideal, which, as we know from other cases, would require rather strong time realism.

We hasten to add that this seemingly minor part of their pathology constituted one of our major technical hazards, as becomes clear when we remember that promise as well as threat, punishment as well as reward, encouragement as well as criticism, have a rather healthy relationship to time as a *conditio sine qua non*, as a prerequisite without which they make no sense at all or are even doomed to make things worse. But more about that later. Just as an illustration of some of the more fantastic time problems, not even mentioning the host of daily troubles along that line, here are two excerpts from records:

We have finally worked out a haircut schedule. It was Joe's turn to go with me today to get his hair cut. This produced quite a reaction in Larry, who burst into my quarters today after learning from Joe that he was going with me to the barber. He demanded that he be taken today and that's all there was to it. I reminded him that we had all sat down and worked out the schedule and that he had agreed to come after Joe because his shopping trip came before Joe's. He was blind to this reasoning, however, completely swept away by his involvement in this particular need of the moment. "Yeah," he whined and screamed at the same time, "Now I'll never git one. I'll never have one, never, never." Again I remonstrated, "But, Larry, you know you'll go tomorrow, we worked it out that way, and I've always done what we planned to do, you know that." "No," he screamed, "I'll never git mine." (Entry: 2/7/47, Emily Kener)

Fantastically enough, tonight, just before bedtime, Bill demanded that we go canoeing. I said "We have that planned for tomorrow after school; you know, we planned that." No, he insisted he wanted to go right now. I tried humor. "Yeah, sure, in the dark, we're going to go and bump each other under those bridges. That would be funny, wouldn't it? Besides we'd have to wake up the guy who runs the place because he's home sleeping now." "You'll never take us," he threatened me, completely unimpressed by my attempt to cajole him out of it. "How can you say that when we were already there week before last and we're going tomorrow?" I asked. Adamantly, he insisted, "Yeah, we know, we know, you counselors never want to do what we want to do." (Entry: 4/6/47, Barbara Smith)

## 16. Assessing Social Reality

The most obvious deficiency of the classical concept of the "ego" as the agent for keeping "contact with reality" lies in the lack of differentiation between physical and social reality. We think that there are two functions here which are not identical and that we may frequently find the one quite well intact, while the other one may be seriously impaired. This means, of course, that this term actually covers a wide range of much more specific jobs to be done by the "ego" than the general term "reality testing" would indicate. We have all seen children who are perfectly capable of figuring out how much weight a skating pond might carry and how far it is wise to venture onto it and are yet unable to figure out at all "what goes and what doesn't go" in a group in which they find themselves. And we also know how often even egos with an enormous I.Q., able to master the complex logical tasks of academic issues, may be helpless and insensitive when it comes to knowing how people around them really feel. And vice versa, of course. With the enormous development of social psychology, sociology, group psychology, and cultural anthropology during the last decade or so, the need to specify the various ego tasks which fall under the term "social sensitivity" has become more obvious than ever, and even the records of our relatively short life with the Pioneers would contain material for quite an ample dissertation on this point. For reasons of brevity it may suffice to list the following areas of main concern to the practitioner, into which the general concept of "assessment of social reality" can be broken down.

*Interpersonal sensitivities*—by this we refer to the skill of figuring out how *another person* may feel about us, what is going on within him, what motivates his behavior toward us, and of predicting how he might act and react toward what we do. This may refer to another child in the group, or an adult.
*Sensitivity to Group Code*—by this we mean the skill of

sizing up what "goes" and what "doesn't go" in a group of contemporaries, on which basis the group will judge one's behavior, what makes one popular, disliked, respected, scapegoated in a certain group under certain conditions. All groups have some "unoutspoken" principles which underlie their behavior toward particular members in particular situations. The effects of such codes can be easily demonstrated, even though the basis and detailed workings of them are still one of the hardest phenomena for research to touch.

*Assessment of collective mores*—by this we refer to the underlying behavior code of larger social situations in which children may find themselves, and we think of items like the awareness of a child as to what a specific neighborhood or environmental setting expects him to do when a visitor comes, when he is visiting somebody else's house, when he finds himself at a public theater performance, along with the larger issues of mores and customs of various segments of society as such.

In a nutshell, the following observations seem to be most important for an understanding of the children we talk about: 1. It would be all wrong to expect them to show generally disturbed functioning of their ego in terms of assessing social reality. We find, rather, that most of these children show an amazingly wide range of contrasting behavior along this line. Most of them show, in some areas, not disturbances but hyperthropic development of this function. We shall discuss their amazing 'acuity of social perception in battle-relevant areas" later on. At the same time, they also show most severe disturbances of this same function in certain other areas, toward certain people, and under specific conditions. Something like a "geographical map" of their distribution of social acuity versus total insensitivity would be a fascinating task for research to tackle, and enormously helpful to the practitioner on all levels. 2. It remains quite important to differentiate sharply between whether the children, in a specific incident, do not see "social reality" or whether they are very well aware of it but simply "don't give a damn" or even enjoy the irrational effect of their behavior with gusto. Only the first case belongs here and the mere reporting of an incident would not allow us to be sure. We would have to know much about what else was in the picture to be certain. The incidents reported below are of that sort. The way they stand they might just as well belong in the other two categories. But we happen to know from living with those children so intensively which was the case when a particular incident occurred. 3. The causes for lack of realism in the assessment of social reality, again, may vary tremendously from case to case and don't really concern us here. However, it might be well to keep in mind that they are basically of three varieties. (a) Some of their "social blindness" is simply part of their basic pathology; their ego is all tied up with it. The child, for instance, who is beset by a delusion of persecution could not afford to see too clearly how people really feel toward him. (b) Some of it is actually more or less the "fault" of the reaction of the world toward them. As long as they are engaged in warfare against adults who really distrust and dislike them, they can't afford to become too sensitive to their surroundings, just as a soldier on the battlefield had better restrict his attention to battle-relevant issues. That part, by the way, begins to clear up as soon as the therapeutic milieu and treatment takes its first effects. When they relax and begin to relate to people, they also begin to "pick up clues" from the adults around them and become more interested in what other children think and feel about them. (c) Some of their social blindness, however, is simply a result of fixation on the basis of neglect. This part can be corrected simply by education, or, let us say, by exposure to interpreted experience. At camp, for instance, we have met many children who were simply stuck on a naive, narcissistic level of earlier childhood, of enjoying reciting a poem or a song with total abandon, with not the slightest awareness of the infantilism of their behavior, which might have brought applause from auntie, but was poison for an audience of tough contemporaries. Such children, exposed to such experience in a protective atmosphere, could be shown easily in a sequence of marginal interviews what was going on, and could then actually become more "sensitive" toward group mood, group code, and a variety of issues involved. 4. The reason why we are so eager to draw attention to this phenomenon of "realism in the assessment of social reality" is that, for the straight psychiatric clinician, it would seem primarily an "educational" issue rather than a clinical one. We think, however, that this would be a mistake. We are convinced that in the job of rehabilitating such children any attack, on any level, upon this phenomenon is of primary importance. For, as long as their social sensitivity is too narrow or disturbed, these children cannot even be exposed to life experiences which otherwise might prove salutary. The very disturbance of their sense of social reality will bring chaos and rejection down on them. In order that the child may live outside the treatment home, and even in order to make use of some of the very experiences which become important ingredients in the total course of treatment, some of this disturbed ability to "assess social reality realistically" has to be tackled very soon after the first chaotic reaction of treatment shock is over. This is what makes these children, for the therapist, so different from the common garden variety neurotic. With the youngster who has a classical anxiety neurosis, for instance, and little else, we don't have to bother much. Freed from the clutches of his neurotic conflict, his ego will breathe "freely" and soon be able to amend on its own whatever it may have missed in terms of social sensitivity experiences in the meantime, though supportive group therapy is often indicated even for him. With the children we have in mind, here, a strengthening of this and other ego functions has to precede and run concomitant with the rest of their treatment, or else the very media of treatment influences are restricted beyond hope.

Most of the disturbance of our children in the line of "realistic assessment of social reality" is obvious all through our recordings, even where we quote anecdotes to illustrate another point. We can easily limit ourselves, therefore, to a very few illustrations at this time.

On the afternoon that he was scheduled to go with me to have his hair cut, Larry was in a transport of joy. He was going around gaily chanting and bragging, "My haircut, my haircut, Emmy's goin' to take me for a haircut." This incensed the group against him and caused a flurry of attacks on him by the others. Joe punished him viciously, calling him "baby" and "bastard," and had to be pulled off him by the counselor. As usual, the sibling hatred of the group was stirred up into open rage by his injudicious bragging. He has been in the same situation innumerable times. So far we have been unable to make him aware of what he was letting himself in for. (Entry: 12/15/46, Emily Kener)

Danny's infantile greediness for adult affection completely blinded him for a long time to the code-prescribed rules for toughness and unity against the adult world carefully observed by the rest of the group with the exception of Larry, who suffered from a similar code blindness. Thus, while capable of extreme primitivity and violence against the adult when he himself ran into frustration-loaded moments with them, whenever there was a group incident involving serious rule breakage or theft of some article, this was almost a signal for Danny to become glucose sweet in his attitude toward the adult, with a smirking virtue that turned the rest against him. It was obvious that Danny saw these moments as an opening for a sudden "affection blitz," which we tried to neutralize as best we could. But we could never operate fast enough to save him from group rejection and scapegoating in the moments. On an occasion when we were having a group meeting about a station wagon incident that Danny was not involved in, in the middle of the meeting suddenly, in dulcet sweet tones, he asked our housemother who was sitting in, "Emmy, do you think we could have our meeting on my special diet now?" (he had a diet for his obesity), thus demonstrating unmistakably, again, his extreme code tactlessness. For here, while the others were on the carpet, so to speak, and angry at the adult, he took the chance to make a virtue bid toward the housemother. The group reaction was instantaneous, "lard ass, fat ass, fat bastard—yeah, Danny, think's he's big shit, etc., etc."

After a rather wild canoe ride at Belle Isle, a large public recreation area, in which, although safely supervised by Pearl, co-counselor, Mike still managed to get soaking wet, we finally disembarked and made ready to go to the station wagon. Mike suddenly began to wriggle out of his wet pants, right out there in broad daylight. He was about half-way through when I wheeled and saw him and said, "Hey, Mike, what are you doing?" Spectators were incredulously looking at this spectacle, and I said to Mike, "C'mon, pull up your trousers and come to the station wagon." "The hell with you, you goddam bastard," he said, "These damn pants itch me and I'm gonna take 'em off." I insisted, and, cursing me prodigiously, he pulled up his trousers and tore over to the wagon. (Entry: 5/3/47, Vera Kare)

## 17. Learning from Experience

If anything can be said to be clearly recognizable as belonging in the chapter of "ego psychology," it is the function of learning, whose main domain is so obviously the cognitive mastery of reality. In view of this, it is amazing and most unfortunate that psychiatry and the psychology of learning have taken such a long time really to try to get together. For even most of the straight psychoanalytic studies of learning disturbances were primarily interested, not in the function of the learning process itself, but in the question as to just what happens to this function under the impact of emotional blocks, neurosis, etc. Much is to be hoped from recent attempts to lure learning theory and psychoanalysis into closer cooperation.[4] At this moment, we are primarily interested in a broader implication of this problem.

Our children had, of course, numerous "learning difficulties" which would easily fit into the whole gamut of functional disturbances described in literature. Their description and analysis would be of interest. Here we want to focus, how-

[4] A most promising effort at such a synthesis of the two approaches may be found in John Dollard and Neal E. Miller, *Personality and Psychotherapy* (New York: McGraw Hill Book Company, Inc., 1950). See also, O. H. Mowrer, "Learning Theory and the Neurotic Paradox," *American Journal of Orthopsychiatry,* XVIII, No. 4 (October, 1948) p. 571–610.

ever, not on the problem of academic learning in any sense, but on one of the most basic ingredients of all learning—the ability to make use of valid inferences from previous experiences. This faculty seems to be "taken for granted" for all but moronic children and adults, and yet it is anything but matter of course. In fact, the proverbial story of a man who sails all around the globe without gaining anything in real insight or understanding ought to warn us how complex and disturbable are the functions we have before us.

With our children, it was quite noticeable that, aside from "having learned too well" the lessons of their traumatic life experiences, they had wide gaps in their ability to learn from what happened to them before. Most children are able to remember an incident in which their behavior was followed by inconvenient consequences without being too bothered by it. Yet, when a reasonably similar situation presents itself, the image of the previous incident somehow turns up, offers a mild danger signal sufficient to modify behavior, at least in parts, in the situation at hand. With the Pioneers, we seem to be stuck in an unhappy alternative with little in between. Previous experiences either have been so traumatic that only their thoughtless repetition occurs as the result of even mild similarities between a present situation and one before, or else no signal of similarities is being given at all, no inferences are drawn for the present from what happened in the past. It seems that these children consume all of their psychic energies so much in the present that little is left for an evaluative process to be used for later on—if such a simple quantity simile is permissible at all. The same is true for pleasant experiences—they, too, seem to be soaked up so greedily when they occur that little trace is left for later reality assessment. Thus, it took our youngsters an exceedingly long time before the harmlessness of some adults, the pleasure promise of some program possibility, would "sink in," and it took an equally laboriously built-up chain of well-interpreted situations of "cause and consequence" before the idea that certain kinds of fun had better be forfeited would even begin to make sense. The implications of this for treatment practice are enormous. But even when they are opposed to friendly adults and happy life experiences, treatment for these children needs the presence of a constant obstetrician of the learning process for anything to "sink in." The necessity for strategic pick-up of learning potentials will be described more in detail among our "techniques."

The following illustration may give the flavor of what we were all up against in our daily tasks.

Our children would inevitably insist on taking their favorite toy or gadget to school with them. With monotonous regularity these things would be broken or totally destroyed in battles with other children or would be lost in the melee of playground activities. Yet they never showed a flicker of concern that anything would happen to these toys as day by day they carted them along with them. Many children will have a hard time not to take their favorite gadget to school and most of them will succumb. We would expect them however at least to verbalize some doubt or show some hesitation. It was this inability of our youngsters to work up even a little anticipatory anxiety which was so impressive as evidence of their inability to learn from experience.

## 18. Drawing Inferences from What Happens to Others

If it is hard enough to help our children make sense out of what directly happens to them, our job is intensified in difficulty when it comes to making them learn from what happens to others. Not that adults don't have trouble with that, too. The denial of reality danger by the argument "It can't happen here" ought to be well enough known to all of us. However, in those cases we usually can assume that the basic ability to draw such inferences is pretty well established—special reasons of anxiety have to be valid to make some life area or other taboo for the functioning of logic. With our children, there were whole areas within which the process of "learning from what happened to others" never was practiced at all. And, where there was any interest in "what happened to others," it was usually stuck on a totally narcissistic, magic, wish-fulfillment level on the basis of fatalistic theories of exceptionalism. Thus, for instance, the fact that one person or twenty others got in trouble for what they did would be waved away as having no implication for their lives, while the luck with which somebody once went scot-free in a delinquent enterprise or a dangerous act would be considered proof of personal tax exemption from the laws of nature or society obliging the rest of the world. Of course, there are instances where there is purpose behind this madness, as we shall point out later—what seems like a disturbance of an ego function may sometimes assume the proportions of a hyperthropic ego skill in argumentation for the wrong cause. Here we have in mind the subjugation of logic under impulsivity and narcissism to such a degree that even skillfully raised arguments fall on reality-deaf ears. And this is the worst of it—if the ability to draw realistic inferences from what happens to others is seriously impaired, not only will such children not learn from what they hear about life and what they see happen to others, but it is even difficult to make use of such incidents to argue with their own "worser" self. For, how do we do "ego supportive therapy" with merely neurotic children? One of our safest standbys is obviously the use of logical argument, skillfully applied by a well-related person. If such argument holds no binding power, we lose one of the most effective tools in our battle against delusional magics.

Sam, an inveterate thief, was describing to the group one day a kid who lived in his neighborhood up north where he was before he came to Pioneer House. This boy apparently was the community thief par excellence and Sam described his exploits with relish. He told how he broke into this store and that house and how he used to treat all the smaller guys to candy which he bought from his nefarious gains. Then, as an anti-climax, he brought out that this guy was now in Jackson prison. From here, he went on to sketch, unable to resist his bravado mood, some of the "jobs" he had pulled, not with this other fellow who was much older and served apparently as a delinquent ego ideal, but on his own. He made no attempt to conceal anything even though the director was around within earshot. In a subsequent lull in the activities, the director called over to Sam and chatted with him about the story he had just told. He said, "So this guy is in prison now," and Sam nodded agreement. Then the director said, "How about you, how do you figure you can get away with it?" His reply was classic: "I'm smarter than he is, that's all." He apparently had no hard feelings about the challenge but acted as though it were a piece of naïveté on the director's part even to believe for a minute that he would get into serious trouble.

One day, the boys were quite excited about an accident that happened to one of the kids in their class. He had been skating in the street and was hit by a car, suffering concussion and broken ribs. They talked about it almost exclusively on the way home and gave the impression that they were in some way quite threatened by it. It was thus quite surprising to us when both Andy and Bill, in defiance of rules, started to skate in heavy traffic in front of the Home just before dinner. The Executive Director called them both into the office and, attempting to make propaganda on the basis of the accident to the boy in their room, a pure parallel, brought it to their attention, saying, "Here, a guy in your class is seriously hurt doing just what you guys are doing tonight and yet it doesn't seem to make any sense for you at all." "Oh, that dumb jerk." Andy said, "He don't know what's going on anyway." The Executive Director argued the point even further, "What do you mean, he doesn't know what's going on?" So they tried to prove he couldn't skate "good" but, when asked how did they know how "good" he could skate, they were unable to submit evidence for their argument. Still they insisted that nothing would happen to them and that we were just "mean bastards" because we never wanted them to do anything that was "fun."

## 19. Reaction to Failure, Success and Mistakes

Even normal adults do not always find it easy to react reasonably and realistically to failures, successes, and the mistakes they make. Failure either seems to discourage the ego or to seduce it into a variety of compensatory mechanisms, many of which are anything but desirable in a total pattern of life. Success has a tendency toward the production of characterological changes in terms of snobbishness, over-confidence, etc., or may lead to a variety of exploitative behavior trends which do serious damage to the acceptedness of a person within his own group. And it is well known that the ability to see, face, admit, and react reasonably to mistakes, and the ability to risk mistakes without having to use compensatory displacement mechanisms afterwards constitute one of the most difficult tasks and one of the most coveted maturity signals for anybody, even in his own realm of professional competence. No wonder that children as disorganized as ours have special problems when confronted with success, failure, or the admission of a mistake. Many of our children are so fatalistically afraid and convinced of the unavoidability of failure that they withdraw from some fields entirely, or develop terrific resistance against even "trying" under the most favorable circumstances. This can get so bad that even the visualization of an otherwise pleasant task, say a game, may call forth the image of failure first, and therefore makes it impossible for them even to want to try. This is often accompanied by a variety of defense mechanisms such as depreciation of the activity as such, pretense at disinterest, proclamation of total inability in this area, etc. Exposure to success situations, however, is no unmitigated blessing either. Sometimes our children, when successful with what they tried, become entirely intolerable for those who are supposed to survive with them. Their egos are so success-hungry that even a mild experience of that sort throws them off all restraint and they begin to act like a conceited, aggressive, reckless mob, eager to seek somebody less successful to mirror their own achievement, with no restraints of tact left. The admission of a "mistake" in turn, is usually met by one of two reactions—either it is considered just more evidence that "I'm no good at that anyway, so what's the use of trying," or the person who administers criticism immediately is pushed into the role of a hostile, mutilating, depreciating adult. But even the overlooking or "tactful ignoring" of mistakes later recognized as such by the child backfires more often than not. It is turned into its opposite, and interpreted as lack of interest in the child's progress, lack of helpfulness, or sheer stupidity on our side. This total breakdown of ego functions when confronted with failures, successes, or the assessment of mistakes, seems to us to constitute one of the greatest hazards of all for the educator, as well as the clinician, who tries to survive with or rehabilitate children of this type. It makes even "good" programs established for more normal children entirely unusable for ours; it is one of the main reasons why the moneyed layman does not enjoy contributing time or financial support toward their rehabilitation, and why even the professional often throws up his hands in despair. Techniques to get at this special angle of ego disturbance seem to be more important than anything else, even though this item does not rank high on the customary lists of clinical priorities.

The boys all had their swimming tests at the Boys' Club to determine whether they could be permitted to swim in deep water or not. The instructor, well briefed in our program, had carefully arranged for no one else to be present at the pool except our own group and even then each boy was taken in one at a time by him while the counselor diverted the others by activities in other parts of the club. For example, while one boy was being tested the counselor was with the others playing pool, basketball, etc. In this way, we hoped to protect the pride of each group member, not only from the observation of outsiders, but even from criticism from members of our own group. The swimming instructor, in addition, was a trained worker with boys and handled the fellows very skillfully. He reported to us after the tests that Henry was unable to swim at all and would have to start in the beginners' section. He assured Henry that he would teach him to swim and that in a matter of weeks he would be in the intermediate group. Still, on the way home, Henry was in a blue sulk. To reclaim his prestige, he did at least two things—he insisted on smoking in the wagon and began to scapegoat Larry viciously. In addition, he propagandized against the Boys' Club—"who wants to belong to that old dump anyway?"—and tried to talk the boys out of ever going back there. It was obvious to the group that he was sore because of his poor showing but because he was top man on the totem pole they didn't take it out on him, which in this case turned out to be quite a blessing, for Henry could have been even more difficult. Even after we got home, he refused to eat, staying in his room. After dinner, he deliberately "knifed" every activity in the back by luring the others into chasing around and finally engineered a real bedtime riot. (Entry: 12/17/46, Joel Vernick)

During the crafts program, Andy painted very carefully, using a brush, and his first design was quite formal. It was a picture of a flower with some clouds floating in the sky. However, when he pressed down the paper the design came off messily because the paint hadn't been moist enough. He became violently upset and with tears of rage he threw it on the floor and stamped out of the room into the adjoining playroom where he sat down in a chair. He sat in depressed fury. This is all the more amazing because Andy is one of the most advanced children in the group in this area. When he does something well we have the reverse problem with him; he infuriates the others with his crowing. Yet, if he fails, he blows up every time. I reminded him how many really good things he had made and put this one to one side, saying that it too would look better after it dried. This didn't help and he would not re-enter the activity, finally going downstairs, and I didn't see him until dinner at which time he still appeared gloomy and detached, but recovered from the acute intensity of his reaction. (Entry: 3/13/47, Barbara Smith)

## 20. Exposure to Competitive Challenge

The ability to react well to a competitive challenge is not at all one of the "primary" and simple ego functions. It is, in itself, a highly complex syndrome of ego functions, each one of which can be separately well developed or disturbed. An analysis of the ingredients of an ego's ability to react well to competitive life situations would, among others, show the following ingredients:

Ability to accept temporary frustration in view of later possible, if doubtful, gain.

Identification with a team (in some cases at least).

Submission of momentary personal needs in favor of long range goals.

Ability to accept the facts of battle without interpreting the adversary's fighting as "hostile," or even the ability to accept some actual hostility in good grace.

Ability to produce aggression in varying sublimation levels without allowing hostility generated toward the persons involved to become rampant.

Skill in the manipulation of pride as a stimulant—without developing superiority feelings or snobbish complacency on the one hand, displaced scapegoat formation on the other.

Ability to manipulate the complex and ambivalent relationships toward one's own team and team members.

Ability to take defeat without disorganization, of enjoying victory without triumphant exploitation, of bearing doubt and insecurity without ego-decay.

Ability to enter the content area of competitive enterprise with adequate sublimation, enjoyment, and actual skill.

Ability to accept the role distribution necessary for competitive task without interference by sibling rivalries, status conflicts, etc.

Ability to accept limits and umpire decisions without delusional pathology.

This is only a sample of some of the ingredients involved in "competitive" life situations, and even their special mixture in content and quantity will depend, of course, on the type, style, level, and other specific circumstances of the competitive challenge involved.

The foregoing analysis might raise the question as to just why a function as clearly composite as this is listed here at all, since it seems that its ingredients should be covered in other points mentioned in this same list. The answer to this is that, psychologically speaking, there is little justification for making this a separate item. It so happens, however, that the societal culture within which we operate puts such a premium on the ability to take competition with grace that the functioning or disturbance of this very process becomes a crucial issue in this culture of ours. It is from the point of view of the cultural anthropologist, therefore, that we would rather see this item elevated to a point in its own right than dissolved into its ingredients. And, besides, since most attempts at therapy are afflicted by the same cultural determinants, the awareness that the "use of competition" in education, group work, or therapy is predicated upon certain very specific ego functions to be taken for granted is of paramount importance.

In a nutshell, how much and what type of "competition" can be afforded or used in life and programming in a treatment home also becomes a clinical issue, not one of cultural custom or even pride.

Picked up the kids after school. They were enthusiastic about baseball at Belle Isle. It was a beautiful, fresh spring afternoon and, although Belle Isle was a little windy, it was nice early baseball weather. Since this was the first game, the kids were rather tense, out of practice, and there was a lot of wrangling about sides. Of course, nobody wanted Larry or Danny, the former because of his sprawling uncoordinated movements which hamper him in all athletics, the latter because of his bulk and slowness. The way it wound up with Mike, Andy, and Bill on one side, fleet and agile as they are, and Larry and Danny on the other, it would have been murder. I suggested that I play on Larry's and Danny's team to even up the sides and that threw the balance way out, too, because then they were afraid of my prowess. Mike began to curse and said he'd be bitched if he'd play, Bill began to look for rocks to throw around, and Andy sneered with his usual *"Jeezus."* I then quite firmly suggested, "O.K., guys, what about a practice session today? No score." This took hold, especially when I began to bat high flies and fast grounders for them, and the afternoon didn't go half badly. After fooling around like this for about forty-five minutes, they got interested in a sandlot team that came over for a practice workout and we watched this for about twenty-five minutes. Danny got very friendly with a mounted cop and his horse and, when he began to bother him a little with his questions about the horse's private life, I lured him away. (Entry: 4/11/47, Joel Vernick)

## 21. Ego Integrity under the Impact of Group Exposure

Our culture makes two conflicting demands upon children, so far as their role as members of groups is concerned. They can be briefly abstracted in the following statements:

Resignation to adaptational modesty.
Renunciation of exploitational temptations.

Educators have described at length what a "chore" group life is for children, since they have to accept many "sacrifices" for the sake of others for the attainment of a decent group role and the achievement of common group goals. We know how even the nursery school child is expected to "share," to surrender some of his demand for total possession of the adult, to make concessions by accepting a less coveted game now so that the group can have its decision realized, with a dim chance of getting one's special wish later. There is much more to it than that, of course, but may it suffice to mention that much "group adjustment" does mean a certain sacrifice in egotistic and narcissistic impulsivity, with some subtler rewards dangling somewhere in the future.

Educators have described less dramatically the other side of this same picture: adjustment also means renunciation of the special chances and temptations with which group life confronts the individual. It is not true that you need only "cooperate and share." You also have to learn how not to exploit a chance to dominate which a confused or weak group throws into your path, how not to use others to gratify your own pathology, ready though they may be to make you do just that, how you must not try to manipulate groups so that they become just another means in your life sphere, no matter what the other members need them for. In short, after group exposure, the renunciation of group psychological temptations becomes as vital a point as the much more publicized virtues of the "share and cooperate" philosophy of life.

We consider both features—the "adaptive modesty" of the individual as well as his readiness to "renounce exploitational temptations"—to be basic conditions for what we call "integrity" of the ego when exposed to group life.

Harry has an extreme oppositionalism, a kind of innate narcissism that flares in moments when adult controls are aimed at a given item of behavior that is important for him to carry out. In these moments, as a part of the pattern of rebellion, he involves the group very neatly in rioting and raids simply as a special tool in his warfare against the adult. Thus, one evening when interfered with in a scapegoat issue against Larry, for whom he developed a special hatred, he deliberately lured the group into a mass walk-out at the moment when the evening counselor was trying to work out a program for the evening. His tactics were amazingly skillful. First he aped boredom. When the counselor suggested this or that, he lolled in his chair, looked up at the ceiling, mimicked a man going to sleep and made them all laugh. Suddenly he jumped up out of his chair, and, agile as a monkey, leaped across the room, saying "follow me, guys" and, without even a backward glance over his shoulder, he ran out into the street and around into the back yard. They followed him at once, excited by his daring, and he exultantly led them to the top of the garage roof where he had them throwing bricks down into the yard in a tremendous state of intoxication with their destructiveness. The garage, which was on its last legs anyway and had several loose bricks, was subjected to many such raids through his leadership and, within three weeks after Harry came to the Home, looked as if it had been bombed.

This, however, is only half the picture. For a healthy "group role," something else has to be added, namely:

*Assertion of one's own personality structure; resistance against becoming a mere "ingredient" in the group psychological scene.*

With all due credit to the importance of the adjustment of individuals to the groups they are part of, a democratic philosophy of life has equal interest in the fact that the members of its group still remain individuals. It would not want to gain any type of group psychological strength at the price of having the structure of the individuals who constitute those groups wiped out in the process. This side of the picture hasn't been promulgated quite as much as the other one but is equally obviously implied. An individual who would allow himself to be "used for anything" just because of his helpless emotional dependence on a group he is in, or members of it, would, obviously, have lost his "integrity" as a person. In short, we do not want children to become mere "tools," either of another group member, of the temporary leader, or even for "somebody else's cause." We want them to be able to "assert" their personality structure, even under the impact of group emotion and group loyalty demands and orgies, and we want them to remain able to resist dissolution of their judgment, their self-directed goal awareness, their thinking ability, etc., under the impact of any "mob psychological" device.

Applied to our children specifically, this means the "ego" must be as eager not to lose its basic functions under the impact of group atmosphere as we know it has to be to make certain sacrifices along the impulsive-demand line.

The danger of this "loss of integrity" by the ego under the impact of group psychological processes has become especially clear to us in the course of our studies in group contagions.[5] What we said before about the impact of "Group

[5] Norman Polansky, Ronald Lippitt and Fritz Redl, *op. cit.*

Psychological Intoxication" as well as "contagibility" belongs here, too.

Translated into the life sphere of our children, this means specifically that we want the following ego functions maintained:

Ability to stand up under the impact of sheer group status ("Johnny cannot make me do this, even though he is the big shot in the gang"). Ability to retain reasoning powers even under the impact of group emotional stir-up ("I still think this is a dopey thing to do, even though the whole group yelled with enthusiasm about what that dopey counselor suggested").

Ability to maintain one's own need rights even in the face of group emotional propaganda ("I don't like to go on no overnight, I am too scared. The hell with all that baloney that we will have a wonderful time").

Ability to set limits to contagibility where one's own personality structure would be impaired (The whole group starts on a wild destructive orgy. Member A, who is otherwise a good sport but does not see any sense in this, is capable of withdrawing from it or making attempts to stop it).

Ability for intelligent rebellion against overdependence ("She always tells us what to do. We want to have a chance to decide for ourselves, even though she is O.K. and usually has good ideas").

There are many more where these come from. What we are trying to point out here, having to forfeit the chance for an anywhere near adequate discussion of group psychology for the time being, is simply this:

Some of the trouble our children get into is due to the fact that their egos do not have sufficient control over their own impulsivity, and do not have sufficient scope to encompass group values and goals into the orbit of their jobs. At the same time, however, some other trouble they may get into is due to the fact that their egos do not have sufficient resistance against the impact of group influence, atmosphere, dependence, and so forth, to maintain their personal integrity against the temporary group current.

Bill comes from a family background which is closer to typical middle class than that of the other Pioneers. He is the only one, for example, whose family unit has stayed intact and who has never been in a foster home previous to placement at the Home. While he has terrific impulsivity problems along hyper-aggressive lines like many of the others, he has, as we might expect, more deeply introjected superego values. Some of the crude sex behavior such as open masturbation and erotic play between the other children, whom it does not bother, really evokes guilt feelings in him and still he is incapable of defending himself against surrender to any prevailing group behavioral sex pattern of the moment, whatever its shock value may be. Dramatic testimony for this occurred one day in the playroom when there was a piece of highly erotic exhibitionism between Andy and Mike going on, which Bill fell into as usual. Suddenly, in the middle of a crude piece of behavior in which he was acting out the fantasy that he was "screwing this corner in the wall—hey watch me guys," he stopped and cried out "Gee, my ass is going to fall to pieces," an obvious castration anxiety suddenly liberated from deep level unconscious regions. But not even this stopped him and, spurred on by the group excitement, he kept right on until stopped by the executive director.

We mean both problems here, not only the much more publicized one of "group adjustment" but also the equally important one of "self-defense of the ego against group psychological impacts." Though of composite nature, either one of those ego functions is of tremendous importance for the purpose of a good adjustment to life, and the educator as well as the clinician must become interested in a more specific analysis of just at which place in which respect a child's ego is unable to do that job. All too long have we propagandized the task of "group adjustment" in general, without specific reference as to just where the specific disturbance may sit.

## 22. The Wisdom of Tool-Appraisal

There is another most typical ego weakness, which our youngsters seem to share with a large number of adults, especially where these find themselves in parental roles. Since this item is easier to clarify with an illustration out of the psychology of parental behavior, let us remember the frequency with which even parents who are perfectly realistic in deciding that Johnny's behavior now should be interfered with are often at a total loss as to how to do any realistic speculating about just what specific ways of interfering would do to Johnny and the purpose they have in mind. We find that some adults may show quite adequate realism in the decision as to when to act. They neither get unduly punitive nor sentimentally soft. But when it comes to assessing just which tool would serve them best, their egos seem to be totally void of any cognitive curiosities at all.

This same complaint can easily be levelled against our Pioneers. Sometimes they acted as an impulsive and not too bright child would act in a workshop. In his eagerness to get the lid of a watch open, he may grope for the most inappropriate tool, which greedily applied finally wrecks the watch for the improvement of which it was originally employed. Of course, we have in mind, here, primarily wrong tool thinking in connection with our Pioneers' reaction to human behavior. That means that often, even though their ego gives them some realistic insight about the problem to be tackled, it leaves them in great trouble by not adding to that any cognitive awareness of the multiplicity of possible approaches, of the adequacy of the approach tried to the situation in hand, of the less visible subsurface results. This phenomenon becomes especially irking where it extends into a certain rigidity of defense mechanisms, so that new situations cannot be appraised as to the modifications in behavior they would require, even where the general direction of response may be adequately sized up.

For weeks after coming to Pioneer House, Mike's chief defense against his insecurity in the new group was a kind of aimless and naive surrender of all his personal possessions. In this "casting bread upon the waters" approach he apparently assumed that he would be rewarded by affection and acceptance from the others. While we might have expected this for the first few days, the length of time that it went on, even after it became obvious to Mike that it wasn't working, indicates that in some way or other this had been established as a pretty deeply ingrained response to outer insecurities and threats. Evidently, in the rather primitive institution in which he had lived between the ages of three and eight, this technique of chronic bribery had been the only one which had protected him against older and tougher children, and having learned this, and this alone, as a survival technique, he used it far past the point of diminishing returns.

Sam, who had chronic difficulties in school all of his life, was a confirmed truant prior to Pioneer House. We openly sympathized with him about his many unpleasant school experiences. Still, he had to pretend he had stomach pains and a variety of physical complaints to avoid going, which we knew had been the kind of excuses he had used in previous home placements where he had attended schools in which he had been mistreated. This was so even when he must have realized that we saw through his defense, since we called in our consultant pediatrician who cleared him medically. This was done deliberately so that he could not accuse us of being "mean" and callous to his complaints. He still refused to go and in interview situations we promised him every immunity against reprisal for anything he might have to say against our present school arrangement. Wouldn't he tell us what he didn't like, what he was scared of, what was wrong? "No," he would say, "Dave, it isn't that. It's just that my belly hurts so." And then, after school was over, he would suddenly convert to good health and want to join the play activities, etc. It didn't even seem to bother him that this alone would undermine the position which he would take again the next morning— that he was "sick" and couldn't go, his "belly hurt" or his "head ached," etc.

## Summary

In looking over this assortment of twenty-two different "functions" of the ego, we are again impressed with the enormous task that still lies ahead of us. For it is painfully obvious that our twenty-two points are a sundry and ill-assorted lot. Some of them clearly are composites to be broken down into many more details; many of them have more inherent tendency toward syndrome formation with some of the rest than with others. All of this leads us into a task which can be tackled only by organized and large scale research, for which this presentation is no more than a prelude.

One statement, however, we would want to emphasize heavily before we leave this point: No matter how imperfect any given assortment of ego disturbances may be, *it is important* to begin to break down the vague concept of a "weak" or "poorly functioning" ego into many more specific parts than has ever been done before. For our work with disturbed children, as well as for daily ego support for the normal ones, we have to know *all the jobs an ego may be summoned to perform in a twenty-four hour day.* The traditional descriptions of "ego functions" view this concept primarily in terms of "basic attitudes toward reality," as seen in fantasy produced on the couch, daydreams observed in the playroom, and "defense mechanisms" toward life situations as such. We think it is important to follow the ego into the scene of *daily behavior control,* and to get a detailed inventory of all the prerequisites which go even into seemingly "simple" tasks.

We hold this because, to find ways of ego support, we first have to know just what jobs the ego needs to be supported to do. There is no path to a more efficient instrumentology of ego support except the one that leads over a more specific knowledge of just what ego functions are to begin with, and what they look like when disturbed.

# Chapter 4

## The Delinquent Ego
## And Its Techniques

THE PICTURE we have so far given of our Pioneers would leave one with the impression of children of high impulsivity, especially along the lines of hatred and destruction, and at the same time of children equipped with totally inadequate "controls." Their egos have been portrayed in the previous chapter as poorly developed, badly functioning, incapable of performing their task.

This picture of deficiency and helplessness of ego function is true enough as far as it goes. It constitutes, however, only half the story. We had better hurry and draw the other side, which looks nearly like the opposite of the one we have just described. The truth is that the ego of these children is as helpless as we showed it to be only in some life situations. In others we are suddenly confronted with ego functions which seem to be hypertrophically developed. Far from being inefficient in the tasks it sets itself, their ego, under those conditions, performs with amazing and exasperating efficiency. The only trouble is that their ego, where it seems too well intact, is functioning in the service of the wrong master. Unable to cope with the task of "civilian life," in battle-relevant areas it suddenly seems to set itself the task of defending impulsivity with a frantic effort.

This is why we want to introduce the concept of the "delinquent ego." We want to sharpen up an issue which seems to us to have been neglected so far.

Being aware of the terminological difficulty connected with such a combination of terms—for the word "delinquent," if used at all, would be more properly attached to the superego rather than the ego of a child—we had better state as clearly as we can just how we want this concept to be taken. Unable to load this book with an adequate discussion of the whole problem of delinquency itself, we shall have to be satisfied

167

with defining the terms as used for our purpose here, and hope for the best.

## The Ego and the Concept of Delinquency

The *"legal concept of delinquency"* simply states which type of behavior is forbidden by law, in which state, for which age group of children, and so forth. This is all it can do. It is obviously no help at all for whoever wants to know just what a piece of behavior means, how it was caused, or what should be done to avoid or cure it. It is worth while, though, to know about legal definitions so that one can assess the reality impact of certain issues in a number of cases.

The *"cultural meaning"* of the word delinquency might summarize all statements indicating that a piece of behavior is in contradiction with the value demands of the dominant culture within which a given child moves. We are aware, of course, of the fact that this definition contains serious faults. We know that there is no rigid system of values which would be valid for everybody in any one given culture. Rather, larger cultural value demands overlap in different segments of smaller subcultures within any one given society. Unable to cope with this difficulty at the moment, we shall try to devise appropriate corrections as we go along.

The *"clinical concept"* of delinquency is not in contradiction with the cultural or legal one but should be considered as an attempt to specify and supplement where the others left off. However, it is of great relevance, indeed, for the educator and clinician. We primarily have in mind the sharp difference we are forced to make between the assessment of the *delinquent behavior* involved in a case and the question of the *basis* on which such behavior occurred. An example may make this clear: Let us assume that we hear about a twelve year old who stole. On a legal basis, this behavior certainly falls into the category of "delinquent." On a cultural basis, too, this act is delinquent, provided the youngster belongs to the middle-class-value-identified society of our country, or is judged by it. The clinician might want to start getting interested from here on, however, in the more closely related "clinical question." He might find, for instance, that in one case the stealing was simply part of a jealousy neurosis; the youngster otherwise was highly "value identified," and his superego plagued him mercilessly after the act. Clinically, we would be inclined to call this "stealing on a neurotic basis." Compared with this youngster, the child who would simply steal because he saw something he wanted, who would "not give a damn" whom it belonged to, would be better classified as one whose stealing not only is a delinquent act in itself, but can be declared also to happen "on a delinquent basis." Such a differentiation, while it would change little in the legal or cultural value of the behavior in question, would certainly make a great difference in terms of what really ailed the youngster and what should be done to cure him and to prevent others from similar thefts. Just what variety of personality disturbances may be referred to when we make a statement that the youngster's stealing was on a "delinquent basis" may vary from case to case. We may think of "characterological disturbances," or we may contemplate the possibility that a particular child is stealing "because of a total identification with a delinquent neighborhood code." We might even find that a youngster growing up under certain conditions would be expected to develop a "delinquent superego" *in identification with* the adults with whom he has lived.

When we talk about the "delinquent ego" here, we have two things in mind:

1. We use the term "delinquent" in its cultural meaning—referring to any behavior which runs counter to the dominant value system within which the child's character formation takes place. Thus, we would include his insistence on "hate without cause," even where no clearly legally punishable act was involved. We mean all the attitudes which will be developed in a child who is about to drift into a "delinquent style of life."

2. As far as the "ego" side of the picture goes, we want to describe the ego in those situations in which it is bent on *defending impulse gratification at any cost.* In short, instead of performing its task of looking for a synthesis between

desires, reality demands, and the impact of social values, the ego is, in those moments, totally on the *side of impulsivity*. It throws all its weight into the task of making impulse gratification possible, against the outside world as well as against whatever remainders of the voice of its own conscience may be left. The amazing spectacle which we have before us in the children who hate lies right here: Sometimes these children seem to act wrong and confused simply because their ego is inefficient and cannot, as described before, manage the onrush of impulsivity in complex life situations. At other times, the situation is different indeed. Far from being helpless, the ego of these children is suddenly a rather shrewd appraiser of that part of reality which might be dangerous to their impulsive exploits and becomes an efficient manipulator of the world around them as well as an energetic protector of delinquent fun against the voice of their own conscience. Just which specific task the "delinquent ego," by which we mean from now on the ego's effort to secure guilt-free and anxiety-free enjoyment of delinquent impulsivity, may have to fulfill, will depend upon other details of a youngster's personality. Some, for instance, are identified with a delinquent behavior code anyway. Their own superego being delinquency identified already, guilt feelings won't bother them. The task of their ego is primarily to make it possible to "get away with things" and to defend their delinquency against the threat of the world around them. Others are not quite that advanced. They still have mighty chunks of their value-identified superego intact; the voice of their conscience still tries to make itself heard. In that case, the "delinquent ego" has the additional task of "duping its own superego," so that delinquent impulsivity can be enjoyed tax-free from feelings of guilt. In still another case, neither value-identified nor delinquent superego allegiances are very strongly developed. Those children are like a "bundle of drives," and their ego seems to have primarily a "reality manipulative task." These details are fascinating but irrelevant here. In all three cases we shall receive the full brunt of an efficient ego, bent on the task of impulsive protection, when we try to educate or treat such children. Far from acting delinquent out of

helplessness or just because of an occasional onrush of unusual impulse intensity, these children have an organized
system of defenses well developed and meet the adult who
tries to change them with a consistent and well-planned
barrage of counter-techniques.

Our term "delinquent ego" is therefore in the nature of an
auxiliary concept, saving us the need to use a long sentence
each time we refer to this. What we really should say each
time would be: "the ego, functioning right now in a planned
attempt to defend non-acceptable impulsivity." Thus, we use
this term as an abbreviation rather than as an attempt to
imply that the whole ego of a child is either delinquent or
not, or that only the egos of delinquents are ever summoned
to perform such a task. On the contrary, the defense of impulsivity against the outside world as well as against too
heavy superego demands is a task which, up to a certain
degree, every ego is summoned to perform at times. But with
these children we meet it in a compact concentration which
constitutes a formidable block to education and to therapy.

Once a child has part of its ego so clearly throwing its
weight toward the side of the defense of delinquency, we are
saddled with an entirely new task. In order to "free" the
youngster of his delinquent urges, we have to take the hurdle
of strategic impulse defense by their ego. With such children,
therefore, the exact study of just how their ego goes about to
defend their impulsivity against their own conscience, as well
as against the outside world, becomes a matter of prime importance. Since the material gained from the psychiatric
treatment of the basically neurotic delinquent has produced
little insight into the "tough defense machinery" we are
referring to here, it is worth while to give it our full attention.
Indeed, the development of a successful "total treatment
strategy" in a residential treatment design hinges upon this
very ability to know their *ego strengths as well as their ego
disturbances.* The detailed tracing of the machinations of the
delinquency-protective ego of our Pioneers would run into
several volumes. We have to restrict ourselves here, therefore,
to a mere listing of the most discernible "ego functions in the
service of impulse defense."

## The Strategy of Tax Evasion

Our Pioneers did not fall into the category of children who simply have "no superego at all," or who are harmoniously identified with a totally delinquent neighborhood code, as the classical "healthy delinquent" is supposed to be. In fact, we never met a child who would fit that description. Even the toughest children with whom we had to deal would reveal, upon closer inspection, that the aggressive front of behavior with which they would surround themselves needed many "special tricks" to be maintained at all. Below the behavioral surface, there would be a great number of little "value islands" left—stemming out of isolated remainders of earlier childhood identification, from the automatic absorption of non-delinquent elements in the general "code of behavior" which even a delinquent neighborhood still has sprinkled around, or out of occasional real ties or dependencies with people which couldn't quite be avoided after all. In short, even the ego of the toughest delinquent doesn't have quite as simple a job as we might assume. While visibly expert in the task of producing delinquent behavior without much concern, it has quite a job to perform in order to keep all phases of that behavior from being "tax exempt" from feelings of guilt. The children we talk about have many such "value islands" in their personalities, and consequently their ego spends much time seeing to it that what they do can be enjoyed without the price of guilt feelings. In fact, they have little trouble "getting away" with a good deal of behavior for the moment. To really "get away" with doing all this without feeling bad about it afterwards, however, seems to be an additional job. It is fascinating to watch the special machinery these children's ego has developed in order to secure their behavior against post-situational guilt feelings.

The techniques described here are very similar to the "alibi tricks" which delinquents use in order to "talk themselves out of it" when grilled about a delinquent job they might have been involved in. What we mean here is not this verbal skill of arguing with the representative of responsibility and guilt from the outside world, but the "system of delusions" which they have invented in order to talk themselves, so to speak, out of the demands of their own conscience—where it is still intact.

The situation carries, of course, a strong analogy to what we know about neurotic symptom formation from other cases. Just as the defenses against anxiety which a person displays only prove that there is much to be "defended against," so the "alibi tricks" our children need to avoid "feeling bad about what they did" are equal evidence for both their ego skill in warding off guilt feelings and also the existence of superego demands without which such efforts would not have been necessary. Sometimes, by the way, a study of these "guilt evasion" tricks is the only tangible evidence for the existence of the values, for the duping of which the whole machinery had to be invented to begin with.

The following is a fairly cursory list of such "tax evasion from guilt feelings" techniques which we could amply observe

*Repression of own intent*

at Pioneer House as well as at camp:

Some of our youngsters have an enviable skill of repressing, right after an incident happens, its actual emotional gain and of course everything that would betray their basic motivation to begin with. This repression accomplished, they can now afford to remember, relate or brag about any other detail of the incident without having to fear that the voice of their conscience might be raised in this process.

One of the youngsters at camp had stolen a wallet from a counselor whom he actually liked a lot, and whose "fairness toward him" he had openly and repeatedly recognized before. The specific child had a perfectly "delinquent" superego as far as stealing as such was concerned, but his own value standard would reject as very "unfair" "to be mean to somebody who had been nice to you." When confronted with this misdeed, he had no trouble remembering, admitting, and discussing freely the details of his theft. When challenged, not along the line of having stolen, but of having been mean to somebody who had been so nice to him, he blocked entirely, couldn't remember a thing about just "why" he might have wanted to do a thing like that, assuring us that he didn't mean to hurt the adult, he just needed the cash in the wallet. As long as he could keep up this separation of issues for himself, he was perfectly safe. He would have liked nothing better than to be punished for the delinquent side of the act, so as to be sure not to be confronted with the real "guilt" as far as he was concerned. It took considerable interview work in this specific case until, much later, the child was able to allow himself to become aware of the full impact of his own love for the adult, of the specific fantasies which had gone into the theft, and could be helped to cope with the feelings of guilt which then, post-situationally, suddenly arose.

By the way, it is our experience that sudden *blocking* in a "grilling" interview does not always mean an attempt to hide from discovery. The inability of children to produce at all, when challenged in a way similar to that of the example, is sometimes a direct indication that we have hit upon an area in which real value sensitivity might still be intact.

### He did it first

We do not mean the case, here, where a youngster tries to ward off blame by shoving it off onto somebody else. We actually mean that the mere fact that "somebody else did it first" would really constitute a chance not to have to feel guilty for something he did. We have pointed at this basic principle of "exculpation magics through the initiatory act" before. We do not claim that we can explain it, but have to state it as a simple matter of fact: Conscience can be assuaged at times by the simple awareness that the guilt-producing behavior was entered in only after somebody else had already openly done what one only intended to do.[1] Needless to point out, this is a most "illogical" way of thinking, and no system of ethics we could conceive of actually supports such argument. For the Unconscious, however, it seems to be a fact that, for "intramural use" so to speak, priority of somebody else's guilt takes away the tax burden of guilt feelings quite well.

[1] Fritz Redl, "Group Emotion and Leadership," *Psychiatry*, **V**, No. 4 (November 1942).

For a long time, at camp, we were fooled by considering the youngsters with the most patent trend to accuse others, as the more "delinquent ones." For some of them that is still correct. We had to learn, though, that sometimes this actually works the other way around. The great need to find somebody who did it first need not come from a need to be revengeful or accusatory, but may, on the contrary, point to the very intact part of the youngster's superego. Only because he would really have to feel guilty for what he did, does a child sometimes seek so hard to find somebody else to blame.

## Everybody else does such things anyway

This is a well-known device even among adult sinners, and easily enters the "self-apologetic" argument of otherwise honorable people, especially where obligations to larger issues are involved. Many people who wouldn't steal one cent from another person's pocket find their morals crumbling if something can be pointed out as "general business practice." This kind of "logic," again, is equally indicative of two facts: that this special person's superego can be easily punctured, and also that there is still something that needs puncturing by a special trick.

Lefty, a twelve-year-old boy in one of our Detroit Group Project Clubs, stole two watches and a ring from counselors. After it was finally established that he had committed the thefts, following a long and stubborn "holdout," he and his caseworker discussed the situation. Lefty admitted almost proudly to the caseworker that he had been stealing for a long time. When the caseworker asked how he felt about this, whether he was bothered at all, he replied, "The only thing that bothers me is if I get caught." Did he believe it was right to go around "swiping stuff," asked the caseworker. To this he replied, heatedly, "There isn't a single boy in my neighborhood who doesn't steal. Everybody steals sometime in their life, even you, I'll bet. Even preachers steal." Nor was this an expediency of the moment. In interview after interview, Lefty used the same argument, thus showing how deeply imbedded it was.

*We were all in on it*

The wonderful drug of "group morale" and "we feeling" is not an unmitigated blessing. Under certain group psychological conditions, it backfires on us. A piece of behavior which goes counter to what a child could ever afford without feeling very bad afterwards may be indulged in without the slightest compunction if it takes place as part of a collective enterprise. It is then as though the ego of the child would use the very fact that so many were involved as a guilt-assuaging ingredient. Under certain group psychological conditions, behavior can be afforded as being tax-free from guilt feelings which otherwise could not. The group then serves as a palliative of individual superego demands.

On one occasion the whole Pioneer group had been involved in a very dangerous and destructive episode of throwing bricks from the top of the garage. We decided to have individual interviews with each of the boys to "rub-in" the total unacceptability of such behavior. Andy, especially, was fascinating in his real indignation at even being approached on the subject. Tearfully he shouted at the Director who was doing the interviewing, "Yeah, everybody was doing it and you talk to me. Why is it my fault?" When it was pointed out to him that we were not saying it was all his fault but that he was responsible for his individual share in the matter, he was still unable to admit the point: "But we were all in on it. Why talk to me?"

*But somebody else did that same thing to me before*

As an open argument, such a statement seems incredible and void of all sense. An efficient delinquent ego, though, knows to what wonderful use it can be put, when the task of warding off guilt feelings arises. In fact, we had many children, after long interview work, really come out with this "theory of exculpation" in open declaration. After we had finally crowded them enough so that they could not any longer ward off the guilt issue involved in what they did, they found a last refuge, in arguing with themselves and with us, in this device. They really tried to prove that their stealing was all right because "somebody swiped my own wallet two weeks ago." Needless to add, only a rather primitive ego can still afford to get away with an alibi trick like that.

Following the closure of Pioneer House, Danny eventually went back to live with his own family, since he was not able to make an adjustment in a foster home because of the unavoidably premature release from treatment. Slowly he began to acquire a stealing pattern. Eventually he stole twenty dollars from a staff member at the School of Social Work with whom he had a very positive relationship during the Pioneer House period, when she had been involved in much of the programming at the Home. In interview, when confronted with this and asked if he really felt comfortable in stealing from this person who had always been so nice to him, he said, "Hell, my stepfather wrecked my cowboy gun two weeks ago. Threw it in the stove. I had to get another one." Even after he admitted that this wasn't the staff member's fault, he still clung to the feeling that it wasn't wrong for him to take the money if his stepfather had been so mean to him.

### He had it coming to him

Using such an argument toward us or to themselves, children usually want to imply that their behavior, the delinquent aspect of which they might have to feel guilty about, was primarily motivated by revenge—which is supposed to make it all right. They argue very much as religious people would have to argue in civilized nations which go to war. While "killing" itself is of course sinful, guilt feelings need not occur as soon as a specific act can be proved to be "revenge for an unjustified hurt."

This reminds us of a rather sadistic child we had at camp who yet was obsessed by a strict self-imposed code of not "hurting anybody who is weaker than you." Placed with a group, all of whom happened to be weaker than he, he was soon in desperate straits. He finally found the way out— all he had to do was wait for the chance that one of the

children did something that he felt unjustified, like dis-
arranging his blanket when climbing up to his upper bunk,
and he could afford a really vicious and dangerous attack
on his intended victim. The superego-directed argument
that this child now "deserved" what he got, took care of
any potential guilt feelings to which his own behavior code
might otherwise have made him vulnerable.

### I had to do it, or I would have lost face

Necessity in an extreme situation is considered an extenu-
ating circumstance even in the general course of ethical argument. The mother who had to steal in order to save her
starving child would not only find society ready to grant her
a point, but might herself, even though a most value-identified person, consider this a case where "honesty can't be
afforded any more" and might use such an argument to
reduce her feeling of guilt. With some children, especially at
the age of pre-adolescence and early adolescence, "status in
the group in which one travels" assumes importance of such
a high degree that it actually is considered as falling into this
category.

We have seen many children in dire predicaments like this:
Exposed to a delinquent gang, the cozy group atmosphere
of which appealed to them, they were caught in a conflict
between their individual superego and the delinquency-
immune code of the group. Soon they would be drifting
into a great deal of behavior which would be quite unacceptable to their own value system, but they realized that
non-compliance with the group demand would be accompanied by a total loss of face. As soon as the first battle was
lost in favor of this issue as a "guilt-assuaging" factor, they
would extinguish, or at least reduce, their individual feeling
of guilt, by the inner argument that they "couldn't have
avoided it without being called a sissy."

### I didn't use the proceeds anyway

For some youngsters, the feeling of guilt seems to be
cunningly tied to the condition that the proceeds of their deed

are actually consumed and enjoyed. This gives the delinquent ego a wonderful way out: simply avoid using or enjoying them, and your conscience has to keep quiet. Thus we found many youngsters actually arguing that their behavior was all right because they gave away, broke, buried, lost, or threw away the stolen loot. Usually we would ascribe such behavior to the "unconscious wish for punishment" or to other neurotically defined needs. It helps to know that in some cases this behavior does not indicate an unconscious need of that sort but rather is a skillful device of their ego to deal with potentials of guilt. The differential diagnosis as to which is the case remains, of course, an important clinical issue.

At camp, one season, Whitey broke into the staff quarters and stole several cartons of cigarets. Many of these were used to buy his way into the favor of some of the tough addict smokers who had high prestige in his group. A few, curiously enough, he threw into the lake. He, himself, didn't smoke any. In interviews concerning this behavior this last point became his strongest argument. "What the hell! I didn't smoke a damn one, did I?"

*But I made up with him afterwards*

A similar trick of the delinquent ego trying to dupe its conscience is to tie the emergence of guilt feelings to the condition that the victim of the act remains hostile or puts up a struggle to begin with. Children using this device feel totally free of blame, if this is not visibly the case, or if they can "make friends" with the victim afterwards. This technique is especially effective if our delinquent hits upon a victim with real masochistic needs, or with neurotic trends toward passivity and self-punishment which play right into our perpetrator's pathological hands.

We had quite a time once at camp with a youngster who had been apprehended just when he had tried a particularly vicious attempt at homosexual rape. The child was an habitual pervert, and of course the sexual side of the picture wouldn't have aroused any guilt feeling in him at that time. He was, however, strongly identified with a group code of "fairness toward those who are weak," so we tackled him on the brutality side of the issue. He put up quite a struggle though, trying to avoid admitting that what he did was wrong. His argument, of all things, was that the particular child bore him no grudge, and he "had made up with him" afterwards. In a similar vein, it was hard to squeeze even a drop of guilt feeling out of our sneak thieves if their victim seemed to be careless about his possessions to begin with, took inadequate precautions against theft, or left them lying around. The slogan "never give a sucker a break" can apparently also be applied for internal use.

This issue may become important in the appraisal of the meaning of a child's behavior along characterological lines. Public opinion seems to support the theory that children who show great concern to "apologize," make amends, make friends, after their deeds, thereby give evidence of the better side of their nature and are really trying to prove their good motives. With the children we are talking about, the opposite is the case: restitutional gestures, appeasement and so forth are meant to *cement* their delinquency against the internal danger of feelings of guilt.

### He is a no good so-and-so himself

It seems that even where the act itself has to be admitted as being guilt provoking, the possibility of being able to *depreciate the victim* involved eases the guilt issue. This type of "logic" which the delinquent ego displays sometimes assumes fantastic proportions. This is especially the case where the very value issue which makes the perpetrator's behavior so obnoxious is used to depreciate the victim himself. Thus, some of our thieves would consider it quite a good excuse for their act that the person they stole from was "only a goddamn thief" himself. They argue, in that case, on the level of adolescent "jackroller" who lures homosexuals into tempting contact with him in order to knock them out and relieve them of their cash. In a treatment situation, the stealing part of the side is usually warded off for a long time as a value issue by sick youngsters—it seems to them justified simply on the basis that the people from whom they steal "are such lowdown despicable bums" themselves.

Dick, who stole a fountain pen from the director's lodge at camp, was subsequently a victim of some of his cabin mates who stole his fountain pen and jacknife. In our discussions with the culprits, they tried to side-issue the interview with the argument, "Yeah, what are you talking to us for? You know what a dirty crook that guy is. Why he came in here and stole a fountain pen last week. What right does he have to complain?" "Did he steal from you?" we asked. Even after they had to admit that he hadn't, it still did not detract from the vehemence or tenacity of their plea. He was still a "lousy crook" and had it coming.

*They are all against me, nobody likes me,*
*they are always picking on me*

The unconscious insight of the delinquent ego into the basic machinery of morality is indeed uncanny and we should have learned from it long ago. It seems that the principle of "noblesse oblige" can be invoked only if there is a semblance of "noblesse" to begin with. The experience of "hostility" from the world outside cuts down on the degree to which individuals feel themselves tied to the "moral code." In fact, the epitome of this technique is obviously the development of clearly persecutory delusions to begin with. We have seen this displayed by our Pioneers in the whole phase of "treatment shock." During this period the children operate, in part at least, on this assumption: if we can only prove that the world is against us, then even value demands within us which we would otherwise recognize as valid can be balanced off and can be forgotten. Short of the consistent use of this principle for "delinquent defense," the next step is an attempt to pick out of reality situations that part which may be interpreted as "an act of unfairness" and use it to wipe the guilt issue off the slate.

It is this technique that delinquent egos use with such skill, when the environment in which they find themselves is really rejective, brutal, or at least unloving. This is why some of them cannot be treated at all without exposure to the totality of an acceptant and strategic design.

In addition to justifying his stealing on the basis that "everybody steals," Lefty also argued that his mother never got him "nothin' that he wanted," that she was nicer to his stepsiblings than to him, and that his step-father was cruel and stingy. In reality these things were all true to a certain extent, as the family story proved. Thus, "if she ain't gonna buy me that Bulova watch I want, I'm gonna steal one, just wait and see." And he did. The fact that his mother, who did reject him, was still not financially able to buy him a watch anyway made no difference. His feeling of rejection from her and the step-father was still enough of an argument so that he could go out and steal valuable items on a guilt-free basis. "How about the guy from whom you swiped it? What did he do to you?" we asked. This made no difference to Lefty who continued to argue in the same vein.

*I couldn't have gotten it any other way.*

This superego-directed "argument" is based on the assumption that an individual has the "right" to certain gratifications, and that value issues stop being relevant if for some reason their attainability is not granted. It is the attitude of "the world owes me this," with the implications that all other considerations, including value issues, are secondary to that.

All the ego now has to do is to classify a specific gratification that the individual's impulse is after as "basic, something he has coming to him," and from then on no holds are barred. In order to abuse this principle as wildly as some of our youngsters do, the distortion of their concept of "the world" and their own superego is usually already a prerequisite.

During the initial phase of treatment at Pioneer House, Sam stole the Director's cigarette lighter. In an interview with him we tried to get at some of his motivation for the theft. His only defense seemed to be, "Well, I wanted a lighter."

When further challenged, "Yes, you wanted a lighter but how about going to such lengths as to steal it from someone?" he grew quite irritated. "How the hell do you expect me to get one if I don't swipe it? Do I have enough money to buy one?" There was no question that, having logically narrowed down his chances of getting a lighter to stealing it, the act itself was quite justifiable to him on a "closed issue" basis: "I want it, there is no other way, so I swipe it —just because I want it."

Two items need to be stressed to avoid a misunderstanding of what we have tried to point out in this whole section on the strategy of tax evasion. One is, again, the importance of differentiating between the mechanisms described here and a use of any such "arguments" in order to fool authority figures or as a semi-legalistic device to soften the punitive implication of a misdeed for which one has been caught. Wherever the latter is being done, the same arguments quoted here may be used, but we then have to deal with an entirely different layer of "defenses of the delinquent ego," which we shall describe shortly. What we have in mind in the section on tax evasion is an actual attempt of the ego to ward off *inner* conflict between the children's own conscience and what they do. That is, their ego uses these devices to make delinquent behavior possible and to keep it guilt free, not to ward off outside consequences. The existence and usability of such defenses always prove both the energetic effort of the child's ego to protect his delinquency from his own "better self," and the existence of some parts of an intact conscience or superego— for the really "valueless" youngster wouldn't need any of this at all, and would simply enjoy his delinquent fun with a defiant "so what?" attitude. As in the case of the emergence of resistance in the treatment of neurotics, the defenses employed here prove both the existence of pathology and the functioning of the ego defending it. Thus, the careful study of such "alibi tricks" would help us in the diagnosis of what the enemy of our treatment effort is doing and, at the same time, also offer us additional insight into those parts of a child's superego which are still intact. The clinician, as well as the educator, might welcome both.

The other item to be stressed here and elaborated upon later on is, of course, the great impact of all this for practice. And this part is relevant not only for the educator of the disturbed child, but also for the parent and educator of his normal age mate. For, what is disturbance later on usually was a perfectly legitimate phase of development at an earlier time. The very type of "alibi tricks" children have to employ in the defense of their search for happiness which will irritate adults gives us a wonderful picture of just which level of superego development they have achieved, which is still to be entered into, where potential distortions might lurk. For the therapist of a disturbed child, the implications of all this are equally serious—for it means that in those cases the problem is not one of "ego support" but one of *superego support* and ego *repair*. The areas in which children act in the way we described are not the ones where their ego is "weak" or "disturbed." On the contrary, these seem to be hypertrophically developed ego functions—only applied in the service of the wrong goal. The result of these hypertrophic ego skills applied for the wrong goal must not be confused with the evidence of other areas in which the ego is weak or disturbed in its functioning, though any one child may, and usually does, show a mixture of both. The differential diagnosis as to just which problem of a child is more indicative of the one or of the other becomes of prime importance, and it is with this in mind that we want to challenge the clinician to give this item much thought.

## Search for Delinquency Support

An efficient delinquent ego is not satisfied with inventing alibi tricks to put its own conscience to sleep. It reaches out more actively for opportunities for the guiltless enjoyment of delinquent gratifications. The following are some of the devices employed with this end in mind.

### Ferreting out the "wrong" type of friends

The skill with which children of certain disturbance types ferret out other children with a similar or a supplementary type of pathology has provoked the amazement of clinicians before. Thus, you can rely on it that the youngster of strong sadistic trends will spot the potentially willing masochistic partner in a group in no time at all. It is also known that youngsters, or adults for that matter, with certain types of sexual perversions will be amazingly keen in the appraisal of similar potentials in personnel around them. The same thing holds true for youngsters whose ego is bent on a support of delinquent behavior at one time or another. They will feel "uncomfortable" with other children who are too allergic to the type of delinquency they show or whose superego emanates too clearly its value demands. They will "pal" and associate on their own choice with children who may be expected to support, supplement, or contribute to their own constant search for delinquent enjoyment. It is interesting to watch how this basic principle often throws into companionship children who, on the basis of other properties of their personality, are really not very compatible at all. They often have little to do with each other or look for much more adequate playmates when non-delinquent activities are concerned. They are quick and eager, though, to search for the supportive type of friendship whenever the issue of a specific type of delinquent behavior becomes relevant. The closest scrutiny and study of friendships made under the impact of this issue is of great practical importance, indeed.

It is always fascinating to watch how within the first three to four hours of the first day of camp the delinquents "find" each other. This cuts across group lines, age barriers, and socio-economic differences. Children who have never met before in their lives and may even live in different parts of the state sniff out each other's delinquency potentials with an amazing swiftness which almost looks like a sixth sense. This acuteness in size-up skill does not apply so much to the non-delinquent type of youngster. One boy from the Detention Home in Detroit and another from the Upper Peninsula in Michigan, not even in the same cabin, were discovered the first night of camp, one summer, skulking around some counselor cabins. From their behavior it was clear that they were "casing" to establish the vulnerability of the camp set-up for future stealing. Both youngsters, in spite of the confusion and chaos of the first day of camp, had already sized up each other's "reliability" as good delinquents.

## Affinity toward gang formation and mob psychology

With the science of group psychology as undeveloped as it is, we sometimes feel full of envy when we observe some of our youngsters developing a nearly uncanny instinct for sizing up group situations for the delinquency support they might render. Such children will naturally drift into the type of group atmosphere which is clearly that of a gang structure, or they will skillfully produce, or at least exploit, the phenomenon of "mob psychology." Without turning this item into a specific treatise on these topics, we want to refer only to the rich possibilities which specific group atmospheres offer to the delinquent child. Especially does the sudden breakdown of inhibitions, reality appraisal, personal affectional ties which even otherwise well-functioning groups suffer under the impact of excitement or group psychological intoxication, lend itself to a masterful pick-up by the delinquent manipulator. He is able to get others and himself into more delinquent activity under those conditions than even he would dare or would be able to devise under other circumstances. This phenomenon is intensified when a number of children with delinquent egos live together in a group to begin with and when they have a chance to solidify their individual delinquent defenses into something like an officially recognized "group code." It is as though those youngsters knew that submergence into a delinquent group code would be the best antidote against the remainders of their individual superego demands, which might hamper their guilt-free enjoyment of delinquent fun.

The difference in susceptibility to mob psychological temptation between the "delinquent" type of youngster and the straight neurotic or normal child was strikingly shown in camp experiences. One night there was a tremendous excitement in one of the cabins of pre-adolescent boys. They were going to "get" a kid from another cabin who had wronged them in some way. This particular group, which had among its members a rather non-delinquent boy, had worked itself up into a veritable frenzy and finally tore out after the victim, chasing wildly through the woods to his cabin. Counselors went after them to bring them back. This one youngster, however, seemed completely unaffected by all of this and instead was grumpily fussing about, looking for his toothbrush and complaining that there wasn't enough hot water to take his shower. He wasn't shocked by this behavior as far as we could determine, but he just wasn't interested. None of the others would have missed such a chance to get in some reckless or cruel behavior which would have gone tax-free because of the general melee.

### Seduction toward the initiatory act

We mentioned before the mechanism by which youngsters manage to consider themselves exempt from value conflicts: if somebody else "does it first," the whole sequence of events after that can be chalked up to the principle of "exculpation through the initiatory act." [2] Some of our youngsters don't stop at using this convenient machinery—their ego is skillful enough to produce such a seducer at the drop of an impulse. What they do is this: they provoke somebody else into an act of aggression, defiance, delinquency of some sort or other. As soon as the other child starts it off, they are free to pick it up from there and enjoy the rest of the anti-social chain as though it had come from the outside to begin with. This trick is especially visible along the line of aggressive behavior or defiance. One boy will "dare" the weakest link in the chain to do this or that, and once the other boy has started off, he will take the clue from there, but now with total abandon of any value compunctions he might otherwise have felt. The alibi trick mentioned before now does the job for him.

At Pioneer House, Henry was extremely skillful in engineering "riots" around bedtime. After the counselor had

2 *Ibid.*

left the sleeping rooms or even while she was still in there, Henry would ingeniously use stimulative language like, "Hey, Andy, Danny fat-ass swiped your comic book. You gonna let him get away with that?" Andy would then tear out of the sleeping room to pound on Danny's sleeping room to get "his comic book back," even though he knew Danny hadn't swiped it. At this point Henry and Joe, a third boy in the sleeping room, would dash out and start wildly chasing through the house. From here the excitement would infect the other sleeping room and soon the whole group was out of control. Henry never could be pinned down on this for he always would say: "Who me? What did I do? Did I *make* him go out? He started it and then me and the other guys did it."

### Hankering for delinquency lure

Some of our youngsters have a great affinity to situations which would be expected to be tempting toward their own impulsivity. With uncanny foresight they ferret out such "temptation potentials" and get themselves involved. It seems that their ego has accepted "temptation beyond endurance" as a valid argument against guilt feelings. All they have to do then is to seek out situations of that sort.

We found our Pioneers time and again magically drawn to activities which, though innocent looking at the start, would invariably end up by exposing them to more excitement and temptational challenge than they could take. They would invariably drift into alleys where irate neighbors might be expected to chase them away, so that destructive window breaking then would be considered an understandable "act of revenge."

They would discover, of all the many basements of the various University buildings, the one which contained a coke machine which seemed to be all too ready to respond to buttons instead of nickels—it happened to be in the Law School of all places, too. Or they would carefully seek out stores whose keeper could be expected to be of a less watchful type, or browse around the rooms of counselors at camp whose tendency to be not too vigilant with cigarettes or cash lying around was known to them. In the cases we have in mind, they did *not* enter those premises with a decision to steal. All their ego did was to drive them toward "situational lure," knowing it could leave the rest to predictable "chance."

### The exploitation of moods

Some of our youngsters would suffer from obvious "moods" or "fits," which were part of their pathology and which, at the time, they really could not help. It is amazing how the delinquent ego of some children even exploits the *internal* opportunities thus offered to them. A child, for instance, with an intense need for sadistic behavior for which he really would feel guilty if committed in cold blood, would skillfully time the gratification of his sadistic wishes with an onset of his uncontrollable pathology. Thus, the fit of rage a child really could not help would be exploited to cover up an act of cruelty to a hated enemy, or an act of recklessness toward an adult, which he could not have afforded otherwise without guilt. Timing it well with the onset of a fit gave him a chance to get away, so far as he was concerned, with the excuse, "Well, I can't help it, once I am in this state." It is important for the practitioner to be aware of this. For, while the outburst itself cannot be prevented until the basis for the fits has cleared up, their exploitation for the secondary gain of guilt-exempt aggression can be counteracted by strategic handling. In the process of treatment this often becomes an especially important item. Some of our children would exploit stages of fits even at a time when that much intensity was not really "needed" any more, and it was important for us to point out the difference between our tolerance of the onset of their attack, which was as yet beyond control, and the point where their ego began to exploit such an attack for behavior which they could have helped, had not their technique of "mood exploitation" been in operation.

Danny, whose severe fits of temper lasted twenty-five to thirty minutes, became very crafty at squeezing secondary gains out of this symptom. On many occasions he would say things like, "Aw, Fritz, you know how bad my temper is. I really couldn't help knocking Larry down and kicking him." This became especially prominent in his exploitation of an understanding that we had with the school to call us if he became aggressively upset there so that he could be removed to Pioneer House. Soon he was noticeably working himself into upsets to force the school to call so that he could be taken to the Home where he much preferred to spend the day. In our interviews with him, pertaining to this issue, he invented many reasons why he was prone to get upset in school such as "the guys make so much noise it gets on my nerves and then I get mad and can't control myself." None of these "environmental" arguments were vindicated by his reactions to similar occurrences at Pioneer House itself.

### Rebel for somebody else's cause

We apologize to Lindner for giving the wonderful title of his book a somewhat willful twist.[3] But there is no better way to summarize what we are trying to refer to here. It is well-known what peculiar twists the current concept of "morality" may suffer if a deed is perpetrated in the service of some special "cause." Many a hero of the "underground resistance movement" would have to feel quite guilty for any of the deeds he committed, had he allowed himself to act that way in the pursuit of his ordinary civilian life. Our youngsters, somehow, seem to be aware of that. Only, of course, they don't pick a "real cause," in anybody's terminology, for their exculpatory acrobatics, but are rarely at a loss for finding some little issue that might be abused that way. One youngster, for instance, may be wronged by a teacher in school. Five others, who usually don't care much about that one youngster, may happily seize this opportunity to "show that teacher where to get off," or they may wreak havoc with the furniture or windows of their school house, considering all this only as the secondary by-products of a quite justified

[3] Robert Lindner, *Rebel Without a Cause* (New York: Grune and Stratton, 1944).

tour of retaliation. The mechanism involved is clear: some-body else's cause is picked as an opportunity for a guilt-free display of behavior which the various individual superegos would otherwise hardly have tolerated. This certainly is a welcome enrichment of the already well-stacked list of de-linquent defenses against personal guilt.

> Frequently when we would take the Pioneer group on a sta-tion wagon ride we would encounter other youngsters who would be standing by the curb wanting to hitch a ride. Of course, for a variety of management reasons we could not afford to pick children up for rides, aside from the fact that usually there wasn't even room. This, however, led to many incidents of baleful reprisals from the members of our own group. "You mean bastards," they would say, "won't even pick up a poor little kid who needs a ride." Then they might begin to throw things at the driver, become aggressively wild in a variety of ways, break safety rules, all on the basis that we were mean to those " poor little kids." This is especially ironic in view of their hostile behavior toward hapless strange children who might have wandered into their yard at Pioneer House.

### The cultivation of delinquency-prone ego ideals

One of the best tricks of the delinquent ego is to deny the desire for actual delinquent exploits, but to hang on to an ego-ideal of a person whose image is secondarily encouraging of delinquent fun. Movies, radio, television, and the comics offer ample stereotypes for those whose creativity doesn't quite enable them to fabricate their ego ideals out of their own ingenuity. The normal child, of course, makes legitimate and quite beneficial use of the same process. Thus, a reckless murder fantasy might produce guilt. Hopping around in the suit of an admired Western Hero and shooting toy guns at otherwise aggression-tabu adults is something different. Or, it might be too anxiety raising to imagine oneself as a thief. Hanging on to the ideal of the swaggering gangster toughie, with bravery and loyalty to his pal in the foreground of the picture, easily covers whatever illegal acts are supposed to go with such a figure as its secondary trimmings. What the ego does here is comparable to the workings of the dream, where we also find side issues put into the focal role while the real issue is being dislocated into marginal details, "not worth the attention of the wakeful mind." In the normal development of children this whole process is quite helpful, for all the ego does is to support impulsivity enough so that it can be discharged in fantasy and play. The delinquent ego uses the same mechanism in earnest to "exculpate" itself from real-action guilt. What started out as a game of "playing gangster" may soon end up in a real stealing episode and with our Pioneers we rarely stood a chance to squeeze any guilt feelings out of them for such thefts. They considered us fussy for making so much of an issue that "really" was only the by-product of a fantasy game. With some youngsters this abuse of ego ideals for secondary delinquent gain may go so far that they actually begin to "play act" the role of their hero so constantly that nearly everything they do from now on is in their fantasy, not the "real self" any more. Needless to say, guilt saving through such a device is, if it is paid for by the child through the surrender of reality relationship to an extreme degree, clearly pathological.

Danny ran away from his own home (following Pioneer House closure). For a few hours he hung around a riding stable on the outskirts of Detroit. He fantasied that he would live in the woods, steal a horse, and forage for food "outlaw" style. Supported by this role play, he went to a nearby small town and stole a bicycle, obviously a symbolic equivalent for the horse. With this he rode into the night and was picked up by State Troopers. Two aspects of this exploit were quite impressive: (1) Usually Danny was very frightened of the dark, yet under the power intoxication of his outlaw self-image he was fearless on the dark, lonely country roads, so befogged that even the State troopers could not understand how he was able to navigate them, and (2) any attempt on our part to emphasize the seriousness of the stealing part of the episode went by the wayside in the fact of his repeated assertions that he was only being an "outlaw," and what did we think an "outlaw" would do when he didn't have his "hoss" to ride? He even joked about it as a "gag" and about how he had amazed the State Troopers with his "daring."

*Delusion of exceptionalistic exemption from the laws of cause and effect*

Some children are not primarily plagued with guilt, but they are afraid of the realistic consequences—physical danger or societal retribution when caught—of their acts. There is one good way of removing that block: if they develop the idea that what might be a normal course of events could not take place in their case because they have exceptional luck, wisdom, skill, or something like a pact with fate, then fear as well as guilt become unnecessary. Those children lull themselves into intensive delusions of inviolability—some of them simply in terms of daring danger, others in terms of "I never can be caught." Not only are they unaware of consequences, like the ones described under "ego disturbances" before, but they go a step farther than that: they make it an issue to believe that the laws of nature and social retribution have no effect on them. They run around like people with a magical charm around their neck and, as with those, actual evidence has no chance to sink in. Some egos, in their effort to protect delinquent exploit, even go so far as to surrender their original function, namely that of reality testing. In order to protect the reality of delinquent fun, they resign themselves to accepting clearly mystical illusion as a basis for their lives. Where this is still a skillfully maintained ego-supported illusion with a purpose in mind and where it deteriorates into actual schizophrenic delusions, is a distinction important but not always easy to make. The safest indicator in favor of the "delinquent ego defense" interpretation we have found so far is that this madness is only active where there is a "purpose" to it, while other reality testing functions remain clearly in the saddle in other areas of their lives.

One of our campers insisted that he was able to see in the darkest part of the woods at night with no flashlight. On many occasions he would be missing from his cabin at night and could be found hidden in the woods near the kitchen which he would be waiting to "raid" after everyone was well asleep. Obviously, his boasts that he "never got lost in the dark" were associated with delinquency ventures and played the role of protecting him against implications of failure or detection since, if he could see better than other humans, he had a better chance in these respects. The fascinating thing is that on still other occasions when he did not intend to engage in delinquency operations of one kind or another, he would also disappear from his cabin at night just to "test-out" and enjoy this "skill" at navigating around in the dark. This same youngster had also a magical belief in his own agility and daring. We were informed on a later occasion by the authorities who were transporting him from one detention home to another that he leaped from a running automobile going at some forty miles per hour to escape from the guards. It so happened that he was not hurt but his belief in his own powers of indestructibility was obviously involved in making it possible for him to try such a risky stunt.

### Dependency on delinquency-tied ambitions and skills

The courtroom argument by hoodlums that "this is the only profession they know and can make a living at, and therefore it is too late to change" is well enough known. In fact, with some of them we cannot deny that, by now, they have a point in their favor. They have failed to develop any of the qualities, skills, taste patterns that it takes to succeed in less illegitimate efforts and we may even sympathize with their hesitancy to surrender a field in which they excel as they do. This, however, is true only if we think of where they are right now. When they started out on their delinquent careers the situation may have indeed been the reverse one. From a variety of then still open possibilities such youngsters managed to pick those skills and careers which would also allow them the enjoyment of secondary gains from delinquent exploits. It is true that, from then on, they spent as much energy, frustration tolerance, and sincere "job enthusiasm" on their endeavor as any ambitious young man or woman might put into his regular career. But their ego obviously played them a trick—and it was a safe trick to play. It tied their delinquent exploits to the safe strings of achievement pleasure, status enjoyment, efficiency pride. These gratifications naturally become so important in their lives that it would be a great sacrifice for them to accept the prospect of what they would consider a bleak, badly paid, and inglorious though "moral" existence.

This could be most clearly seen in our pickpockets at Camp. We were impressed with the hard struggle they would have with their intentions to mend their ways. For they had much actual gratification involved in their nearly magician-like skills, and the admiration they elicited even from their disconsolate victims offered such a rich diet of narcissistic gratifications that there would hardly be another endeavor that could anywhere equal this satisfaction promise. If their ego wanted to secure this type of gratification for good, it couldn't have done a better job. Really, when under a self-imposed diet of restrictions, deprived of the practice of their skills, these youngsters seemed to suffer like a musical genius who isn't supposed to touch his instrument for a while.

## Defense Against Change

It is impressive to watch what an efficient delinquent ego can do to still the voice of conscience by the hypodermic of its alibi tricks; it is fascinating to observe the delinquent ego in its helpful efforts to seek out and cement the opportunities for delinquent fun. But if you really want to see what it can do, try to tangle with it more directly. Try to expose it to a situation which is meant to bring about change—and you will see a display of all the fireworks at its command.

Needless to say, such opportunity is best studied when delinquent egos are exposed to a full frontal attack in a residential treatment design. There they really have to fight for their existence. Our chapter on "Treatment Shock" will give an illustration of such a fight. Let us now list separately the various techniques involved by the ego in its defense against change:

## Confessional constipation

Some children get flustered, embarrassed, somehow blocked, and suddenly can't talk even if they would like to. This is not what we have in mind here. The youngster we are thinking of also suffers from sudden language blocks, but there is a plan behind it, though not necessarily a conscious one: he "clams up" on you entirely on the very issue in which he would, if talking, bare a vulnerable spot in his defensive armory. These children clam up, not when they are ashamed, but when they are cornered—thus carefully avoiding a chance that they might have to become ashamed or guilty, two emotions feared like fire by a good delinquent ego.

Innumerable times at Camp this scene would repeat itself: a youngster or maybe even the whole gang would sit in our office in a gripe session during which we tried to get them to admit just what they stole where on that trip to town. That was all. No punishment involved, no further trouble if they would only "come clean." In fact, we promised them that we would even take care of the return of the articles to their original owner, so there was nothing to worry or fear. Sometimes we even promised to pay for the damage done by them with no other questions raised. This, of course, was our trick. For in reality we were trying to expose them to a situation where the very absence of punishment would have to make them admit that adults were "fair," could not be accused of being "hostile," and that maybe in this place their stealing was mean or silly or both. Yet—no chance for such a trick to work with delinquent egos. They know too well where the real danger lies. We would have got our loot back more easily if we *had* threatened punishment—for that would have been "internally safe." The danger of being put in a situation where they might have to admit we were fair was well sensed by their vigilant ego. Result: it had them "clam up." Their loot was literally sticking out of their pockets, they knew we knew they had it, they would even have gained by letting us handle it from there on. Yet— a total "clam up."

And, of course, their ego was one hundred percent right from a strategic point of view. For their clam-up forced us to be the ones to insist that they stole the stuff (which made us distrustful enemies in their eyes). We finally had to take the things out of their pockets (which put us in line with the most hated bullying, third degree cops) and we were forced to take them back to their owner anyway (which made us mean so-and-sos of adults who don't want children even to have a little bit of fun and even take their toys away from them which weren't worth much money to begin with). In short, their confessional constipation, seeming so "senseless," is obviously the most expert trick their delinquency defensive ego could have displayed: reversing the tables in one swoop. While losing the loot, they are winning the battle of triumphant evidence of hostility against us.

Our Pioneers, by the way, had both forms of inability to confess, even where confession would be a reasonable way out. Sometimes it was due to real embarrassment or guilt blocks, like those of the neurotic child. At other times it was the type of confessional constipation as ego defense described here. We had quite a time learning to tell the two apart, which, of course, is a prerequisite for adequate clinical handling.

### Escape into virtue

The delinquent ego, like any good military strategist, makes ample use of camouflage and strategic retreat. Sometimes, when things get really dangerous, the safest stall is to produce some of the changes the adults seem to be so keen on, without real surrender.

At Camp we would often get amazing "improvements" after an unusually short time, sometimes of whole groups. Only the naive ones among us, of course, were fooled by such maneuvers. What this really meant was that these children caught on to where the real danger lies. And as long as they showed surface improvement along the lines that seemed so important to us, they would be safe from too much "interviewing" and they would be sure to be "left alone." The same trick is well known to work in detention homes and jails. It is not only true that you get less punishment and more privileges if you make a "good adjustment" to institutional routine; you are also "safer" from the more delinquency-dangerous aspects of reformatory life. If you just let down on your symptomatology a bit, or show one special "cooperative" behavior here or there, neither minister nor priest nor psychiatrist will bother with you nor does the salvation-hungry educator have you in for long talks. In fact, even parole boards can easily be fooled that way because they basically judge you on your "adjustment to the institution," having little chance to know what bigger jobs you really prepare in your fantasy while "in stir."

With our children, such "escape into virtue" could happen on an individual basis, or as a collective phenomenon. Sometimes whole cabins at Camp might really be full of cooperative activity interests, and function much above what the numbers possibly could keep up for long. Such collective "escape into virtue" offers the individual member an additional item in the armory of his defense.[4]

### Group ostracism against those who reform

This was one of the greatest nightmares we went through in our early experimentation with group therapy for children who hate, at the Detroit Group Project and the Camp. We seemed to get such amazing results in one way. Previously totally unrelated youngsters, who didn't seem to care about anybody or anything, did, with skillful handling, soon develop something like group psychological ties, interest in each other, even something like a more organized structure in their group life. Yet, the more "cohesive" their groups became, the more we realized that we had a monster by the tail. For soon that very cohesiveness of the group was turned full steam against us. Cohesive groups develop an intensive behavioral group

[4] Fritz Redl, "Resistance in Therapy Groups," *Human Relations*, I (1948), 307–313.

code, adherence to which becomes an issue of member loyalty. Like the sorcerer's apprentice, we had started more than we at first knew how to control. Still proud of the successful development of group cohesion where there was chaos before, we suddenly had to recognize that this same "group pride" became one of the greatest blocks against change we could have feared, and that we ourselves had so happily contributed to its development. The most important items, with high priority, in a delinquent "group code," were, on the one hand, the avoidance of all behavior which might have the tint of adult-submissiveness, of faint-heartedness in value issues, or of "ratting" on a pal, and, on the other hand, the production of clear acts of "daring." There is tremendous group pressure brought to bear on each individual along that line, and severe ostracism follows a breaking of this code without a hearing. Like all systems of tyranny the delinquent gang has a chronic "loyalty board" operating, which keeps the less recognized delinquents in constant terror, not only of being found guilty, but of being misinterpreted. By this sharply defined and strictly kept group code and the use of the technique of ostracism for its enforcement, the delinquent gang offers the individual member an additional defense against the remainders of the voice of his individual, civilian conscience, should it make a delayed attempt at being heard. The "delinquent" part of the ego of the individual youngster, in turn, uses this well-known danger of ostracism in a most efficient way. It gives heavy—and justified—danger signs at the slightest impulse to commit a non-delinquent act. The mere wish, for instance, to enjoy adult counselor love openly or to allow oneself to be seen in a "friendly private talk" with such an adult, would send shivers up a would-be toughie's spine, and if he ever gave in to such a temptation, he would make sure that none of his pals was around. This source of "fear of being loyalty suspect" constitutes a pretty good safeguard. It actually cuts down the volume of "adult friendly" behavior and forces the child into a higher display of rebellious and daring behavior, primarily produced "for no reason at all"—which in our case means: to please the loyalty board.

Shorty, a ten-year-old youngster we knew at camp for two summers, had a strong need for group approval from the delinquent type of youngster. Ambitions to be tough and powerful, built up as a protection against fears and anxieties aroused in him by a psychotic mother with severe paranoid delusions who always frightened him with her stories of "attackers," provided the case history background for this pattern. At the same time Shorty also wanted to have a close relationship with the adult but his other need to receive support from the tough group always superseded this. Every time he would try to come around, perhaps to spend a half hour in the director's lodge talking with him or just being near him while reading a comic book or listening to records, his actions provoked a group criticism: "Baby, Fritzie's pet, lookit 'im." Swayed by his sensitivity to their feeling, Shorty, in spite of help we tried to give him, never quite could make the hurdle or accomplish some synthesis of his needs. Even regrouping him with a less tough group doesn't work because this meant he could not have supportive proximity to the tougher youngsters that he needed for an ego-ideal, so, to prove his power to himself, he would then brutalize weaker children.

### Avoidance of delinquency-dangerous personnel

We, of course, mean by this phrase dangerous to the delinquency of the child. From the child's point of view this might include: kids who are really nice and who might make you feel bad if you act too rough in their company, adults who are really friendly and a lot of fun, so you would have to feel bad if you acted too mean—and you might even get lured into being interested in some of their programs—foster parents or house mothers who are swell, don't punish unfairly, give you a break, and are really decent folk.

The basic machinery operating behind this phenomenon reaches far down into the most fascinating and involved problems of group psychology. Our studies on "contagion" have time and again confronted us with this issue; we met it in the form of "shock effect" there. This paragraph cannot possibly even describe the full problem. Suffice it to say that we think we have ample evidence that this peculiar phenomenon is a well describable fact. At camp, too, we could watch the same spectacle time and again.[5]

The youngsters with a really good delinquent ego were usually easier on us in the beginning. They still thought we were just about as "dumb and mean" as the average adult, and they were perfectly secure in their knowledge of "how to handle bastards." As soon as they began to see us more the way we wanted them to see us, their delinquent ego began to be on the alert. This, by the way, is a crude but quite effective diagnostic criterion for the difference between the youngster with a neurotic basis to his stealing and a real delinquent one —the neurotic child relaxes this general warfare against you when he feels you are all right. The delinquent one has to increase it then, for that means you become really dangerous to his need for remaining delinquent.

The technique of "avoidance of delinquency-dangerous personnel" is a good safeguard against the educator and therapist, as it has been for centuries against the representative of religious ethics. The same technique is, of course, also employed against other children whose behavior or whole outlook on life might mysteriously "threaten" the delinquency-prone youngster. Grouped with age mates who are "regular enough" guys so they can't easily be warded off through simple ridicule and contempt, but who are openly value-identified in essential points, the delinquent ego usually gives heavy signals of being "ill at ease," and avoidance of such company is usually the result. It seems that the "company you avoid" may be as characteristic, if properly interpreted, of course, as the company you keep.

At Pioneer House, Henry, easily the most seasoned and "professional" delinquent of the group, was the most pleasant for a while. When he began to feel the impact of the real positive adult interest and visualized the high gratification potentials of the Home, however, his rebelliousness increased. He was markedly uncomfortable in many moments, for example, when a positive program structure might be going on, and the group was having a good time.

[5] Fritz Redl, "The Phenomenon of Contagion and Shock Effect in Group Therapy," in Kurt R. Eissler, *op. cit.*

In those moments he would snipe at the adult and try to start some trouble to break up the gratification pattern because these activities in combination with the leadership of the benign adult were delinquency-dangerous. There was an interesting shift in his attitudes toward the same activity— e.g. a game of cards—when it was not being dominated by an adult figure. Then he did not necessarily try to break it up, even if he himself did not participate. There was something about even short range acceptance of the adult by the other children which threatened him and which he had to destroy. Here we see this technique of avoiding delinquency-dangerous personnel spread out to protect a delinquent leader's hold over a whole group.

### Refusal to give up delinquency-prone life factors

Everybody knows about some peculiar cases which had social workers puzzled for a while but are no longer a mystery to the field. We refer to the youngsters, or adults, for that matter, who seem to "function better"—at least, and only temporarily—where life is rough on them, and who seem to run away or become hopelessly restless when they really "get a break." One of the types belonging in this category is the youngster with a vigilant delinquent ego. Such a delinquent ego knows very well "what the score is." Moving from a tough neighborhood into a "nicer foster home" means the loss of a lot of indirect delinquency support, even though food and clothes may be better. Staying in a really tough reformatory gives a chance for expert practice in anti-social fantasy and group leadership skill quite different from what is given by a friendly institution where you would yourself feel out of place for acting too rough.

In short, uncannily aware as to where the real danger to a well-sustained delinquent philosophy of life comes from, such a delinquent ego holds on for dear life to the very conditions which favor its fomentation and avoids having to surrender them even at quite a price. This is why some children will run away from the friendly foster home, while they toughly stick it out in the punitive institution which feeds their wonderful delusion of persecution with constant supply.

Among the minor and partial factors in any youngster's life which are indirectly supportive of the chance for delinquency, a few can be listed here. Some of our youngsters withstood for a long time all efforts to make them budget their pocket money more wisely. This, of course, could have many reasons. With some of them we were sure that what was going on belongs in this category: having enough cash on hand would reduce their temptation to bargain, cheat, steal, or feel sorry for their poverty, and thus reduce temptational chance as well as alibi tricks. A vigilant delinquent is aware of that. In other cases we think that the frantic effort to remain a failure, a reject, a "dumbbell" in school, which some children put on quite in contrast to their ability potential, belongs in this chapter, too. Getting kicked out of class, or suffering from unbearable boredom because of non-involvement, or being scapegoated by smarter children or achievement-proud teachers, offers a wonderful inner alibi, if such is needed, for tough behavior, truancy escapades, revenge tricks, and so forth. On a minor scale, the hesitance of our children at Pioneer House to surrender temptation-loaded gadgets before going to school or at bedtime belongs in the same category. Flashlight, gun, toys, yoyos, a newly made drum, and what not, are wonderful temptations for abuse. Surrendering them means the reduction of a chance at non-acceptable behavior. It is important, though, to differentiate this case from the one where those props are needed for reasons of anxiety assuagement or because of other, symbolic concerns.

A youngster we had for one session at camp later got into severe delinquent difficulties and was placed in the detention home. Upon being visited by us there, he amazed us by speaking most positively about the guards, the food, and the activities. At camp where he had plenty of freedom, where people were really nice to him and where his activity diet was most elaborately planned, he had been negative, critical, abusive, and certainly unappreciative. In the detention home he even looked relaxed and quite happy though the negative, restrictive atmosphere, the callous and even brutal treatment by the guards, were quite obvious.

*Strangulation of love, dependency, and activity needs*

Diogenes proclaimed that the safest way of not getting involved and remaining "free" from disappointment and unhappiness is to stop wanting anything. Our youngsters don't go quite that far, but some of them actually develop a fakir-like ability to go without what they really covet, provided that this saves them from the risk of involvement dangerous to their delinquent outlook on life.

Parents of normal children have often observed the same process in pocket edition. A youngster, for instance, may have been repeatedly punished for misdeeds by being sent up to his room. Amazing, how many children actually develop, as a counter technique, a real withdrawal from activity need, a taste for passive daydreaming which, once developed, makes them safe. They don't have to change; they just don't mind this form of punishment any more. The same is well known about children stored or actually jailed for long stretches of time under obviously stupid conditions of boredom or isolation. Some of them crack up, it is true. Others simply learn how to "take it," how to drop their normal desires for a normal boy's or girl's group activity fun, and how to be happy by newly discovered pleasures of daydreaming, dozing, or the proud planning of future revenge or delinquency escapades. René Spitz's pictures show how very little children, handled by disinterested institutional personnel, actually lop off their normal child's need for response from adults and become listlessly depressive, pathetically passive in posture and look.[6] The delinquent ego of our children, where it is in action, is capable of similar performances which are all the more surprising since they are in contradiction to what we have said about them under "ego disturbances." For, usually, those children have a short frustration span, are incapable of having their behavior defined by long range goals, are addicted to the pleasures of the moment beyond reason, and so forth. All the more surprising, then, that where their basic delinquent trends are really threatened, their ego suddenly develops all these

[6] *Grief,* a silent film produced by René Spitz, M. D.

capacities so obviously lacking in the less anti-social exploits of their lives.

Mike was about the most "impulsive" youngster in the Pioneer House group; his inability to wait for anything, his immediate-gratification greed, his short attention span, his restless fidgeting, were well documented in every phase of life. What a classical case of "low frustration tolerance!" Yet, this same youngster, we may remember, was able to ignore and deny his own wishes for food for stretches of twenty minutes at a time, when we stood in front of him, waving a three-decker sandwich literally under his nose, holding out a glass of milk to him, offering him both friendly, temper-soothing gestures and words. The reason why he would refuse to eat is obvious in that situation: he needed to maintain the "delusion of persecution" by us on various grounds. However, what a feat to perform, *what admirable ego strength all of a sudden* in a child who would usually be classified as "hardly having any ego at all," just because it is needed to maintain his anti-adult outlook on life.

We have had a chance to marvel at similar features of "strangling their own love needs" performed by many toughies. We have seen the greedy and jealous eyes with which they watched their more adult-related companions allow themselves to be tucked in after being brought back from a rained-out overnight, while they would stubbornly pretend to themselves that they wanted none of that. From its own point of view, their "delinquent ego" is consistent, of course. It knows that the greatest danger in terms of a final surrender to adult value demands would lie in becoming dependent on needs only friendly adults can really supply. So it takes all precautions against "getting soft."

## Mechanized Warfare with Change Agents

A vigilant delinquent ego cannot be satisfied with defending itself against the temptation toward change. Over and beyond this, it will be confronted with situations where "change agents" are thrown into its life in the form of educators and clinicians who make a frontal attack on its position. In those instances it has to be ready to deal directly with any personal effort at change—and it is. A good delinquent ego usually has a whole "mechanized" arsenal of direct defense techniques at its disposal, some of which will be listed here.

### Diagnostic acuity in battle-relevant areas

Disinterested or blind as the ego of such children often may be to what is going on around them, or how adults feel about them, when they become cornered in their delinquent exploits these same egos often develop a most astounding acuity of perception of at least those factors which are directly relevant to the issue. This is what makes any general statement that their egos lack in social perception or in contact with the outside world so obviously ridiculous for the cases at hand. For in these moments these same, otherwise cognitively deficient, egos develop hypertrophic skills for which even the professionally trained diagnostician rightfully envies them. Some of our youngsters, for instance, developed an astounding skill in such moments of being able to appraise exactly just when an adult would be "safe" or "dangerous"; they knew exactly just what modulation in the tone of voice meant the end of our patience, or what physiognomic and gestural combination on our side still meant we wouldn't "do anything about it," no matter how frantically we thought we signalled the end of our permissive attitude. They were on to all our whims and weaknesses, predilections and assumptions. Some of them even "sensed" in no time what type of argument would appease or divert or fool us most easily, what cajoling or affection-seeking behavior on their side would throw us off the scent most effectively.

The same statements hold for their appraisal of other children in areas of their delinquent exploits. Time and again we were put to shame by the uncanny personality appraisal such children could make of each other, where we ourselves, with all the elaborate tests and case history material at our hands, were helpless. At camp, for instance, some of the youngsters would not only "case the joint" in no time with an uncanny sharpness of vision for just where people could hide things, which adults were negligent about their cash and which were not. They would also "case the personnel." They would unfailingly know which child could be trusted to hide stolen loot without squealing until the noise blew over, which other one might promise secrecy but tattle in a sentimental moment or betray himself by slip actions in a pinch. Some of them even were able to make as sharp differential diagnoses as the one between a good thief and a thief on a neurotic basis, and, like the personnel department of an adult enterprise, would be eager and often able to screen out the "psychoneurotics" who couldn't be counted upon from those who were eligible as reliable members of a tough gang.

Such amazing skill in factual and psychological insight is certainly not compatible with the vague statements about "lack of reality testing" which we usually make about these children, but demands the admission of an expert reality appraisal in some moments of their lives. It is true, however, that such acuity of perception usually is limited to the area of their immediate delinquent realm of interest and cannot be extended easily beyond that. The co-existence of contrasts in the same child would baffle us no end. Thus, one and the same youngster might obviously be unaware of the question whether we liked or disliked him, but would at the same time miss no clue as to what might make us angry or compliant in a specific situation. And a child who seemed to care little about what other children felt and thought about him, so that we complained about his obvious "social blindness" most of the time, would suddenly surprise us with the most insightful appraisal of another child's reliability index in delinquent warfare, or of his unconscious desire to reach out for affectionate adults. This same "uncanny insight" into the unconscious of other people and their own has often been remarked upon about adult schizophrenics, too. But most of the time we confine ourselves to marvel amazedly, and then still continue to call these people "reality detached." If perception of any form of reality is a legitimate function of the ego, such casual gliding over these facts won't do any longer. We had better begin to take it seriously and begin to wonder how the same ego, in some situations so obviously poorly reality-related, can all of a sudden become so reality-sharp. We think a partial answer to that question is the assumption of the skill of the ego which tries to defend a youngster's delinquency from interference by developing "professional sharpness" of vision where such is relevant.

Biff, a pre-adolescent with a very well-developed delinquent pattern, stole a flashlight and then cunningly "parked" it on one of the very young children. He told the youngster he could play with it for a few days. Then "when the heat was off" he went back and said, "Hey, gimme back my flashlight now." In discussing it with him, he was asked why he had selected this particular child to "park" the flashlight. We even pointed out another one at random and said, "Why not that one?" To which he replied, "Oh, that guy (meaning the one we had selected at random). Sure I'll give him the flashlight and he'll be happy and play with it. Then at night he'll get homesick and the counselor will have to sit with him, special, and she may say, 'Oh, where did you get the flashlight?' and then he'll blab all over the place. The guy I gave it to is different."

## The legalistic mind

We had a similar surprise coming when we began to watch more closely the interview reactions of children in the marginal talks we had with them in our group project, at the camp, and later on at the treatment home. In general, the clinician is inclined to have a quite low opinion of the interview capabilities of youngsters of the sort we are describing. Most of them are quite well-known to be the "non-verbal" type, talking about things seems to mean little to them, and many of them have an obvious hesitation about getting involved in anything like an intimate interview situation around personal problems at all. They remain non-expressive in such interviews. They are not ready to produce associations or to offer any personal feelings or explanations whatsoever and avoid such situations as best they can. This general impression of the behavior of such children in interview situations had to be modified a great deal, however, when we began to have marginal talks with them around actual issues which came up in our group life with them. While totally unproductive in their regular case work or psychiatric interview, some of those youngsters seemed to develop the most uncanny skills of counter-interview techniques when it came to a grilling situation or to an attempt on our side to lure them into a confession of a misdeed or to confront them with a particularly untenable piece of behavior or to try to shock them into the admission of guilt, unfairness, or what not related to a specific incident in their group. In such instances, while the seemingly dull, or at least non-communicative, children still didn't talk very much, they seemed to be aware of all the ropes and shenanigans that the most skillful attorney-at-law could hope to call his own. With unerring scent for strategy they would move into a position most favorable for them, they would catch us in the slightest inconsistency or tactical mistake in our own argument, and they seemed to be familiar with all the tricks of counter-argumentation of a person on the spot that could be found in any of the books. Over and beyond this, it was most fascinating to see that these youngsters actually seemed to believe in something like a basically agreed-upon "duelling code." That means, for instance, that, any time they caught us in an inconsistency, or a premature attempt to call their bluff before we could prove it, or an insinuation of a motive for which we did not have enough evidence, or any similar trap, they reacted as though this proved us in the wrong. They seemed to imply that from now on, since we made such mistakes, we had no right to try to make the point we were trying to make no matter how obvious the real situation was to them, as well as to us. On the other hand, it could be observed that if we learned how to be skillful enough to avoid such traps, how to work within the duelling code which they themselves seemed to set, the mere fact of allegiance to it seemed to undermine their morale. We found youngsters, for instance, who would stubbornly refuse to admit anything just because we had made a technical mistake in our argument. They continued in their obstinacy from then on. While at other times, if we were arguing skillfully, the mere impression of our obeying all the laws of argumentative duelling seemed to break down their resistance against surrender and they would finally admit what it was all about, would concede the point to us even though this put them at a disadvantage at the time.

The implications of this seemed to be enormous. One of them is obviously that some of the basic rules of interviewing which have been developed on the basis of psychiatric work with the neurotic middle-class child have to be thoroughly revised for some of the work with some of these children. Another one is that youngsters who are so capable of most reality-geared argumentative duelling cannot possibly be called "reality detached" no matter how much evidence of the latter trait they give in other areas of their life. We think we must assume that in battle-relevant areas the delinquent ego suddenly is capable of using an amount of cognitive skill and ego strength which it seems to be lacking in other moments of its life. To know the strength of their defenses and to take adequate counter measures on our side seem to be as much of a condition for skillful interview technique with those youngsters as knowing the unconscious of the anxiety- and compulsion-ridden neurotic is for the psychiatrist.

Some illustrations for some of the most typical sorts of defenses and strategic moves which our youngsters skillfully made in arguments will be given here:

JUST BECAUSE I AM A CROOK . . . Whenever we caught our youngsters in the repetition of a misdeed which was nearly identical with one they had been caught at before, they were immediately aware of a beautiful technical advantage over us. For they had us sized up in no time for the kind of adults we were, namely, people who wanted to be fair to children, who wanted to give a sinner a break, and who certainly wanted to convey an atmosphere of trust and confidence as an item of encouragement. With flash-like appraisal of our peculiarity, they would in such cases immediately turn the argument away from the actual facts to a counter accusation against us. They would chant furiously and accusingly that they didn't get a break, that just because they had a bad record or just because they had been caught in something before, now even we didn't trust them any more, didn't believe a thing they said, etc. The effrontery with which such strategic reversal of the argument would be pulled on us was equally as amazing as it is effective with the less sophisticated adult or with the adult who is still caught in the concept of interview techniques as developed for their more anxiety-ridden neurotic contemporaries. This technique had another advantage to it: even if it didn't get them anywhere because we had the evidence in our pocket or out-maneuvered their denial attempts, they still could ward us off psychologically. For even when proved wrong, they would triumphantly withdraw behind the argument that "nobody trusted them nohow and what was the good of it anyway." Thus the ego acrobatically finagled even surface defeat into psychological victory over the educational adult.

I FOUND IT . . . Equally amazing is the skill in the "rules of evidence" which such youngsters displayed without obviously ever having had any legal training. They have clearcut concepts of just what constitutes admissible evidence and what does not and they have a very well-developed code about that. Whenever they were holding out on the admission of anything that might involve guilt, they were out-maneuvering us as long as it was possible to confront us with the fact that in the terms of their evidence code we didn't have "enough to go on." This left us "holding the bag" even though we knew the facts and they knew we knew them, too. The most typical and first reaction of our youngsters, for instance, in cases of stealing is not denial of possessing the stolen loot, if there is a risk that that is known to us, but the simple statement, "I found it," with a triumphant stare at the interviewer implying, "So now what are you going to do about it?" It sometimes takes a long time of skillful step-by-step fencing before we can break down the likelihood, the possibility, or the logicality of such an assumption and the interviewer has to avoid carefully making the wrong accusation which he can't prove yet or pulling in witnesses whose reliability or potential hostility to the child in question might constitute a problem. Only after all this, can a further attack on the question be made. At camp we ran into a variety of youngsters who, even when called in simply because a postcard or a package had arrived for them, would immediately greet us with the defensive remark, "I ain't done nothing, you can't pin it on me, I wasn't even there and I can prove it, too, see." Again, this whole move primarily means a shifting from the potential defensive to an attack, forcing the adult to produce evidence and thus allowing the child to wait carefully for any flaw in the evidential procedure which might be used for actual argument.

O.K., SO YOU ARE GLAD NOW YOU GOT ME IN TROUBLE . . . Coupled with the previous reversal from defense to attack was another device which consists of the insinuation of hostile motives on the side of the interviewer. It was an attempt to shift from the evidence of actuality to the argument about inter-personal relations, a naturally less tangible and therefore more easily misinterpretable ground. The advantage which this technique offered again obviously led in two directions. If we were stupid enough to fall into the trap and to try to assure the youngster of our sympathy with his difficulty in contrast to the importance of getting facts clear so that we could help him with his problem, he would have us exactly where he wanted us. He could have us on a side track leading into less and less provable ground and in an area in which he could easily counter any one of our arguments of affection by a simple statement, "That's what you say," thus insisting sulkily on his original accusation. That meant he would have us on the defensive and off the track for good. If, however, we ignored his attempt at side tracking, we would still leave him with the possibility of using the very fact that we did as a new argument in his favor. He would then insist that, while admitting his deeds, he obviously was right in his insinuation of our hostile and triumphant attitude toward him, and would turn the factual defeat into a psychological victory in terms of a triumphant paranoiac interpretation of our behavior.

HE HAD NO RIGHT TO DO THAT TO ME . . . Another one among the skillful "strategies of the irrelevancies" is the diversion from the real issue to the one item in a total incident in which somebody else got himself in the wrong. A

barrage of moral indignation against the weakness on somebody else's part is stirred up like a dust cloud to hide or
confuse our vision about things that actually count. Thus,
for instance, when we would try to pin a youngster down
into telling us about some of the most impossible, extreme,
and atrocious behavior he afforded at school that day, he
would, sensing what was coming, harp on another item
where either another youngster jostled him, or where
some time ago the teacher accused him wrongly of something of minor importance, or where, in the process of
struggle of the frantic teacher with the extreme behavior
of the youngster in his tantrum, the adult might have made
a minor mistake. In short, the youngster would skillfully
pick up any such issue and now become the accuser, either
against people or against the injustices of life. He would
try to put us into a position either of giving sympathy or of
failing to be able to out-argue his accusations. At the very
least, he would gain time to get away from the issue at
hand. Again this maneuver has a realistic as well as a psychological advantage for the child. For, if we fall into the
trap, we may easily find ourselves in a most difficult position with the roles entirely reversed and the youngster
safely escaping the issue that was important, or if we don't,
the really skillful delinquent ego rarely misses its opportunity even then to complain that we do not pay enough
attention to the youngster's accusations or protestations of
having suffered an unfairness or injustice. This, again, will
be used against us in the long run even if the youngster has
to concede the point at hand. The interview will end up
perhaps with an admission of the point we are after but
also with a strategic victory of the child over the basic issue
we are trying to demonstrate to begin with. For he has
found a beautiful excuse now to hide again behind the feeling of "nobody likes me, nobody cares enough about what
happens to me, even you don't listen to what I have to say,
nobody gives a damn anyway. So why should I bother?"

A detailed list of all the legalistic and psychological skills
which the youngsters developed in the defense of their posi-
tions when under fire ought to be studied in great detail and

would be a fascinating project in itself. These are only a few illustrations; some of the details will become clearer in later excerpts from our records. The implication of this, however, for practice we should not miss right here. It does mean that the "arguing" with youngsters, even in the process of simply tying them down to admitting what they did or clarifying issues which happened in their lives, is far from being a minor job to be done by untrained people or to be relegated to the grilling in a police station. It may become one of the most important fencing grounds of the clinician with the acrobatic skills of the ego so well trained in the defense of its psychological position. In terms of treatment of such youngsters with such hypertrophically developed ego skills in the service of the wrong cause, the very task of anticipating and out-maneuvering this defensive barrage of the ego in argument becomes an important part of the job of ego repair. We shall try to elaborate on that issue later. Needless to say, the strategic advantage of being right on the scene, having an actual role in the youngster's life, and being able to time such marginal interviews strategically at the moment which is most advantageous for the treating adult rather than the defensive child, becomes a very important issue indeed.

### Expertness in the manipulation of people and of chance

Once the ego has thrown its weight into the defense of impulsivity "at all costs," it often goes all the way. The development of great skills of diagnosis of delinquency-relevant issues and of the just described tricks of the legalistic mind is only half the story. To be really successful and safe in its exploits, the delinquent ego also encourages the practice and development of the skills of handling people, maneuvering the world around it, and making the most of opportunity. This probably constitutes the most amazing contrast to the common description of those children as "poor in their reality testing," and as deficient in all the normal ego functions described before. Coupled with deficiencies of such functions which cannot be denied is a concentrated skill expertness of a degree that takes our breath away. In fact, the feats of "influencing people" and "maneuvering life" these youngsters may display sometimes cause the envy of the professional, who has a hard time keeping up with them. What they seem to "know" about people and how to handle them—including ourselves—often puts current research in such matters to shame. Some of these youngsters are experts in accurate "timing." They pick exactly the right moment, not only to get away with things, but also to score a point against us in a subsequent grill- or guilt-squeeze session.[7] Have we ever thought of what subtleness of reality appraisal and awareness of the future this involves? Others develop a nearly acrobatic skill in "handling" us. Not only do they know exactly just which behavior would make us most vulnerable to their wiles, they also know and practice strenuously how to produce it with just the right "feeling tone" to it. Some of them are experts in the "soulful and helpless" stare, which makes us misclassify them as anxiety-ridden neurotics who need a chance to cry on our shoulders; others know exactly how to display behavior that looks like the "child finally snuggling up to the kind adult for help" variety. These youngsters, so "uncontrollable" in their temper at times, have, at others, such tremendous "control" over tone of voice, physiognomy, and posture that they fool us for longer than we are eager to admit. They are equally skillful in manipulating life situations on the non-educational scene. They know how to act "cute" in public, how to wheedle things out of suspicious storekeepers, how to make a prison guard feel that he is "the only person they really trust." Their skill as manipulators of the group psychological scene has roused our deepest envy. They become experts in touching off "contagion chains" at just the right moment which catches the adult group leader unawares and makes it impossible for him to blame them at the same time. They know exactly how to approach a tempted but still superego-ridden child so as to crumble his defenses, how to threaten another one so that the threat will work even if they aren't around to make sure. Their skill of "group composition" and group leadership is yet unmatched by anything our textbooks contain, or our professionally trained group leaders could produce.

[7] See Fritz Redl and David Wineman, "Techniques for the Clinical Exploitation of Life Events" in *Strategy Against Childhood Confusion,* soon to be published (Glencoe, Illinois: The Free Press.).

Not only is all this fascinating and "cute," it is important for the total strategy of treatment and sometimes dangerously powerful. More relevant for this item, however, is that all this is evidence that the general statement that these children are ego-disturbed or have a weak ego or are poor in reality testing or handling is ridiculously over-generalized and inadequate. For the behavior which was described and for which ample evidence is at hand obviously requires a wide range of most specifically developed and well-oiled ego functions which even the normal ego has trouble to produce on such an expert level. It is rather evidence that these children combine with the disturbedness of their ego functioning in some areas the hypertrophic over-development of others in different areas.

Harry always fascinated us, during his stay at Pioneer House, by the ingenuity he had for stirring up group psychological excitement. In the matter of programming, for example, he would always capitalize on those moments when he sensed the group didn't want to go along with the suggestion of the group leader. At such moments he might suddenly jump up and say, "Follow me, guys," and literally, like the Pied Piper, lead wherever he wanted. He never bothered to try this if there was an enthusiastic group response to the suggestion of the leader, however. He always seemed to know when to pull the "initiatory act" so that it would have the effect he desired.

Baldy, a professional delinquent whom we observed at camp for three summers, had a beautifully worked-out, well-oiled approach to adults to ease them in their "suspiciousness" of his pursuits. Invariably he greeted all adults by pleasantly shaking hands, saying, "You're my pal, ain't-cha?" This was not done in a plaintive or pleading manner, but always jocularly as though he realized that the adult realized it was a kind of "gag" but the effect subjectively that it produced upon the adult was very pleasant. He especially selected adults who had top responsibility in camp for these pleasant attentions, showing, of course, a keen nose for hierarchy and power stratifications.

## Absurdity of demand

Another trick which the delinquent ego has at its disposal, whenever the treatment skill of the adult becomes dangerous, can be described in the following way: It is obvious that one of the basic policies of an adult in a treatment home is to show friendliness, confidence, and affection, and to prove to the children that they are accepted and liked even in such moments when frustration or interference is realistically indicated. This very basic policy of a treatment home has one disadvantage, which we already mentioned before. Some of the youngsters with disturbed ego control are confronted with so much onrush of previously unfulfilled desires and with such an intensity of sudden greed of affection and gratification that they are thrown into a frenzy. What we have in mind, however, goes one step further than that. We are talking now, not about the case where a youngster is flooded with the impact of gratification desires because of our permissiveness, but where the youngster's ego planfully and purposefully maneuvers that very technique of ours "ad absurdum." That means that the fact that the adult insists on being affectionate and gratifying is being exploited strategically by making demands of such degree and intensity that they cannot possibly, and should not realistically, be lived up to by the adult. This is done in order to use that very fact then as a wonderful argument cementing the delusional assumption of a hostile world. Thus, for instance, youngsters would insist on such degrees of recklessness of behavior that interference would be necessary. Then they would jump on that fact of being interfered with and use this as an argument that we actually had lied to them, that we were "as mean as detention home guards," that we didn't want children to have any fun either, and so forth. Or, sometimes, the happy enthusiasm of some of the youngsters who wanted promises from the adult about special program, activity, or fun, who would make demands like, "Let's stay up late tonight," something which was still within reason, would be picked up by the more ego-skilled child as a wonderful chance to strike an efficient blow against our basic policy. Such a youngster would never miss such a chance to increase those demands to impossible degrees and then triumphantly point out to the other youngsters how wrong they were in trusting us or assuming us to be permissive at all. Continuing the type of illustration we started, such a youngster might at that moment exclaim, "Yeah, let's stay up all night and not go to school tomorrow." If such a challenge would be met with an obvious drop in enthusiasm by the adult, as it naturally had to be, this would be immediately picked up then by the rest of the group as evidence that the adults were "no fun anyway, they didn't really want to go out for a good time, what the hell, let's stay home anyway to begin with." This "absurdity of demand" theme can be traced throughout all aspects of life from toys, presents, possessions, money, cigarettes, sex license, etc., to the insistence on the display of over-affectionate gestures by the adult. What they do is somewhat similar to the act of the very little child who may ask the adult pleadingly, "Do you like me?" and follow up an affirmative to that question with, "Do you promise to marry me, then?" Needless to say, it is clear that this technique of "absurdity of demand" can be used for two purposes. One is to put the delinquency-dangerous adult into an embarrassing position at the moment. The other is an even more skillful long range use. Well-timed and careful exploitation of these techniques is used to undermine the basic policy which the staff and the design of a treatment home try to convey. The great importance which the skillful handling of such issues implies and the fact that anybody that happens to be with the child at the time, whether psychiatrist, cook, or janitor, has to be aware of the total treatment policy and well conversant with the question of how such situations have to be handled create quite a challenge for practical work.

At Rouge Park, a public recreation area, the following occurred on a sledding expedition during the Christmas holidays. Joe and Sam at first were quite content to slide down a safe hill. Then they decided they wanted to slide out over the Rouge River. It had been rather warm for the past week and the ice was soggy. It was really a dangerous idea; there were even signs especially put up by the recreation department warning all children to stay off the river.

Countless numbers of children, with and without adult escort, were around and no one else was going on the river. Yet, Joe and Sam insisted. When the counselor actually stood guard down by the bank of the river to stop them, they grew especially abusive. "Yeah, you bastards say we can have all the fun we want at Pioneer House but look at you—won't even let us slide on the river."

## Anticipatory provocation

This technique seems to be a side piece to the one mentioned before. The "absurdity of demand" technique tries to exploit our affectionate tendencies toward the children to a point where they become strategically absurd and can be turned into the opposite. The technique of "anticipatory provocation" skillfully plays on the other side of the ambivalent relationship which the children rightfully expect therapeutic adults to have for them. That means that they try to produce aggression, fury, wrath, attack, or even punishment from our side with a real strategic issue in mind. The principle underlying this is one well in line with the basic philosophy of a hostile interpretation of the world which we have already shown those children to possess. Threatened by an adult attitude of acceptance and friendliness which might force them to admit our fairness and make them feel ashamed or guilty, they try to make us angry, make us act in a way which they can easily interpret as being hostile. Then the threat of our acceptance and morality-demanding behavior is easily warded off. It is important, of course, not to interpret all provocative or aggressive behavior of our children on that basis. Some of it is plain aggression, meanness, destructiveness, and nothing else. Some of it is the other side of anxiety, insecurity, and fear. Some of it is thrown at us from the depths of the history of their earlier development. It has little to do with what we are and what we stand for. Some of it is a temporary displacement or the result of a wide variety of mechanisms too specific to list here. With all that granted, however, there are cases where the aggressive, provocative, and destructive behavior of the youngsters toward us or toward the house in general can be clearly demonstrated as having a specific strategic issue as a basis. If they can just get us to do what the mean, hostile, child-rejective, revengeful adults would do, then they are safely back where they were before and the danger of what we try to convince them into through the way in which we live with them is successfully avoided. It is especially interesting to watch how effectively many of the tough children when stored in institutions with not very well-trained personnel make use of this counter technique. It is also interesting to watch how skillfully some of the youngsters, the so-called "ringleaders," exploit this very trick whenever they see some of the other children in danger of falling for the adult, of surrendering their toughness in favor of a happier child-adult relationship. In such a case the really tough ones with much more vigilant and well-equipped delinquent egos invariably manage, sometimes even at great expense to themselves, to produce the provocative situation which forces the said adult into aggressive, punitive, or at least interfering behavior, and to use this very scene, then, as wonderful evidence to the members of their groups, as though they were saying to them, "See, this is what you nearly fell for. Do you admit now how right we are when we tell you adults just ain't no good?" The admirable skills, especially of the more delinquency experienced or practiced children, in choosing provocative behavior for this very purpose constitute one of the most difficult problems in the framework of institutional treatment.

Most striking among all of the anti-adult campaign tricks of Henry were his devices to lure other children away from surrender to the adult on stealing or other misbehavioral issues. Whenever another child would be interviewed in the Director's office about some possible stealing or aggressive acting out, Henry would literally post himself outside the door and "heckle" the interview. He would shout morale-building exhortations to whoever was inside, such as, "Don't tell 'im, let 'im guess, heh, heh, heh. Old man Wineman (if Wineman was doing the interview), old man Wineman, whatcha gonna find out?" Then he would make "raspberry" sounds through the keyhole or shout obscenities. Invariably the Director would have to leave the interview and interfere with Henry, who might even work himself into a tantrum to involve the Director in some form of physical restraint. By this time the other child would have been so replenished in morale and hostility against the Director for so interfering with Henry that the original interview goal had to be abandoned.

## Organized defamation

If adults cannot be provoked into aggressive behavior, then the delinquent ego has one trick left to fall back on which isn't quite as good as anticipatory provocation but can serve as a temporary substitute for a while. That means that all you have to do is keep up a careful campaign of gossip propaganda along the line of purposefully misinterpreting the motives for what adults may do. Thus, there is usually one youngster, at least, in any group of tough children, who will be expert in seeking out opportunities to "argue away" the implications of the behavior of basically friendly and fair adults. Such youngsters will either deny the fairness and affectionateness of the motive out of which the adults acted or they will actually invent the most absurd, negativistic, and hostile motivations. They will have an enormous skill, like all rumor mongers, in thinking of exactly the type of argument that will hit the potential conflict area most safely. Thus, such children will at regular intervals proclaim generalized stereotypes like, "Those goddam sons of bitches, adults ain't no good, don't ever trust none of them," or "They are just trying to save money in this goddam dump," or "Yeah, do you see how mad he was, but he didn't have enough on us this time," and so forth and so on. Or, they will try to ridicule behavior which is clearly affectionate, making it out to be the weak helplessness of a disinterested adult. This type of propaganda is especially skillfully made by children with great acrobatic ability in the initiation of contagion chains. Thus, when a friendly adult will want to say something reassuring to a group or a child after incidents of conflict, this type of youngster will always immediately be able to think of something funny or clownish to say or do so that the scene which was meant to be one of mutual relationship in potential insight becomes an impossible riot with the adult in a ridiculous rather than in a kind role. Or a particular youngster, afraid of seeing too many of his potential companions in delinquency yielding to adults who reach out for them, may actually quite skillfully engineer a variety of little scenes in which these adults lose face, are helpless, or feel themselves obliged to perform special acts of kindness which can then very easily be interpreted by these children on the basis of "those dopes are scared of us," or "they just didn't know what to do, see, I told you so."

By the way, the same technique is also useful against other children, that is, group members whose too openly acceptant gestures toward the adult become somewhat dangerous. What the youngsters really do in that case is defend themselves against the effect of "positive contagion." [8] They are afraid that either they themselves or other children in the group might finally be swayed in their defiant attitude to adult personnel if the children who act friendly to them, or are "good" and more reasonable to adult demands, are allowed to demonstrate openly such behavior time and again. They are well aware of the basic laws of contagion and of the terrific danger that the clear visualization of reasonable and friendly behavior toward adults might finally break down the barrage of artificially produced provocative negativism. These children develop defamation as a planned counter technique. Thus, the youngster who is "nice" and reasonable is not only not recognized as such, but is immediately accused of being a sissy, a coward, of being yellow. The youngster who more openly shows his need for personal adult affection in a variety of infantile gestures or demands and who seeks parent substitute roles from the adult is derided as being a crybaby, a mother's little boy, a fraidy-cat, and what not. This general defamation is sometimes reinforced by an actual provocation of the victim into negative behavior in order to gain additional material for defamatory propaganda practice. For instance, a youngster with an open friendship toward an adult counselor will be "dared," by the tougher members of the group, to do something mean, nasty, silly, and reprehensible to him much beyond what that youngster's actual delinquency range would permit him to do. If this works, they can't lose. Either they

[8] See footnote 5.

get the youngster to do it and thereby create a sharp conflict between him and the adult as they hoped they would, or the youngster refuses and does not pick up the "dare," which gives them a chance to throw at him the barrage of defamatory propaganda with great vehemence. In group work with such children, it is especially important to be aware of the relevance of such processes for the problems of group hygiene. If not handled well, the gossip and defamatory accusations hurled in groups may really begin to define member behavior more severely than the actual relationships between children and adults would otherwise justify.

A gripe session was being held at camp with one of our groups. The issue involved their having taken some boats "illegally," i.e., without counselor knowledge, into the middle of the lake where they actually engaged in some very risky practice which might have resulted in a drowning. Much of the discussion had been devoted to just getting them to "settle down" and admit the seriousness of what had happened so that we could "rub in" its unacceptability. Just at about the point when most of the group had settled down, Red, the undisputed boss of the group, pulled one of his characteristic stunts. He ran over to a nearby table, pulled off a mug sitting there and pretended to drink whisky from it, and put on a real "goofy" drunk act. This sent the group into a wild derisive mood and, of course, made Red's next move very easy. "Yeah, those goddam counselors," he exclaimed, "sure they say 'now let's have lots of fun, boys' but if we take a boat out they act like we was all babies. All they do is lie to you about having fun. Shit on this camp."

*Friend without influence*

Anybody who has ever had a hand in training young and enthusiastic teachers or group leaders will remember that one of the most difficult jobs is to help them become realistic about the difference between love and identification. The theoretical issue is clear and hasn't changed much since the earliest days of psychoanalytic conceptual development. In a nutshell, this is the situation: in order for an adult to get the child really to incorporate any of the values he stands for and thus to gain real inside influence over him, it is important that a child like the adult. As long as hatred blocks the channels of human communication, real influence, as distinguished from simple outside pressure, cannot be established. Thus, the basis for any good educational relationship is, of course, a feeling of being accepted by the educator, on the part of the child, responded to in kind by a feeling of affection and love for the educator. This affectionate, friendly relationship, however, is only the basis for and not yet the achieved end of value transmission. An educator may be loved by a child, may even be the object of a crush, may be extremely popular with the children, but may still have not the slightest "influence" over them. Real influence is dependent on the emergence of the second process after the first basis for affectionate, friendly love relationship has been secured. This is commonly called "identification." According to the classic pattern, it basically means the same in all the million varieties which can be observed in life. The child renounces some of the intensive demands for counter love from the adult and replaces those exuberant love demands by a readiness to incorporate part of the personality of the adult into the ego ideal and finally into the superego. What originally were value demands coming from the outside from another person toward the child are now established as superego demands inside him.

We sympathize with all the criticism of over-simplification to which this model of "identification" has been subjected over the years, and we realize that many modifications and specific additions should be placed in the picture so that it may make any sense for the practitioner. Basically, however, the story still holds for all of us. As long as the youngsters just like us, this affectionate tie reserved for people who are nice, pleasant to be with, or whom it is nice to know, have near, possess, etc., will not lead to a process of identification. We really remain "outside" and our influence on the child's life is negligible. In the training of young teachers and group leaders this difference between love and identification constitutes, as we said, one of the most difficult items to be got across simply because the personal love demands and narcissism of the adult get easily involved, because the smoothness of the process of being liked by and popular with the kids is more gratifying than the arduous and highly ambivalent relationship with children who begin to surrender gradually in terms of a process of identification. Mainly, however, it is hard for the young practitioner to become aware of this difference because of the general confusion in the field, which does not always see that difference clearly either, and because of the great symptomatic difficulty. For, from the outside without special diagnostic criteria, it is not easy to know at each phase of development of such a relationship just what is going on. The youngster with an enthusiastic love relationship or friendship to the adult looks from the outside more like the really successful victim of basic changes than the youngster who goes through the arduous struggle of renouncing his love demands in favor of an identification process. The development of criteria for a clear appraisal of this difference is one of the most needed tasks yet to be done in the field of teacher training, group leadership, supervision, as well as in all educational practice.

While the professional practitioners and even the theoreticians seem to have trouble with this process, the toughies we are talking about have none. As in so many other areas, the vigilance of their ego has equipped them with an acuity of perception which the professional field cannot match and compared with which our current research looks utterly bleak and naive. For it seems that some of the toughest, most recalcitrant, and, in other areas, most insensitive youngsters have the sharpest perception for this very issue at hand. They are totally aware of the strategic implications of this difference and on top of that they have discovered the wonderful advantage for their position if they only use this insight correctly.

At first sight, the safest defense against the danger of love and its implications seems to be a barrage of hatred and of hostile warfare. That way a delinquency-identified child wards off the adult and his attempts at influence most effectively. However, this is true at first sight only. The more vigilant delinquent ego soon catches on to the disadvantages of such open warfare. First, some adults are wonderfully persistent and the attempts to provoke them into the aggression needed to maintain one's hostility are met with such a continuous reservoir of affectionate strategy that the open battle in the long run seems to contain more advantages for the adversary than for oneself. Second, it is a very time- and effort-consuming job, hard on the nerves of all involved, and not everybody's business. On the basis of that insight, those youngsters suddenly discover the great advantage of a "co-operative deal." As soon as the delinquent ego is aware of the basic machinery involved and cannot be fooled about it any more, it asks, why not use that insight for more effective protection which has the added advantage of fooling the opponent even better? That means, since the therapeutic, as well as the educational adult seems to be so eager to like and be liked, seems to be so naive in the delusion that an affectional tie once established solves all problems, why not offer it to him? Besides some of those grown-ups are pleasant people to live with, deserve some kind of recognition, are decent and quite different from some of the other enemies with which the delinquent has to deal, so that in the long run it is hard for him to keep up a constant hostility barrage, anyway. Why not enjoy certain friendly relations on both sides, save one's energy for more delinquency-relevant issues and live with more relaxation than the constant heavy-weapon warfare would allow? In short, these youngsters begin to realize that a surrender to the personal relationship of affectionate friendship with the adult is safe as long as they only make quite sure *that it will never lead to identification.*

Thus, the hostile and hateful barrage of warfare is suddenly dropped, the adult is accepted up to a high degree as a friendly person, a pal, a regular guy, and is even allowed entrance into many of the intimacies and details of one's own feeling, emotion, life, and secrets. At the same time, an unspoken rider seems to be attached to the pact. This says: I am your friend and will treat you as such; I accept your friendship on an equal level and will cherish this as such as long as we both know "where we are at." For, while I like you as a person, I want none of your advice; while I accept your help in "civilian matters," I want you to keep out and stay out from any issue connected with the basic delinquent warfare. The adult who does not know his "place" in such a pact soon becomes uncomfortable, is considered too dangerous, and the friendship offer is withdrawn in favor of a return to the previous warfare or to other techniques mentioned before, like that of defamation, etc. As long as this pact is unconsciously accepted by both parties, the outside picture looks so close to success that it is understandable that time and again we fall for this delusion.

We want to make it quite clear, by the way, that we do not imply at all that this type of "friendship" is not sincere, and that the child actually is only putting up a barrage of feelings he does not have. On the contrary, we actually postulate that the "friendship" part of it is very sincere indeed and quite genuine. These youngsters do allow themselves real feelings of love to such adults; they permit quite genuine feelings of friendship and gratitude to blossom on a strictly interpersonal basis. In fact, they can afford this just because their unconscious reservation that this love must never lead into identification is so clear. It is just because of the real sincerity of the friendship and feeling side that the practitioner is so easily fooled and that even the experienced professional frequently falls into a trap which he thought reserved for the unsophisticated lay public. In fact, we had better admit right here and now that in situations where we had less of a possibility of total observation and intensive life with the children involved than in Pioneer House, we too could recite many cases where the symptomatology of a positive relationship of a previously tough child to the educational adult easily fooled us into confusing it with the establishment of a real identification process.

We assume that almost anybody who has worked intensively with children of the type we are talking about has, as we do, a whole collection of customers on his hands with whom he had partial success but whom he later lost track of for one reason or another, who obviously were not really cured but returned under the pressure of reinsertion into the old neighborhood to delinquent symptomatology and finally drifted around and ended up as customers in various jails with a high mobility between jails of the different states. Among them are youngsters who, sometimes only later, discover a great friendship for us who tried to be therapists or helpers in their early years. It is these youngsters or young adults who usually will remember us when they move from one jail to another, when they get out of or into jail, when they are in trouble, or when they are proudly engaged in a period of temporary good adjustment. It is an irony that it is sometimes those "grateful customers" who make the best propaganda for us as therapists, whose lasting "friendship" with us as persons seems so astounding an island in the total scene of unrelatedness and aggressive warfare between those people and the world. While considerable achievements in themselves, therapeutically speaking such friendships are without value. They are the first steps on the road to a real change and unfortunately some of the egos of the more psychologically sophisticated delinquents know how to keep those first steps for good. From a human value angle, there is something nearly romantic to some of those "friendships" which otherwise hateful youngsters occasionally offer to adults who are decent and fair to them. For the person who is seriously engaged in an effort to rehabilitate and really change the basic philosophy of a child engaged in a delinquent career, it is important to remember that while we need their friendship we want to be sure we do not remain "friends without influence."

## Summary

We have described a wide variety of what we call "techniques of a delinquent ego." Since the description of these techniques has led us so far afield, it might be wise to remember just two things before we pass on to another issue altogether. One, let us not forget for a moment that all of these "techniques" are not to be considered as rigid categories and let us not strain the theoretical assumptions involved in their establishment too heavily. While established on the basis of some theoretical considerations, our primary object here was to pull together observations and insights which would be fascinating and of help to the practitioner. It might be wise to realize the tentativeness of all of our knowledge in this area at this stage of the game, to consider all of these headings more as titles to focus our thoughts around than as actual theoretically sharply defined categories. The other reminder which might help us to put this whole chapter into place is related again to the implication which the term "delinquent ego" might assume, which we hoped to avoid, but which still has us worried. In the extreme case, the techniques described come close to being something like an armory of the well-cemented delinquent character in his fight against the world. However, we want the basic mechanisms described here to be considered applicable to a much wider range of situations, even to such where the word "delinquent" in its original meaning loses its sense. That means that what we described here under the title of defense techniques of the "delinquent ego" are actually techniques of defense anywhere, *whenever an ego makes up its mind to stick to impulsive demands or to its pathology against changes which the educator or clinician is trying to bring about.* The reason for this assemblage of defense techniques, as compared with the usual list of "defense mechanisms" well-known in literature, is primarily that we have to deal here with the well-entrenched, aggressive ego trying to protect impulsive gratification chances against the world outside and also against remnants of superego demands within itself. In the process of warfare of the ego against anybody who tries to touch socially unacceptable gratifications or clinically repudiated pathology, any one of these techniques may be employed with greater or less intensity and they may turn up in a most fascinating variety of combinations. This means that while the list described here constitutes the armory of "children who hate," the ego of any child, especially the normally growing pre-adolescent and young adolescent, will at times have jobs to perform similar to those his more disturbed contemporaries have on a larger and more chronic scale. This further means that the same basic ingredients of ego defense against educational surrender and change can be observed by all teachers and parents and the technical issues of just how to go about meeting the ego that defends itself against change becomes as relevant as it is for the clinician in a treatment home. Only the type of illustration used, the scope of the problem, and the sharpness of focusing to the clinical issue, make the things described here different from what the parent and educator have to live through in their tasks of daily life. With slight modifications which we may easily leave to the imagination of the reader himself, what we said here is postulated to be applicable to the normal child in the normal pursuit of daily life with the adult.

# Chapter 5

## The Pathology of a
## Sick Conscience

WE HAVE FOLLOWED the ego of our children through its moments of helplessness and despair, when it finds itself unable to perform its task. We have also traced the tricky way in which it sometimes scurries to the defense of delinquent impulses against the world around and against the "voice from within." It is time to ask this additional question now: just what happened to the voice of their conscience? What is their superego really like, provided they have one at all?

Let us begin once more with a short glimpse at the concept of the superego, since that term is used in so many different ways, has so many controversial issues attached to it, that we might easily be misunderstood. By the way, we are using the words conscience and superego synonymously here. Theoreticians will tell you that this isn't quite correct, and we agree. For the purpose we have in mind, though, this distinction is negligible. In both cases we talk about that part of the personality whose job it is to represent value demands, to stand up for them in case our impulses try to get out from under their implications. Various schools of thought differ in the extent to which they attribute certain well-known functions connected with these value issues either to the ego or to the superego. Some would want to make the superego the seat of all value issues, loading it not only with the task of representing values and standing up for them, but also with the power of subduing recalcitrant impulses in case of a value conflict. Others—and we have joined them for reasons of conceptual economy—have decided to ascribe all actual "power functions" to the ego, leaving the superego with the task of identification with value contents and with the job of giving adequate danger signals when value issues are involved. Since all this is really auxiliary theory, it would not make too much difference which of the two versions is adopted. In short—

and we know our non-psychiatric reader will be happy that our terminological compunctions approach their end—in this book we shall assume that it is the job of the ego to decide whether a given value danger signal will be obeyed or not and to muster the force to subdue value-opposed impulses into submission. The superego, as referred to in this book, will be expected to fulfill a double task. It will be expected to "represent certain values." It will also be expected to give "value danger signals" whenever a conflict between value and impulsive strivings (id) is imminent, or when a violation of value issues has taken place.

## Just how does a conscience become what it is?

The early psychoanalysts, after Freud had presented them with this concept of a superego, primarily concentrated on the task of finding out just how a child goes about establishing "within himself" parental value demands, originally made upon him "from the outside." The general assumption was—and still is—that parents unavoidably and wisely make certain demands upon their children and, through their attitudes, represent certain "values" toward them. The child "incorporates" the original parental value demands through a complex process called "identification." He then establishes as a "department within himself" what previously was a demand from the outside. The proverbial cookie jar illustration is still to the point. Originally, the fear of punishment would deter the child from gratifying his oral greed. Eventually, he ought to end up as a person who has a "voice from within" tell him what is forbidden even if parental discovery or punishment is not to be feared.

This early concept of conscience or superego is still a good enough model to use, but it is important to add some of the details of its development discovered over the years.[1] For the practitioner who is not primarily concerned with psychiatric or sociological theory, we shall make a long story short and

[1] One of the most comprehensive books on this topic is Edmund Bergler's *The Battle of the Conscience: A Psychiatric Study of the Inner Workings of the Conscience* (Washington: The Washington Institute of Medicine, 1948).

confine ourselves to listing only some of the later contributions of exploration and research to this issue. We assume now that the original incorporation of parental value demands through the process of identification is not all that counts. In fact, we know that some of the original value demands taken in by the little child must be discarded in the process of normal growth. At the same time, a variety of new value demands will have to be added over the years, which become important later but would have made no sense when the child was still young and therefore were not made. Moreover, other sources besides the original parent figures add their influence. The child's ego ideals, for instance, may receive nourishment from images of heroes, saints, explorers, great men, or from actual persons who play a role in his real life and with all of whom he may identify later. The content of the value system of an adolescent is certainly also influenced by the "group code" of the gang with which he travels. Furthermore, sociologists and anthropologists have shown us in detail how many items which constitute part of the so-called "customs and mores" of a community in general are finally incorporated by the growing child into his superego, where they are added to older value demands and become hardly distinguishable from them. Just how this later incorporation takes place is still a theoretical puzzle. Some of it seems to happen via the detour of a relationship to people who represent such value issues and become important in the child's life. At other times it nearly looks as though whole value contents were "picked up out of the air" by dint of sheer exposure to group life.

However this may be, by the time we get the children we are talking about, their superego is already an assortment of a variety of value contents derived from a variety of sources, assembled at different developmental stretches and through different processes. The original act of "identification with the parent figure" started it all off, though, and often leaves a deep imprint in spite of many other factors at work at later times. The complexity of this development and the detailed analysis of the various parts of a child's conscience constitute a clinical problem far beyond the scope of this study. What counts at this moment is the fact that, no matter when assembled and where derived from, these various value demands are by now not dependent on outside reality pressures any longer, but have become a solidified "voice from within."

## What tasks has a well-functioning conscience to perform?

It obviously isn't enough for the superego or conscience to "represent value demands," with which a child has "identified." It also has to let the child know whenever a value issue is or is not involved. It is the legitimate function of the superego to give what we might call "value danger signals," just as the ego has to give signals of physical danger in case of a conflict between impulsive wish and reality threat. In short, the voice of conscience ought to start nagging *before* the child gets through with doing what he shouldn't, so that the ego, taking its cue from there, can get going with its power function and prevent the imminent "sin." It also has the obligation to signal frantically after the deed, so that a too unvigilant ego will be jolted into greater temptation resistance next time. We usually ascribe the ability of jolting the control system into more vigilant action and of making the ego aware of value conflict to "guilt feelings." The conscience or superego uses the production of feelings of guilt as a pre-situational or post-situational signal of value conflict to the ego. The job of actually "doing something about it," of manipulating recalcitrant desires, wishes, impulses (id-strivings) we have, in this book, ascribed to the ego and its power function, discussed in previous chapters.

The real story to be written now would be the history and description of the superego of our children. Just what values did they or did they not stand for? Just what was wrong with their superegos? Just what did we plan to do about it? Fascinating though this would be, it would mean a new full volume, for it could not possibly be condensed into a chapter. So we have omitted the full story, but we must try to fill the unfortunate gap in our picture at least by a few condensed and abbreviated sketches to create an awareness of the complexity of the job to be done with the children who hate.

## Conscience on Second Boulevard [2]

The statement that a specific child simply has no conscience or superego at all is being bandied about rather freely these days. In fact, some quite elaborate terminology has been invented to label such far-reaching claims. Frankly, we think that this is the bunk. Among all the hundreds of children who were supposed to be without a conscience and with whom we lived quite closely for varying lengths of time, we haven't yet found one to whom such an exaggerated diagnosis would apply. We admit, though, that we were often tempted to make such a statement about a particular child, especially when we were angry at him, when our own middle-class sensitivities were rubbed the wrong way by what he said or did, when our lack of familiarity with his natural habitat made us blind to the fact that his conscience simply talked to him in a language different from the one ours would use, including four letter words. The concept of a "child without a conscience"—the so-called "psychopath" is supposed to belong to this category —can be maintained only in the artificial seclusion of individual interview practice. Whoever follows a child through the totality of a residential life situation, into every nook and cranny of the trivia of the day, is bound to discover that such a concept is an oversimplification which makes no sense. As far as our Pioneers and the type of child which we think they represent are concerned, the statement that they have no superego would be entirely misleading. The full truth is much more complex and also much more challenging than that. However, we cannot avoid asking, just what is the matter with their consciences?

### 1. Peculiarities in value content

As far as the content of specific values goes, our youngsters showed three clearly differentiated peculiarities rather than just an "absence of superego." The first one might be described as *clear identification areas with a delinquent neigh-*

[2] Our title alludes to the location of Pioneer House.

*borhood code.* By this we imply that our youngsters have accepted some value demands from parents and from their surrounding community, but it so happens that these value demands are themselves of a delinquent nature. From the outside, this may make our children look as though they had "no values at all," but the clinical difference between that and what we really had before us is enormous and of great relevance. Some of their proud display of crude violence, which the middle-class clinician finds so embarrassing to watch, and some of their open bragging about acts of theft or about their deceit in "getting away" with thefts are openly contradictory to the value system by which we would judge. And often enough such behavior simply meant that our youngsters were "value blind" or "value defiant." It would be too easy, though, to shift the whole problem onto this simple explanation. We observed many instances where we were quite certain that such attitudes were *not* expressive of value defiance against the system in which they operated, but that their behavior was really "innocent." By this we mean that they acted that way because they felt in line with the value scale of their own parents and their natural habitat. Thus, when bragging about crude and unjust violence and when proud of a cleverly gotten away with theft, these children were sometimes not only not rebellious, but actually value-conforming as far as their natural habitat goes. Doing things like these, they did what any good child, obedient to his elders and conforming to the mores of the community, would do. The only trouble was that the parental and communal values themselves were out of focus with the general middle-class value scale. Clinically speaking, though, this makes such acts not acts of value rebellion but acts of value conformism. The conflict in those cases was between the standards of their natural habitat and ours, not between the child's impulse and his superego. It is clear that it is clinically very important indeed to differentiate between the genuine internal value conflict or value rebellion, on the one hand, and the sheer sociological value conflict *around, not within,* the child, on the other. Such differentiation implies sharp on-the-spot diagnoses and becomes one of the most important clinical issues for our concern. Since both value rebellion and value blindness, on the one hand, and sociologically value-conflicting conformity, on the other, look so much alike from the outside, any action which is based on vague general value definitions instead of this sharp differential diagnosis becomes clinically invalid.

In other moments of their lives, our youngsters did not give the impression of nearly total value absence or conflict. Sometimes they showed a sudden emergence of what we might term *"childhood value islands"* which was surprising to watch.

This means that, tough as they were, they would suddenly display very obviously non-delinquent, quite middle-class-like value issues which emerged out of nowhere. The fact seems to be that even a delinquent neighborhood in which children may grow up is not so consistently delinquent in its behavior code, so far as children are concerned, as it may be in its adult affairs. Toward their own children even the adults from tough neighborhoods sometimes practice a much more "civilian" type of behavior code than in their own lives. Also, the fact that children were rejected, had nobody to love and identify with, is rarely true to as high a degree as such overgeneralized statements seem to imply. It seems that even neglected children rescue some one or other "relationship memory" out of the debris of their infancy, and that occasional "identification loopholes" pierce the seemingly impenetrable wall of human coldness and disinterest.

As far as our Pioneers go, there were moments in our otherwise conflict-studded life with them, when individual youngsters would suddenly come through with unexpectedly value-identified statements or attitudes. "You see, that comes from not doing what Emily told you," one of the otherwise most recalcitrant ones would be overheard saying to his pal. Sometimes one of them would suddenly be ashamed when caught in some especially vehement swearing, and would explain his feelings by saying that "Kids aren't supposed to say such things in front of adults." Occasionally, the appearance of a visitor, which usually led to a great display of exhibitionistic toughness, would surprisingly throw the group or individual members of it into scenes of "Let's introduce our guest to our dear housemother, who is so kind to us all." Especially in moments of child-adult happiness, primarily focused around child-housemother, or child-cook, relationships, real value concern or guilt around an act of unfairness would crop up freely, seemingly from nowhere. Such value islands would emerge much too early for us to think that we produced them. They obviously had been there all the time, and now began to emerge out of the debris of general value warfare, as a remainder from earlier times.

Even more fascinating than those "childhood value islands" was the appearance, out of the fog, of whole mountain ranges of *"value sensitivity and value respect"* on the horizon. We refer to these as distinctly different from actual "value identification," a difference which we think needs to be emphasized much more than it has been in the past. This, in brief, is what is being referred to here: If a person visits a household of an entirely different style of life, or a church of somebody else's denomination, he may run into "value demands" with which he is not identified at all. They are obviously not "values" to him—in fact they may affect him as strange or slightly ridiculous—and he would not ascribe power over his own life to them. Most of the time, however, he may still sense that there is something of the nature of a value demand for somebody else at work, and he may respect this fact as having the power to modify his behavior somewhat. Without accepting the values as such for himself, he will usually show a certain amount of "sensitivity and respect" in their presence. He will try to pick up cues from his surroundings as to just "how one is expected to act in such a sase." He will either be polite enough to live up to expectations for the time being, or at least show eagerness "not to offend." What actually happens in those cases is something between actual value identification and value blindness or value rejection. The person we have in mind has *not* incorporated the specific content of the values in question into his conscience. But he has incorporated into his own value system the demand "to be sensitive to and respectful of" other people's value systems to a certain point.

Our children showed whole chunks of "value sensitivity and value respect" to be still intact at times, even while they were engaged in wholesale value warfare in other areas of the battlefront.

Once Larry took Danny and Andy to Sunday service in the church of his own denomination. Both of the other children

belonged to a different one. The two youngsters, otherwise
as obstreperous and mischief-bent as can be, behaved with
perfect tact. They carefully tried to take their cues from
their host as to when to kneel, get up, bow, and so forth.
Only Danny, whose heavy build got into conflict with the
narrow pews, complained afterwards that he wouldn't go
back there, because kneeling down so much and so often
"hurt his goddam knees."

After we were able to re-awaken some such dormant value
sensitivities within our children, we would often find them
objecting to each other's behavior under certain conditions.
In two children whose basic volume of extreme and obscene
swearing would be about equal, we could often find differences, after a while, in "value sensitivity under certain conditions." Thus, while still having no guilt or concern about the
act itself, one of them would begin to feel uneasy if the other
one would produce too wild swear words "in front of a
visitor." Also, our demand to keep eating situations at meal-
time free from too obscene orgies obviously reached something within them. For even while some of them would pay
no attention to our demand as such, when interfered with they
would consider our argument as "justified." The discovery of
just which stretches of "value sensitivity and value respect"
are still intact or can at least soon be revitalized constitutes a
clinically most important issue.

Putting all this together, it can easily be seen that our
youngsters could not be accused of "having no conscience at
all." Rather, we would complain about the spotty value area
coverage of their superego, the occasional blind spots in their
value system, or the identification-based conformity to the
delinquent values of their original habitat. At the same time we
would have to unearth and revitalize but admit as existing
even before our arrival a wide range of "childhood value
islands" and a considerable amount of "value sensitivity and
value respects," at least under favorable life conditions.

## 2. Inadequacy of the signal function

The pathology of a sick conscience does not necessarily
have to lie in the inadequate value content coverage. It may

have its main trouble in a disturbance of the job of "giving value danger signals." These, indeed, were often very weak in our children. Where a normal child would feel some anticipatory pangs of conscience, even before he decided how he would act, our youngsters would have only a very dim awareness that what they were about to do wasn't so good. Thus, even in areas which were covered by value identifications, the very weakness of the voice of their conscience would often mean that it remained unheard amidst the noise of temptational challenge. This made it easy for their ego to ignore it entirely whenever feasible. Sometimes our youngsters seemed to suffer also from another incapacity of a sick conscience, but one which is more often found in the neurotic rather than the delinquent child. They seemed to have what we might term a "post-action conscience." A superego suffering from this disease is of no help at all. It is value identified, all right. But it does not raise its voice in a moment of temptation. It confines itself to screaming all the more loudly after the deed has been committed. Colloquial usage tends to throw this type of disturbance in together with the previous one, referring to both as a "weak conscience." Yet, clinically speaking, we have obviously an entirely different disturbance before us. This type of conscience acts, in fact, as many of the parents of such children acted earlier in their lives. They were, initially, too disinterested or rejective to care much how their children fared, or to give them any help to go straight. Then, if something went wrong, they would literally descend upon the child with the full blast of their revenge for the discomfort the child had caused them. This, in turn, would be followed by another stretch of disinterest, of lack of supervision and care. In some moments of their lives, the conscience of our youngsters would react in exactly the same way. It would produce some feelings of guilt after a too obvious misdeed, but would still give no anticipatory value danger signal in the next temptational situation. This special disease of "post-action conscience" constitutes an important challenge to the task of superego repair. While the behavioral results are the same as with the child who has no conscience to begin with, its cure needs to take an entirely different path.

### 3. Deficiencies in the identification machinery

The development of a healthy and adequate conscience is a complicated job. The basic internal process by which it takes place has as its core the process of "identification." This runs somewhat like this. A child develops a positive relationship to a person (we would like to add, or a group). He then surrenders his affectionate claims upon that person in favor of establishing that person's value demands within himself. Instead of wanting to possess and love the parent or teacher, he begins to want to be the kind of person himself that that parent or teacher would like him to be. The trouble with our children was that they have not often and early enough been in a position where such a process of identification would have been encouraged, and most of the identifications they had made in their earlier lives were flimsy and incomplete and had deficiencies of all sorts. The reasons for this are too manifold to be listed. Among them was the lack of persons who would love the children enough to elicit from them enough counter-affection, and the inconsistency of the behavior of the adults who played a role in our children's lives, so that there was little reason to transform love into identification, even where the former had been produced. There was also a paucity of adequate models with whom we could want the child to identify to begin with, and a great turnover in mostly disinterested or even outright hostile personnel on the changing scenery of their lives. In short, by the time we got them, many of these youngsters hardly knew how to like new people any more, and they had to start learning what it means to like, and especially what it means to identify, all over again. This, by the way, is the reason why only a total treatment design can do the job for them. For once the machinery of identification is misdeveloped or underdeveloped, it requires a great display of "total strategy" to build it up anew. This is also the reason why the layman or ordinary foster parent finds such children so disappointing and intolerable to work with. A normal child, with a stretch of happy childhood behind him, even though somewhat out of gear right now, usually has a good deal of "identification readiness" in him, just waiting for the right person around whom to unfold. All you have to do in his case is to enter his life, give him affection, carry yourself in a way children understand and consider fun, and add perhaps an occasional bit of love-blackmail or bribery, and you won't find the child hesitating long before he accepts what you stand for and identifies with some of the values you hold. Our Pioneers had little of that *"noblesse oblige"* principle built into them when we got them. At best we got them acceptant of our love, and even that was a hard struggle for a long time. Any demand to really change their affection toward us into a desire to improve and identify would rather frighten them back into their original custom of living for the day without moral implications of any kind. The disturbance of the identification machinery as such seems to us one of the most severe diseases of the conscience, and one which needs the most complex and elaborate clinical strategy for repair.

## 4. Guilt displacement, model-rigidity, and other superego disturbances

Along with the three types of superego pathology described above, our youngsters also showed in many moments of their lives the usual assortment of superego difficulties found in the pathology of other children and of adult neurotics. Space allows us to list only a few of those. It seems to us that the difference between the "neurotic child" and the one with "no conscience" has been drawn much too superficially and sharply to date. While the basic superego disturbances of our children seem to fall into the wayward or delinquent category, they are certainly not free from some of the pathology usually described in cases of highly value-identified middle-class neurotics. By "displacement of guilt feeling" we mean the fact that, even where the youngster's superego is vigilant enough to raise value demands, it may miss the goal in terms of the life situations to which guilt feelings are being attached. Our children would sometimes act as our unconscious is known to act in some of our dreams: a deed which in itself is totally harmless produces nagging guilt, while life issues which are really guilt-loaded seem to leave us entirely happy and free from concern. By "model rigidity" we mean inability of a person to experience guilt unless the situation is directly tied up with the original persons who made the first value demands, usually the parents. A case in point is the openly delinquency-identified car thief who feels no compunction about value issues so far as his stealing is concerned, but whose letters to his mother literally drip with sentimental guilt display for minor childlike infractions against her demands. During the phase in which our youngsters first allowed themselves an open regression to their childlike love hunger, we got a great deal of such display of "guilt" in connection with ourselves. But we triumphed too soon. While we thought we finally had their "value sensitivity" stirred up, we soon found that we had only revived old guilt models, the rigidity of which did not make them usable at all in present and real life. In those phases our youngsters sometimes did show "guilt," as younger and more normal children would, in relation to us. But it was the shadow of an infant's guilt, and we had a long way to go before new and real value sensitivities could be developed.

All these and other disturbances of superego functions must be reckoned with. But they constitute only a "marginal pathology" with the youngsters we talk about. Their main line of disturbance—and the major demand for strategy of repair—must be sought along the lines of difficulties described in the first three points.

## The Complexity of Superego Repair

In this chapter we have isolated the "superego" or "conscience" of the child as though it were a part all by itself. This was unavoidable for the purpose of a crude sketch and rough outline of its main functions and their disturbance types. Before we forget the real complexity of our clinical task, though, we had better hasten to put things into context again. For, were only the superego of our children disturbed, the task would be comparatively simple. In fact, most normal and neurotic children also show isolated disturbances of their conscience as we have described them here, and we can often cope with them along the line of re-education, case work, and psychiatric treatment. The children who hate constitute a special problem over and beyond all that. Their deficient and sick conscience happens to coincide with a deficient or delinquent ego. That makes for a combination which seems to defy our usual treatment channels, and which taxes even the most ingenious "total treatment strategy" to the utmost.

Let us assume for a moment that we were lucky or skillful and discovered an old value island or even inserted a new value identification into Danny's life. What a clinical triumph that would constitute all by itself! Yet, where would it lead us if we achieved that much before we were able to bring his "ego" up to par? If Danny, for instance, suddenly feels guilty for acting "so mean" toward us—and what a healthy feeling that would be—what does it get us, so long as his ego cannot cope with even a normal feeling of guilt? From our description of that type of ego disturbance we can easily forecast the chaos in which this will result. Feeling guilty for having been unfair to us, Danny will have to have an anxiety attack or a temper tantrum, or he will have to destroy things which remind him of this obligation or guilt toward us. So the behavior result will be wild, even though we obviously scored a great therapeutic success so far as his superego goes. Or, to raise another complication, let's assume that we "strengthen" Joe's ego enough so that it suddenly is able to be more perceptive of the reality around him than it has been before. Where does that get us unless we also give his conscience more power over his life? For ego strength *per se* is a small gain, as our chapter on the "delinquent ego and its techniques" ought to have shown. On the other hand, how can we get Joe even to see the implication of his earlier deeds unless his ego is first strengthened to be self-perceptive enough of his own motives and to be socially sensitive enough to stop his delusional persecutory fantasies by which he defends himself from the impact of love?

The worst combination of all, though, is not that of superego deficiency and ego deficiency, but of superego deficiency and delinquency-identified ego strength. With the children who simply suffer from a mal-developed conscience, we would have only one area of sickness to combat. With the children

244 / Children Who Hate

who combine such pathology with the impressive ego strength of the "delinquent ego and its defenses," as we described them under that heading, we have an indeed formidable combination arrayed against us. How can we ever get "value identifications" across against such hypertrophically developed defensive skills? What good would the breakdown of such defenses be to our clinical goals if we could not pull the value switch equally fast? Breaking down their ego defenses without supplying them with livable values at the same time will only leave us with ego-deficient children, not with the product we are supposed to deliver.

In short, ego support and ego repair must go hand in hand with value surgery and superego repair. There will be partial priorities along the line, as in many other clinical issues. The timing and the decision about sequence will be as important in this job as in any case of complex physical pathology. Likewise, temporary success on one of the fronts may have to be paid for, for a while at least, by great behavioral chaos and breakdown on another. Or, the benefits to be derived by a job well done on another front may not be reaped until other side jobs are finished. We know this by now in the field of physical medicine. We expect that the successfully operated upon foot may remain unusable until a simultaneous heart condition has also been removed, and we expect the patient to deserve total care as long as any essential part of his pathology still needs to be taken care of.

In the field of human behavior, such clinical realism of thinking is far from commonplace. Public opinion and even the enthusiasm of the one or other professional discipline in isolation from the others often pressure us for a quick exploitation of partial results. With the children who suffer from a combination of ego and superego disturbances, not to mention the pathology of their impulsive life, the need for a total treatment strategy with careful timing of sequence of all part-operations becomes one of the most important therapeutic challenges. It was with this challenge in mind that the complexity of the total issue was unfolded in this book.

# Chapter 6

## The Phenomenon of Treatment Shock [1]

OUR descriptive study of "children who hate" would be somehow incomplete if we did not focus our attention for a while on what happens to them when they are first exposed to the treatment environment. The initial response of our Pioneers to the vast shift in total climate involved behavior phenomena that were different from what had been and remained their basic pathology. During the first three months we saw in fascinating bas-relief how new pathologies in them were stirred and mobilized by our attempts to create a friendly, gratifying, and supportive relationship with them. Actually we observed a violence and vehemence of reaction which took on the character almost of a shock response. The previous adjustment patterns of the children could not help them to accommodate to the implications of the adult who loves, the program that gratifies, the experience that does not traumatize. We are quite sure that such a phenomenon occurs with most children who are sent into a treatment design which challenges their previous mode of adaptation and that they must go through a phase of treatment shock before the therapeutic relationship becomes stabilized. Especially does this apply to the children who hate because they, among all disturbance types, are so peculiarly the products of a social wasteland in which few, if any, of the positive things in life have been experienced.

The shock type of reaction which was the total behavioral pattern in response to the treatment milieu can be broken down diagnostically into the following rather distinct cate-

[1] In part, material on which this chapter is based can be found in David Wineman, *Early Clinical Experiences at Pioneer House* (University of Michigan Institute of Social Work, Ann Arbor, Michigan: An unpublished thesis).

gories: *transference phenomena, fear of love,* and *"neglect edema"* in the *"land of plenty."*

## Transference Phenomena

Historically, in psychoanalytic psychology, the term transference is used to signify the shifting of impulses and strivings from one object to another.[2] It was readily observed in the psychoanalytic treatment of adult neurotics that impulses originally felt toward one or the other parent become reactivated during the therapy and focused upon the therapist. Thus, for instance, positive expression of affectional strivings frequently occurs shortly after the initiation of therapy. Following this stage of the positive transference, there usually occurs an intermittent period when predominantly hostile impulses, also belonging to the early relationships with the parents, become reactivated and assume dominance over the love impulses, forcing them into repression. This received the name "negative transference" and does not signify that the transference disappears, but rather that its valence changes from positive feelings to negative feelings toward the analyst. In psychoanalytic work with children, it was Anna Freud's contention that true transference does not take place in the same sense that it does with adult patients, since children are still attached to the parents in a real sense and the feelings they have toward them could not be said to be reactivated since they have never disappeared. This notion applies to children who are receiving therapy in the office situation but who are still living with their own parents. However, Anna Freud points out that, for children who are physically separated from their parents, something more clearly resembling classical transference does seem to occur.[3] Further, in the

[2] Otto Fenichel, *The Psychoanalytic Theory of Libido* (New York: W. W. Norton & Company, Inc., 1945).

[3] Anna Freud, *Psychoanalytical Treatment of Children* (London: Imago, 1946). Our observations of the Pioneer group certainly lead us to concur with Anna Freud's contention that children who live apart from their parents, e.g. in an institution, develop more classically transference-like behavior toward the therapist.

case of our Pioneers, the core of the transference reaction observed seemed to be destructive, hostile impulse strivings which these children had originally felt toward former adult objects with whom they had lived and which, in a residential setting, were expressed toward the clinical adult.

It is important to keep in mind, when we speak of transference, that the central idea involved in this concept is that through the transference the patient tends to reproduce his characteristic style of behavior, that he wants and strives to behave toward the transference object or objects as he has behaved toward emotionally important objects in the past. When somehow, either explicitly through a verbal suggestion or implicitly through gestures, personal reactions, etc., attempts are made to change this characteristic style of self-expression, then the phenomenon of resistance is encountered. This resistance involves defenses ranging from simple repression to the most elaborate and complex ego behavior against the recognition and modification of one's own impulses. The main psychological goal of these resistance techniques is to retain the original mode of behavior. This, too, was observed in classical formation with respect to the reactions of the Pioneer House group, who struggled intensely and dramatically to retain their hostile behavior pattern toward the adult, especially during the first three months of exposure to the residential therapy situation. From the viewpoint, therefore, that we were struggling with transference and resistance and attempting to manipulate these two major mechanisms in the therapeutic life situation, our task, clinically, resembled that of the psychoanalyst engaged in the traditional practice of therapy in the office situation.

As pointed out, however, the residential therapy setting provides some actual differences, so far as transference dynamics are concerned, from that of the office setting. These were mainly in the direction of transference volume and transference intensity. Since we were actually living with the children, we anticipated and obtained a much greater volume of transference than if we had seen them in an office setting for an hour a day or three times per week. Further, the intensity or concentration of transference that developed was stronger since, with the exception of the public school personnel, we were the main adult objects in their lives. In addition to transference elements in the relationship of the group to us, we became involved in strong emotional discharge because of the realistic role we played in their lives. It is thus impossible to be able always to distinguish clearly, when viewing it from the outside, which aspect of the behavior we observed was in fact transference, which mainly reality-conditioned. In this discussion of transference, however, we are focusing on that aspect of their behavior which we believe to be at least strongly conditioned by the transference factor.

Practically from the outset of exposure to the clinical milieu, the behavior of the group, although individually variable from member to member, increasingly took on the character of a mass evacuation of all the hostility which these children had stored up within them. The hatred was not always necessarily directed against the adult in explicit and concrete terms. Their "range of fire" was against the total environment: the adult, the house itself, toys and other program materials, the other children. When we speak of transference in this respect, we mean more than a simple transfer of hostile impulses, which, indeed, these children could have produced and did produce in a variety of other places and points of contact with the outside world. In the Pioneer House milieu, it took on the added dimension provided through the children's conception of the degree to which their behavior would be tolerated. For we should remember that counter-aggressive punishment from the adult, in the outside world, had acted as the only inhibition toward unbridled primitivity. Having, through our clinical approach, lost the adult as a specific inhibitor, the children were stimulated to express hating mechanisms in themselves, more than they would have been in the outside world. Hatred originally felt against the "mean" adult in their prior lives became broken down into various forms of action expression which looked like a total destructive revolt against the whole environment. The following two examples taken from the first week's record material illustrate the confused chaotic pattern of this initial transference of hostility.

After dinner, bedlam broke loose. The group chased each other all over the house; there were wild fights between Sam and Joe; their language was nothing but a stream of obscenity and they hurled these words at anybody—including staff. Danny just sat or stood around simply reeling off choice terms at any opportunity, and even without an opportunity, and seemed to be getting obvious satisfaction out of this anal word play in itself. They are words which one usually would use if extremely angry but he only smiled or grinned fatuously when he was saying them. The youngsters tore into a wild chase upstairs and, seizing the mattresses in the attic, threw them downstairs and hopped on them. Joe discovered an old airplane and ran with it through the house, finally crashing it and then breaking it into pieces. (Entry: 12/4/46, Fritz Redl)

Our group of six has been here for five days now. There is hardly an intact toy or piece of recreational equipment left in the upstairs playroom. The impulse of the children just to smash everything in sight is almost incredibly omnipresent. I have seen any one of them, with the occasional exception of Henry and Sam, go into a room and react to the mere sight of a toy on the floor by immediately jumping on it or destroying it in some way. They scarcely, if ever, pause even for a moment to use it for the purpose for which it was made. (Entry: 12/3/46, David Wineman)

Along with this generalized eruption of hostile behavior which seemed to be an over-all diffused pattern of expression, there emerged more specific varieties of hostility which were more clearly object-aimed and more characteristic of certain classical types of developmental conflict. These involved primitive fantasies and wishes belonging to early psychosexual development which, in more classically neurotic and normal children with strong defenses already present in the ego, could not have emerged without months of patient undoing of the whole defense pattern.

It was necessary to sit with both Danny and Joe at bedtime since they were both causing much disturbance in the sleeping room. I took them downstairs and arranged them each on one side of me. In the course of just quietly sitting there with them, not saying anything to either of them, but not permitting them to leave until I was sure they would quiet down, they were stimulated to weave the following fantasy about me: They would both be in the basement and I would come down. Danny would heave a hammer at me and crush my skull. At this point, Joe looked at my hands and said, "Look, he already has wrinkles in them and he is going to die soon." There were further variations of this "shrivel away to the point of death theme," all anticipating my early demise. (Entry: 12/4/46, Fritz Redl)

The boys were doing a tumbling routine upstairs in charge of one of the counselors. A staff member was not on duty at that time and I watched them. Suddenly Sam insisted that we go away since they wanted to have a meeting of the recently formed secret society. I knew they were only going to start throwing things around the minute I left, so I said, "You can have your meeting; we won't listen." Andy picked this up immediately, "Well, if you don't listen, then we can talk." Then followed a joint name-calling and aggressive fantasy against me with the following theme: "We're going to cut Fritz' dick off. We're going to murder him. We're going to kill everybody." It was all in a playful mood, with the group constantly assuring themselves that we were not listening anyway. (Entry: 1/13/47, Fritz Redl)

Here we can see the primitive attitudes toward the father in their original unmodified form. Concurrent with this type of fantasy there appeared a variety of erotic-obscene fantasy material built around unresolved psychosexual conflicts stemming from the early oedipal stage. The erotic relationship between the mother and the father together with the expected rivalries, hostilities, and anxieties which this creates, was dramatically projected onto the housemother and director of the home, who served as the central mother and father image. Then it was further displaced onto all of the clinical personnel, whom the children paired off, so to speak, into a veritable cluster of mother-father images, with accusations of sex relations between them, rejection of the children, and reservation of affection only for each other. A typical episode in the group behavior along these lines in the early period of treatment follows:

> "Yeah, yeah, look at Emily and Fritz. (Emily was the housemother and Fritz the director.) All they care about is fucking each other. Emily and Fritz are in there fucking. Emily and Fritz are on the bed. (Roars of laughter and obscene shouting.) Now Joel (counselor) and Barbara (counselor) are on the bed. No, they can't be on the bed because that's where Fritz and Emily are. They're on the wall. Dave (executive director) and Vera (another counselor) are on the chandeliers, etc., etc."

This stream of revilement and obscene accusation ran a turbulent course during the first three months of exposure to the Home. A rather fascinating type of condemnation and elliptical form of representation evolved which was purely group idiomatic and which they used to refer to and describe their fantasies. If one of the group members would say "on the bed," "on the wall," or "on the chandeliers," everyone immediately knew that this meant that the adults were being suspected of having sex relations. Further, the geographical designation—bed, wall, or chandeliers—had a specific meaning such that "on the bed," meant "Fritz and Emily," etc. At this stage of treatment just the word "bed" used in a certain way by one child would send the others into a barrage of obscene accusations. The degree to which these most primitive oedipal feelings continued to flood the transference reaction was quite amazing.

> Tonight, just before bedtime, there was a display of group revolution against going to bed in which Sam and Joe co-starred. The usual scheme of an aggressive raid through the house was afoot and was timed to begin right after, or during, the last few minutes of treat. Sam and Joe were provoked by quick interference on my part into a premature attempt to rally the group and only the hesitation of the rest of them to follow Sam and Joe, because of my very strong demands, avoided a group riot. Because they could not arouse any group support, the two boys, and especially Sam, began hurling perverse sex insults and

invitations at me. Sam lowered his pajama pants and exhibited his penis; he invited me to "suck him off" and, when I ignored this, he got wilder and wilder, finally stirring up so much excitement that I had to take him into the office. He then lay down immediately on the floor, face downward, and insisted in an hysterical squealing voice that I was going to "fuck" him and chanted it over and over again, making coitus movements towards the floor. I asked him why he was doing this and he said that I was making him do it. When I expressed amazement that he could even think such a thing, he switched to saying the devil was making him do it. When I asked if he really heard the devil talk to him, he tittered and replied that I was talking silly. (Entry: 12/27/46, David Wineman)

Here we can see much of the unconscious imagery which is involved in the libido attitudes toward the adult. We must first understand that the night time raid has a special meaning with respect to the separation from the adults, enforced by the sleeping routine which also has the element, in fantasy, of liberating the adults for further intimacy toward each other. The following incident may make this important theme clear:

In the course of today's visit to my apartment they were lively, but not extremely so. Henry rummaged around and found a bottle of brandy that I reserve for guests and sneaked a slug of it into his coke. Since nobody got wise to it, he had to brag about it. This led to the others chiming in and bragging about being drunk. Many of their jokes (about drunk drivers who go to jail, etc.) depicted me increasingly in the role of the drunken father who comes home and forces the mother into sexual intercourse. Later, back home at bedtime, they were beginning to act up and told their counselor: "Fritz can't come up now, he is too drunk to move." Then from Andy, "I'll cut Fritz' dick off so he can't fuck Emily while we sleep." (Entry: 12/26/46, Fritz Redl)

The aggressive raid can be seen as a further outpouring of the unconscious fantasies around the sexual intimacy of the parents. The group fantasy and behavior involved in these raids are highly significant. The children invariably tried to pillage the ice box and then, brandishing their flashlights wildly, meanwhile fantasying them as guns, they conducted a spirited search, like a lynch hunt, under the spell of which they careened madly through the house in a perpetual merry-go-round search for a fantasy enemy whom they were stalking down to destroy in the shadows. We saw many of these raids and often it was necessary to interfere sharply since the group intoxication which ensued was almost impossible to handle. In some of them we felt that all that was involved was a quite ordinary aggressive search for mischievous fun. In others, however, accompanied by fantasies such as the above, a rather clear symbolism seemed to be added: the mother is triumphantly seized while the father is hunted down and killed.

This material seems to indicate that the children are here most strikingly re-enacting some of the classical hostilities belonging to the oedipal stage of development with the further distortions which seriously rejected children can give to the inherent conflict of this period. In this connection it is seen that the jealousy of the children is clearly bivalent.[4] They are jealous both of the father for suspected preference and possession of the mother and, in reverse, of the mother for preference and possession of the father. It is as though they here conceive of a pact on the part of the parents to banish them from love. It is not at all clear that this implies only sexual love, even though the verbal form of their attack on the parents is of the crudest and most obscene type. Indeed, we would suspect that children who are overtly rejected, as these were, have little incentive to go beyond the crudest, most primitive imagery with respect to the nature of the relationship of the parents toward each other. To begin with, they are deeply deprived from birth with respect to libidinal gratifications from the parents. Further, practically all they visualize on the libidinal scale between the parents is a rather open, crude sexual tie. Seldom do they observe tenderness, feelings of mutual consideration, helpfulness, or concern. Thus it is quite understandable that the very image they have of love

[4] For an important insight into the bivalent character of jealousy see Richard Sterba, "Eifersüchtig Auf —?" *Psychoanalytische Bewegung,* XII (1930), 167.

*per se* is couched in sexual terms. Sexual relations between the parents thus come to represent the love they do not have themselves and in a way climax the deprivational life experience to which they are subjected.

In the case of Mike, his mother and father fought bitterly and the father would be absent from home on periodic bouts of drinking during which he wandered about the country. Upon his return, he and the mother would "make up," which meant that they indulged in further sexual contact with each other, only to break up once more. Their living circumstances were very primitive and Mike was aware of the sexual relationship from very early years. Thus the only "love" relationship he observed was the sexual aspect.

We can readily extrapolate from psychoanalytic findings among neurotic children what such an orientation would do to the oedipal development of the child. We can infer through this approach that children such as these would have to have a very primitive oedipal pattern and that their premature sexuality and easily aroused sex primitivity are really desperate devices to right the libido imbalance which has distorted their whole development. In the service of this need, they focus many of the deprivations belonging to the presexual stages of life onto the sex level which, as stated, is in most cases the only form of libidinal relationship they have observed in the relationship of the parents to each other.

## Fear of Love

The primitive nature of the transference reaction displayed by the children was etiologically rooted to either poorly managed or totally absent affectional relationships to adults from early infancy. These primitive behavior patterns remained intact within the personality because, in their previous lives, adequate adult affectional rewards for the surrender of this type of behavior were not offered to the child. The concept of primitivity does not limit itself, however, to the mere existence of a generally hostile type of self-expression. Most importantly, it also implies that such children are oriented toward the self as emotional objects, that they have not moved along the developmental scale to such a point that they can take on other human beings in a positive emotional sense. This is why, obviously, they can adhere to a style of life in which the "me first" slogan is the heart and soul of their value system. It is well known that this is the earliest conception of life that a child acquires in his emotional development and from which he is pried loose in the process of socialization when this occurs in a normal way. Yet, children like these, obviously, do not remain frank infants. Even though their whole philosophy of life is grounded in infantile narcissism, at least by the time they are in pre-adolescence they have acquired a veneer of awareness of how life should be lived. They know that hatred and aggression are not justifiable when one is well treated and they are capable of guilt feelings when they find themselves unable to respond with counter-affection to the loving adult. Love coming from adults, therefore, constitutes a threat to their whole adaptation system, which is built on primitive self-love. Thus, the exposure to love creates a crisis which, in the beginning of treatment, takes the form of a dilemma:

Should the new love triumph over the old adaptation pattern, the internal sanctions for narcissistic exploitation of the outside world would be removed. Conversely, should the old pattern prove triumphant over the new love, they might lose new gratifications derived from this source.

The children attempt to resolve this dilemma during the initial stages of treatment by denying the premise around which the dilemma is built: namely, they attempt to deny that the new adult in their lives actually does offer them love and security of a caliber which would prove destructive to the old value system. If they can be successful in accomplishing this, they can, in turn, justify the continued existence of their behavior symptoms.

This evening Joe heaved a bowling pin at Danny in a fit of rage and barely missed his skull. His counselor quite firmly told him that we could not permit such dangerous behavior here. "Yeah," he shouted, "for the least little thing they beat, I mean bawl, the shit out of you!" (Entry: 12/4/46, Vera Kare)

This incident, occurring on the fifth day of the group's exposure to the treatment milieu, shows the acuteness of the children's diagnosis of the adult's attitudes, their quick perception of the limits beyond which the Pioneer House adult would not go in restraining or disciplining them. In order to ward off the perception of the adult as benign and friendly, a variety of hostile behavior patterns were developed. These represented the struggle to devaluate the clinical adult so that he would more resemble the old punitive adult and thus not stand in the way of the untrammeled expression of ancient hostilities and aggressive exploitation of the outside world. Provocative defiant behavior, clearly aimed at luring the adult into punishment traps, was seen on several occasions.

It was bedtime and the youngsters finally quieted down enough to be given their treat. They dawdled so long, however, that finally I had to insist that they hurry and get into bed. Joe said he was going to take his pop to bed with him. I told him he could not and that he would have to finish it down here. He snarled at me, "Dammit, I won't, you bastard," and presented a perfect picture of defiant, provocative revolt. Finally I had to take the bottle from him because he started upstairs with it despite my demands to the contrary, and I knew from experience what a problem this would raise with the other children. He repeated his insult and tried to snatch the bottle from my hand. I isolated him from the others and he went into a paroxysm of aggression. After he quieted down, we talked. I explained to him that there were certain things that we let the group get away with but there were others that we would not tolerate. I mentioned examples of both. Joe reacted to this with the following: "Why the hell don't you hit us? That would have effect." (Entry: 12/6/46, Fritz Redl)

In this sequence, it can readily be seen that the violent acting out by Joe is an invitation to physical punishment which, when not forthcoming, actually forces him to verbalize his need for it. The verbal, explicit request for punishment was, however, rare. The acted-out invitation was more frequent than its verbal equivalent. Thus, one of the children who had been the victim of chronic beatings by an alcoholic father, desperately tried to put us in a position where our behavior toward him would resemble the experience he had had with his own father.

I have observed Danny in at least twenty-five incidents during the first month at the Home where either the director of the Home or I have had finally to resort to physical restraint (holding) in order to quiet him sufficiently so that he could be allowed to mingle freely with the rest of the group members without risk of physical injury to them. Each time I have been impressed by how he goads and insults us. When this proves insufficient to provoke us, he finally begins to attack us physically or smash furniture and other equipment so that, in order to prevent either physical injury to ourselves or unlimited destruction, we have to hold him. (Entry: 12/30/46, David Wineman)

In addition to actual attempts to lure the adult into behavior which could be interpreted as punitive, the children developed other defenses for avoiding the responsibility for change implied by love. A type of "regurgitation" pattern occurred in which the children would defiantly "throw up" in our faces, as it were, already accepted affectional tokens. Through this mechanism they then could release themselves from the obligation to be more cooperative which the acceptance of the tokens would have implied.

Mike became furious today when I insisted that he stop throwing food at the table. For quite a long time he lapsed into a sullen sulk and then began working himself up into a real temper outburst in which he went upstairs, gathered all of the belongings which he had accumulated during his short stay here (he entered only nine days ago), and threw the stuff in my face, saying that he didn't want our "god-dam stuff, etc." (Entry: 2/8/47, David Wineman)

## Neglect Edema in The Land of Plenty

The treatment shock phase is a function of a third and fascinating variable. The children who hate, we must remember, are the children of neglect. They have been chronically traumatized through repetitive frustration of many of their basic needs. Indeed we might speculate that they suffer from a disease entity directly stemming from neglect itself which, for want of a better term, might be called a "neglect edema." Their frustration swells and festers, as it were, until even frustration which is minor and painless in terms of the "normal" threshold for frustration tolerance becomes for them an intolerable challenge to control which they cannot meet. For each frustration, no matter how small the issue may be, is lumped together with the chain of frustrations out of the past.

Today the group was scheduled to go swimming at the Boys' Club, but the trip had to be postponed because of the breakdown of the station wagon. The group was quite angry about it and made various wild accusations against us to the effect that we never do anything for them, that it was a dirty trick, etc., just as though we had deliberately planned that the station wagon should go out of commission. Larry, in particular, was very upset and raved and ranted for about thirty minutes. He did not have a wild psychomotor tantrum, but his verbalization was extremely hostile and most interesting because of the distorted reasoning with which he supported his charges against us. The key note to his attack was, "How come we can't never do nothin'?" It was useless to point out to him that we had been swimming on three or four other occasions as scheduled and this hardly means that we "never do nothin'." He was not even temporarily stopped by this counter-argument and simply went on, screeching out his accusations over and over again until he finally wore himself out. There is more to his special ideology than just simple situational frustration. I have observed him on a score of occasions during these first six weeks when he will use the same argument that he never gets "nothin'," or can never do "nothin'," etc. in relation to having been refused, temporarily, a request. (Entry: 1/30/47, David Wineman)

This intense pessimistic fatalism seems to be a deeply ingrained ideology which has been built up out of previous repetitive frustration and disillusion. The need and peculiar ability of the ego to deny certain aspects of reality which come into conflict with this ideology indicate definitely that any treatment should unquestionably involve heavy satisfaction dosage combined with verbal manipulation of the ego's conception of reality.

We take such children and transplant them into our treatment environment, for them a veritable "land of plenty." And neglect edema in the land of plenty is transformed into a longing for much more than can be granted. First, the proximity to new and varied satisfactions acts as a powerful stimulant for the total demand system. Second, the perception of the benign adult, even though part of the child's ego, as we have shown, is heatedly denying the very quality of his benevolence, provides a base for an almost delusional expectation pattern. Exaggerated ideas of the loving adult's ability and willingness to accept all impulse expression are built up. If the hostile adult of the past was one who thwarted pleasurable experience, then the loving adult is just the reverse, i.e., categorically permissive. The underlying emotional slogan becomes: "If they love me, they will give me anything I want, let me do anything I wish." Love, in other words is perceived narcissistically, aided and abetted by the neglect trauma of their past lives. Thus, the ego of the children is caught, as it were, in a pincer movement between two frustration pressures initiated by the treatment situation:

1. They build up an intolerable greed tension because of the proximity to an abundance of new gratification chances.

2. They cannot cope with the inevitable disappointment that the clinical adult, although benign and gratification-oriented, does not conform to the implications of their delusional attitude toward the loving adult, i.e., that he be totally permissive.

Inevitably, therefore, a certain proportion of the hostility which emerged as a part of treatment shock derived from the frustration of wishes and strivings tied to these twin pressures. Especially can we expect this type of response since we are dealing here with egos whose reaction to frustration has predominantly been an aggressive one, which, by the time they come into treatment, has become almost a built-in mechanism.

In their aggressive reaction to the frustration built up in this sector of the treatment shock reaction, the children were driven to insist on concessions from us, and hostile bickering and bargaining persisted with a chronic vehemence.

> After the group came home from school, Joe came into the office, saying he wanted to talk with me about cigarettes. As soon as we sat down, he began in high crescendo and with various aggressive tactics to demand ten cigarettes a day. I refused, reminding him of our deal calling for five cigarettes and how we had clarified that we would not increase the number of cigarettes beyond what he had originally claimed he "had to have" to avoid stealing or getting them illegally. Here he burst into tears and called me a string of anal obscene names, claiming I had promised him more. Without waiting for me to reply, he worked himself up to a veritable frenzy. "Yeah, you say you will give us whatever we want. Shit, bastards, fucker." I reminded him again that this was not what we had said. He could have five cigarettes because that was what he said he needed to begin with. He reacted by hurling threats at me about what he would do if I didn't give in. He would smoke behind my back. He would insult our cook so that she would leave. He would destroy my desk with tools from the workshop at night when I was asleep. I said, "You're very upset and angry. Maybe you're really not used to being given a good deal. I understand how that can be. But we can't go any further on the number of cigarettes. Here, if you want your five, take them." Finally, after sitting there for a while, glaring at me, he got up and, slamming the door, went into the living room. There he sulked for ten minutes, and then came back in, much more under control,

and asked for his cigarettes, which I gave him. (Entry: 1/10/47, David Wineman)

Here we see Joe, a "good" delinquent, trying to terrorize us into yielding to a demand for more cigarettes. We have made a "deal" for five cigarettes. As a delinquent he has grown up to respect at least one code, the code of the "deal"; and yet even this is not strong enough to offset the delusional thinking that creeps into his argument with us: "You say you will give us whatever we want." And, if we do not live up to the delusion, if he cannot terrorize us into yielding the five extra cigarettes, the frustration so engendered is at least enough basis to continue to hate us, to rationalize acts, as well as threats, of aggression.

## The Task of Overcoming Treatment Shock

While we wish to avoid here going into elaborate details with respect to our total treatment program at the Home, the flavor of the treatment shock response will be more sharply conveyed if some specific consideration is given to the treatment demands of this period. The uniqueness of this stage of our clinical experience lies in the fact that, although the behavior we have described involved original pathology which the children brought with them, so to speak, it was in itself a distortion of it at the same time. There was an intensity and out-of-focusness about it that was inherently rooted, etiologically, in the adjustment challenge of the clinical milieu *per se*. Thus, in addition to any clinical measures that were to be directed toward the original symptom complexes of the children, still other steps had first to be taken to cope with this aspect of their response itself. For, unless they could be helped to work out the treatment shock reaction, real treatment had very little chance of ever getting started. It is this clinical task with which we concern ourselves here, and only in summary because of space considerations imposed by the intended scope of this book, which is not primarily focused on therapeutic design.

### 1. Meeting Ego Tensions through Programming[5]

Before proceeding to an analysis of the program techniques of this period, it is necessary to comment upon the psychological implications of adult-supervised play with the Pioneer House type of child. To begin with, in the minds of most children, and especially the Pioneer House children, the period in their lives when adults play with them and think up things for them to do is when they are "babies." So, a resistance is immediately formed against cooperating with this type of program, because of pre-adolescent prestige values which proclaim proud independence from adults. Secondly, the Pioneer House child, as has been witnessed from record material already presented, had acquired a strong hatred of adults which induced strong resistance toward cooperating with any adult-sponsored program, out of pure suspicion and aggression. So, at the outset, it can safely be assumed that the adult group leader was regarded as an intruder. Thus, in analysis of programming, it will always be necessary to keep in mind that the reaction of the group to activities proposed by the adult had at least three determinants:

The intrinsic appeal of the activity itself to the taste pattern of the child.

The conflict-loaded attitude toward the adult.

The group composition and member-to-member interplay.

Group reaction to an activity was affected by such things as which child in the group accepted it and how much this child could condition the other members in their attitudes. Usually this was, in turn, related to status levels among the children, which were quickly established even during the earliest stages of group formation, so that, if a child with high status in the group rejected an activity, it influenced the reaction of the other members adversely. Incidentally, if a child with lower group status showed interest, this even had prejudicial effect

[5] A great part of the material presented in this section is taken from a study by Barbara Smith, *Programming in a Treatment Home for Disturbed Children* (Wayne University School of Social Work, Detroit, Michigan: an unpublished thesis).

on the accepting child's status, since the other group members felt threatened by this violation of their own code.

The analysis of the therapeutically planned program during the initial period at Pioneer House can now be focused upon specifically. From the description of treatment shock, it may be seen that one of our main problems was to find ways and means of draining some of the enormous impulse pile-up which accrued from the reaction itself. Activities had to be devised which would provide immediate impulse satisfaction and quick goal attainment. These would place little demand upon the children for postponement and would be primarily on a motor level of functioning. Through this, a general tapering off of impulse needs was anticipated. A comparative study on programming at Pioneer House during the first six months reveals that, during the first three months' period, important shifts took place in activity popularity, which were in accordance with a trend to move from less to more structured ego functioning.[6] Data abstracted from this study are presented in Table B.

### TABLE B *

*Activity Acceptance Rankings*
*By Percentiles During First Three Months of Treatment*

ACTIVITY                    PERCENTILE

| | December 1946 | January 1947 | February 1947 |
|---|---|---|---|
| Toys | 40.60 | 36.00 | 18.50 |
| Active Games | 17.80 | 3.78 | 11.00 |
| Sports | 16.50 | 16.60 | 16.20 |
| Quiet Games | 9.50 | 25.40 | 37.00 |
| Music and Dramatics | 8.40 | 11.30 | 10.40 |
| Arts and Crafts | 1.80 | 2.27 | 4.60 |
| Trips | 5.40 | 4.65 | 2.30 |
| Total | 100.00 | 100.00 | 100.00 |

* Total number of instances per month:
December 460
January 264
February 216

FIRST MONTH. Inspection of Table B shows that, during the first month, those activities which were most popular with

6 *Ibid.*

the group were play with toys, active games, and sports. These three kinds of activities have in common the provision of channels of discharge for motor achievement of quick impulse satisfaction.

THE USE OF TOYS. It has been seen from previously presented material that much of the play with toys was really a mass destruction with very little real use of toys for the actual purpose for which they were made. This use of toys specifically fulfills the definition of unstructured activity, but even the non-destructive use of simple toys falls logically into the realm of quick satisfaction discharge, since the toy itself provides visual and manipulative satisfactions within time spans compatible with short frustration tolerance. This would not apply to complicated mechanical gadgets, but these were in a minority among the toy "population." In cases where the use of a more complicated toy might have involved frustration reactions, there were occasional modifications of the function of the toy to fit the need pattern of the child.

Larry played with the electric train. When the transformer did not work, he was perfectly happy to run the train back and forth on the track. (Entry: 12/1/46, Barbara Smith)

While toys were usually destroyed in the end, there were short periods prior to destruction when the actual intent of the toys was recognized and when their use was legitimate. Also, many toys such as guns, flashlights, and other power-symbolic materials were actually used in the development of wild fantasy play which built up into game patterns which permitted the required release of tension during the first period.

Today I played "guns" or "flashlight hide and seek" with Sam and Larry. Our equipment—a gun and a flashlight each. We darkened the upstairs playroom and stalked each other in the shadows. We each took turns being the hunter and the hunted, with one of us being hunter and two others always being the hunted, although the latter two were both on their own. A man was "shot" when a beam of light from the flashlight fell upon him without him being able to defend himself through "shooting" of the other fellow. (Entry: 12/25/46, Joel Vernick)

Improvised games such as these were common with toys like the machine gun and other materials through which the release of hostile and aggressive impulses could take place.

GAMES. Games which did not require the use of materials grew out of body contact types of expression like tumbling and wrestling, both of which were quite popular during the first month. One of these which showed an interesting combination of fantasy and physical expression was "Tarzan and the Leopard Man." The ideational content of this game obviously grew out of comic books. This fantasy game occurred at least ten times by actual count during the first month and was equally popular with catch football, indoor bowling, and "guns."

> There was an improvised game between Henry, Joe, and Andy. Joe and Andy pretended they were Leopard Men and Henry was Tarzan. They pretended they were stabbing each other. There was a switching of who was Tarzan, because he could not be hurt. This began to break down toward the end into a pure form of wrestling, which finally became serious when Andy began to scream that Henry was hurting his neck. Counselor interference was necessary. (Entry: 12/11/46, Vera Kare)

In this game, the distribution of the omnipotent role (Tarzan, who could not be hurt) is interesting. Actually, in everyday life, Henry was the most powerful. For him to yield his power in the fantasy seems to be acceptable since he knows that he is not really weak and since he is achieving enjoyment out of other elements of the game, perhaps even his essentially despotic yielding of power. For Joe and Andy, the power gain through the Tarzan role is important as an equalizer to Henry's superiority. However, the weakness of the fantasy structure as a control is shown in the breakdown of the fantasy into actual wrestling and the final reality emphasis by Henry of his real power when he begins to hurt Andy.

SPORTS. Wrestling and tumbling were used more frequently than any other single activity during the first month with the exception of toys. Here, the acceptance of definite rules for wrestling was very low and counselor supervision had to be acute in order to prevent actual injury to the weaker children. The satisfactions of tumbling were obvious: immediate gain in power expression and exhibitionistic satisfactions. Tumbling was also very important therapeutically for, in order to pursue it, definite acceptance of reality rules and counselor control had to take place, since the youngsters were technically unskilled and had to be taught rudiments in order to succeed at all. Also, it forced waiting for turns (postponement) and acceptance of differences in skills (competition tensions), since not everyone could tumble at once and there were obvious differences in the degree of innate skills which the youngsters showed. It was one of the few activities of the first month where adult participation was welcomed on two levels:

(1) Teaching—being taught how to tumble.
(2) Audience—showing off skills.

OTHER ACTIVITIES OF THE FIRST MONTH. The other activities which show much lower incidence during the first month are nevertheless important to discuss.
*Music and dramatics.* Use of music during the first month was mainly through recordings and group singing. Although it was never possible just to expect the group to cluster around the phonograph in a passive listening attitude, which accounts for the small frequency in the count of music as an actual program activity, the phonograph was a very happy supplementary activity, frequently being used while other activities were in progress. Thus, one youngster or a small subgroup could be hovering around the phonograph, vacillating between this and more active forms of play such as wrestling on the floor. The use of the phonograph just to make a good deal of noise was important in expression of aggression and excitement, regardless of the content of the record.

Danny has been frequently observed to go to the phonograph or radio and increase the volume to almost deafening pitch as a substitute for an actual blow-up, either against the adult or against other youngsters. What determines whether he uses this device or whether he permits the blow-up to occur, we have not been able to ascertain. He always gives the excuse, when he does this, that he cannot hear and, although he does have some hearing loss, still the time of his utilization of the phonograph or radio volume as an aggressive channel is too well coordinated with other behavior to believe that this is the only, or even the chief, reason. (Entry: 12/28/46, Individual Record on Danny, David Wineman)

The content of the records, too, had some value for serving as aggression- and excitement-release devices. Western, cowboy, and frontier experiences (such as "The Story of the Pony Express," "Billy the Kid," etc.) were very popular because of the themes of violence and daring. Group singing was possible during the first month mainly under conditions where the group was compressed into artificial cohesiveness through the need to stay physically close to each other by external conditions. For example, rides in the station wagon where they were all together were favorable for stimulation of group singing. Usually, the suggestion would come from the adult leader, and instances of total group participation were quite high. Here again, the favorites were army, camp, and outdoor songs, whose allusions to daring and aggression were obvious. *Arts and crafts.* There was very little ability to use arts and crafts programs during the first month, although repeated efforts on the part of the staff to introduce them were made. Value was seen in trying to stimulate interest, even in the face of the group's failure to accept the activity idea, in order at least to establish an expectation pattern and to sharpen staff diagnostic perception for which aspects of given arts and crafts ideas were appropriate, which inappropriate, to the group needs. Thus, although the group may have been unable to follow through because of lack of technical skills, loss of patience with mistakes, and lack of familiarity with materials, they still developed a strong awareness that these things were available, that they always would be there to use if and when they were ready to participate. In this way, occasional participation by less blocked youngsters was achieved and encouragement to others expressed.

*Trips away from the house.* Trips were used very frequently during the last month. The purpose of the trips was threefold:

(1) To neutralize house boredom and the feeling of being chained down to one small physical unit.

(2) To provide some form of mobile activity with a maximum of group control.

(3) To give experience with sharp goal perception from the very inception of the activity. Thus, to know that "now we are going skating at Palmer Park" or "now we are going to Belle Isle and shall be there in thirty minutes" had a structure-giving effect.

There were two types of trips: Trips whose main goal was to provide sightseeing and exploration experiences, and trips which contained elements of the first type but where there was, in addition, a special goal such as ice skating, visiting a museum, bowling, indoor roller skating, etc.

There was usually group resistance to starting off on trips, but, once the hurdle from the Home to the station wagon was overcome, they usually enjoyed the outings. The staff was quite insistent on each youngster coming along, although when very determined resistance was expressed on the part of the child, arrangements were made for him to stay at home. The theme of the adult insistence was "Oh, come on, everybody is going, we'll have a swell time, etc." rather than "You have to go because we say so, etc."

*Quiet games.* The group was able, during the first month, to use quiet games (cards, checkers, bingo, riddle games, jigsaw puzzles) more easily than arts and crafts and music-dramatics; in most cases, their utilization seemed patterned after past experience. Thus, cards were more popular than checkers and checkers more than bingo.

*Summary of first month activity behavior.* The activity behavior of the Pioneer House group during the first month indicates a relatively high dependence upon activities which permitted the youngsters to achieve what has been referred to as "quick impulse satisfaction" and, as such, had high "drainage value" for tension-dominated impulse patterns.

THE SECOND AND THIRD MONTHS. Within the same range of activity possibilities, the second and third months at

Pioneer House show an increasing popularity of quiet games and a diminishing need to use the unstructured, highly excitation-loaded type of activity. The use of toys, active games, and sports appears to be replaced by a greater ability to derive satisfaction from the quiet, more psychologically complex activities such as cards, jigsaw puzzles, and riddle games.[7]

## II. Protective Interference

Activity programming, successful as it was, was not the answer to all of the impulse excitement stemming from treatment shock. For not all impulsivity could be discharged in this way. Besides, the very exposure to program activities unavoidably produces new quantities of impulsivity for the manipulation of which the ego of the children may not yet be equipped. Also it often becomes clinically important to stop activities or behavior which is itself acceptable before the excitement produced by it reaches such intensity that the children will be overwhelmed by anxieties and guilt. In all such cases interference tactics of various kinds must be used. Thus, our second main strategy for coping with treatment shock involved the development of various techniques for such interference. Broadly speaking we have lumped such techniques together under the common name of "protective interference." By this we mean that such interference tries to cope with impulse behavior without traumatizing the child through brutality or terrorization of any kind and in such a way as to protect him against having to keep it up either as a defense or as a primary expressional need. In this way, protective interference is designed as a direct form of support to the ego in moments when it suffers severe loss of function and is thus not directly aimed at removing causes for pathology. Especially is this true of the treatment shock period, for, as we have stated, the behavior of the treatment shock phase is such a unique response that no measure taken as a step for

[7] Rich material concerning a similar use of programming is contained in Gertrude Wilson and Gladys Ryland, *Social Group Work Practice* (Boston: Houghton Mifflin Co., 1949), Part II, and in Gisela Konopka, *Therapeutic Group Work with Children* (Minneapolis: The U. of Minnesota Press, 1949).

coping with it could be basically construed as a therapeutic approach to long range pathology. It is with this in mind that the following strategies are discussed, with the intention of exemplifying the type of interference we utilized.

DECLARATION OF LIMITS: RULE AND ROUTINE INSISTENCE. As we have seen, part of the treatment shock reaction involved a delusional expectation that the benign adult would be totally permissive. To counteract this we simply have to show them that "It ain't so." We realize that, as we do this, we are crossing swords, so to speak, with the paranoiac side of their response to us. The latter keeps them hopefully on the lookout for us to take over interference tactics so that they can misconstrue them and accuse us of being "mean bastards" who are just like the other adults they have learned so well to hate. But this challenge has to be met, for only in part are they so deluded about the adult anyway. Only in part do they believe that we will let them get away with everything. For we have ample evidence that, if we do not stop them with some few basic rules and routine patterns, they will go even farther in their delirious aggression against us and get toxic with guilt and anxiety. Even though they are involved in misbehavioral warfare, still they fear that this very misbehavior will eventually exile them permanently from adult love, but they themselves are powerless to stop it. So it is against these two interwoven motifs that our first rule and routine policies are aimed, namely, fear of loss of love because of unstopped aggression and an actual delusional confusion about how permissive adults want them to behave.

RULES. In speaking of "rules" we have two levels in mind. The first is that of reality rules. Obviously, regardless of any consideration of the love or affectional needs of the children, we had to show clear-cut insistence on observation of rules against dangerous aggressive behavior against others or the self. In spite of the fact that we had been careful to select children who were not totally reality-blind, there were many moments when dangerous behavior occurred and had to be stopped on the spot.

In many of his upsets at the table, Danny would furiously throw any eating implement within reach blindly about, having no particular target in mind. This, of course, gave no assurance that he could not seriously hurt any one near and we always had to remove him from the table in those moments regardless of our knowledge that this would produce the most violent of thirty-minute tantrums.

Such a display of interference on our part had implications for the treatment shock response, for it proved to the group that there were some things that simply could not be permitted even though at the same time there were no punishment implications involved. There was, so to speak, a "ceiling" on aggression. Along with a consideration for physical dangers went also concern for psychologically dangerous behavior. Thus a fight would have to be carefully refereed and stopped at that moment when it looked as though serious damage to the morale of a youngster, or repetition of case history trauma through physical hurt, might be inflicted.

In the beginning, Larry lured out all of the most vicious sibling hatred that most of our tougher kids had stored up in them because he was so fixed on the adult, so obviously hungry for lap crawling and caresses. When the teasing and baiting of him became most infuriating, Larry would sometimes lunge out in a reckless counterattack of primitive fury which one would never have expected from this detached and infantile child. These fights could not be simply stopped in the beginning because in this way some of the sibling hatred was directly discharged. But we had to be very alert to call a halt when it looked as if Larry was on the verge of being overwhelmed by his more skillful opponent—and they were all much more scientific than he simply through more experience—because a severe beating would have (a) made it impossible for him to return to the adult at such a price and he needed to have that period of adult caressing and fondling, and (b) would have retraumatized him through physical pain after the history of sadistic treatment from his own step-father, who, like our children, resented his infantile claim upon his mother.

On the second level of rules are those involved with social, rather than physical, realities. In connection with table behavior, for instance, after the first week passed by and we had actually "got acquainted," we were quite insistent on limiting obscene language and acting out at meals. For the combination of crude sexual obscenity and eating, especially in a situation involving sitting around the table with adults, would have been unacceptable even in their natural habitats no matter how lax their eating habits may have been. Permitting such behavior would have created a confusing seductive challenge. Thus, if a child insisted on carrying through an obscenity orgy at the table in spite of our counterinsistence that he stop, we removed him together with whatever was left of his meal to another room where he ate privately. A counselor always went along and finished his own meal with the removed child whenever necessary. Not frequently, during the treatment shock phase, we might have three of our group eating in three different places supervised by three different staff members. There were no punitive implications or other consequences other than removal for this behavior, the only "unpleasure" being that which may attend not eating with the group in the regular dining room. This was put to the child as inevitable because of the degree to which his behavior had gone while he was at the table.

ROUTINES. As a counter-measure against the chaotic implications of the rampant impulsivity of the treatment shock period, a "hold the line" policy on some few high priority regimes had to be followed. The mere fact that there is a certain time to eat, to sleep, to take showers and to have fun, etc., creates a sense of boundaries and limits which provides insurance against total disorganization and chaos. It seems to us that this is obvious without further elaboration. Our problem here was to implement this principle of at least minimum routinization, to really "hold the line" and yet to do it "protectively." It was possible only under conditions of exorbitant staff-time and energy consumption (and ingenious handling of our own counter-aggression) as the following example will show.

At first, bedtime was pure and unadulterated bedlam. The kids realized that here they 'had" us. For what was more innately pleasurable than chasing about the house from one room to the next, making your counselor call after you, having her try to hold you, and breaking away when she became distracted by three of your pals who were meanwhile jumping out through the window onto the sun porch where it was freezing cold? We soon realized that two counselors and one "over-group" representative (one of the two directors) were not enough. There were too many for us. So each evening for a week the whole staff went on emergency duty at bedtime (7 adults). As soon as there was any disturbance from any child in the sleeping room, he was "bounced" by any available adult. Each bouncee was carefully isolated from any other bouncee for, even with two adults in the same room sitting with them, they could "contage" each other indefinitely through hilarious dialogue with each other whereas, when they were alone with an adult who was quietly sitting with them, they soon calmed down. In this way we actually "broke" the night time raid pattern. By pure insistence backed by multiplicity of forces we drained the pleasure value of it down to the point where they finally were willing, with only minor flare-ups, to go through more of a semblance of routinized bedtime behavior.

We do not pretend here that we are handling basic problems in this way. But we do think that our insistence on some simple essential routines again acts as a support to the ego and a counter-agent to treatment shock, since we did not have to continue our "D-Day" tactics after they got the point that we could and would stop them in this particular kind of exploitation.

ROLE CONSISTENCY AND ROLE CLARIFICATION. One of the big troubles the ego of our childen encountered under conditions of "treatment shock" was to retain the ability to see the adult at all as a loving, benign person in spite of the delusional struggle against love and its implications. This is even more accentuated by the fact that very frequently in the beginning we had to hold children during temper tantrums because of the regression of communication levels in moments of ego breakdown. Under such conditions, it is of vital importance that as few adults as possible become involved in the carrying out of interference so that we can keep as hostility free as possible the relationship channels to most of the adult figures involved in the clinical situation. Thus, when "first aid techniques" by the activity leader were ineffective and gross temper explosions occurred around an activity, it was necessary to use strong limiting techniques to insure safety to other children and to prevent severe destruction. Such interference, quite obviously, plays into the case history delusions of the youngster, no matter how antiseptically it is carried out. Because of this, the activity-identified adult whom we wanted to keep as free as possible from hostile projections on the part of the child was not usually involved in major interference tactics. Rather, under such conditions, the directors of the Home functioned to implement limitations on unacceptable behavior.

Tonight the activity program involved work with decals (little designs that can be transferred on to sheets of wood). The boys all wanted to transfer them to their wooden chests. Each boy snatched his work box. Danny immediately flew into a temper because a spool of thread was missing from his box. He stamped about, shouted insults at me, threw the box on the floor, and broke it beyond repair. He then snatched from me the sheets of decals and some of the construction paper we were using for making frames. I asked him for them, explaining that he could have only those belonging to him, just as the rest of the group had to do. He then developed a perfect rage, swore more vehemently, threw his chair around and began slamming the doors. I made no attempt to restrain him, dodged the things he was throwing at me, and continued to insist verbally that he stop. A few minutes after his extreme behavior began the director came in and took Danny into the office where he had to hold him in order to calm him down. After a lengthy period in the office he came out and quietly joined the activity, working quite cooperatively the rest of the evening. (Entry: 2/11/47, Emily Kener)

In this instance, the activity leader can be observed to refrain carefully from attempting to impose the heavy interference which was necessary to cope with Danny's outburst. She clearly shows her wish that he should stop and indicates freely that she feels that he is being unfair to the group, but beyond a certain threshold of limitation she does not go. The strategic removal and subsequent handling by the director deflects Danny's aggression away from the activity leader and through this resumption of integrated group and activity behavior is initiated. The activity leader also is quite careful not to over-sympathize with Danny against the director which would, if not carefully watched, lead to exploitative playing off of the "good" and "bad" adults against each other.

We have here abstracted some examples showing the basic policies behind the process of "protective interference." This in no way answers the question of just how such "interfering" is carried out. Far from being a simple device, protective interference raises a host of cautions and for each technique to be used there are also as many counter-indications. A detailed display of the "techniques for the antiseptic manipulation of surface behavior" will be presented in a separate publication.

## Summary

Here, in our description of the first three months at Pioneer House, we have tried to show the complexities of the initial reaction to treatment. We have had, of course, to eliminate many things on account of shortage of space. However, what has emerged, we hope, is some picture of the distortions of their original pathology in our children's personality functioning in the face of the shock to their whole previous adaptation pattern produced by the clinical milieu with its baffling exposure to adult love and new gratification horizons. This initial discharge of conflict in the treatment setting is seen as a necessary beginning point in therapy with these children. Perhaps, had we not ourselves been groping with the workings of a brand new clinical design, we might have been able to prevent some of the volume and intensity of the treatment shock reaction. That it always would occur in some proportions we may be quite sure of, however, so that it may well have been an advantage to see it in such macroscopy, which otherwise might not have been possible.

We have tried, too, to convey illustratively some of the peculiar treatment demands of this period. Basically, the two main strategies for coping with treatment shock devolve upon a very elastic activity program, on the one hand, to provide as much free drainage of ego tensions as is possible, and various styles and strategies of protective interference, on the other, to facilitate the actual surrender of certain aspects of impulsivity.

# Chapter 7

## The Clinical Dilemma

IF THE TECHNIQUES designed to cope with the special confusions and extra volume of aggression which our children display during the phase of "treatment shock" are only a "prelude" to what is really needed to cope with their disturbances, what then can we do for a long range approach to their pathology? If it is as difficult as this to survive with these children without taking recourse to clinically impure methods of control, if it is so difficult to handle their initial exposure to a treatment climate, what should be the design for real therapy?

This question must not be answered hastily. So far, the picture we have drawn of the "children who hate" is still quite incomplete. We haven't followed in detail the question of just why they "got that way," nor have we even tried to offer an itemized account of the history of their various emotional conflicts, of the misdevelopments of instincts and drives, of their distorted desires and misled fantasies, all of which push them into behaving the way they do.[1] What etiological suggestions were expressed can hardly be called more than "hints." We mainly relied on the hope that our examples will suggest to the reader just along which lines their basic pathology may lie, that our "entries" may furnish color to the one-sidedly abbreviated sketch of their disturbed "controls."

Yet, from all we have seen about these youngsters, two conclusions may be drawn: They are beyond the reach of education and they are below the grip of the psychiatric interview technique. This is not much of an answer in itself, but it may help us to stop being misled by current popular illusions and may thus put us onto the more realistic path toward a way out.

---

[1] The type of sensitive socio-psychological analysis found in Allison Davis and John C. Dollard, *Children of Bondage* (Washington, D.C.: American Council of Education, 1940) could profitably be applied to further preliminary studies of the children who hate.

## Beyond the Reach of Education

According to general assumptions, it is expected that disturbed children should improve if they are exposed to a good educational setting and surrounded by friendly people who handle them with wisdom and affection. Let us say this in more detail. It is believed that disturbed children should be given adequate recreational facilities and sufficient channels for "constructive fun." This ought to help them drop their confused and destructive urge for mischief. It is also assumed that a good deal of their irritability and hatefulness could be avoided if they were exposed to experiences which fascinate and challenge them and to learning methods which give them a chance to succeed and to experience mastery and achievement. Moreover, we take it for granted that the sight of the happy and desirable behavior displayed by companions who are less disturbed than they should make bad children eager to mend their ways, especially if they find out that they can gain love and approval of friendly and generous adults by doing so. Besides, we assume that the mere absence of the cruelty, abuse, insult, and embarrassment which these children have experienced before should give them a chance to blossom out into feelings of warmth, acceptedness, and happy security. Insofar as the simple exposure to such an educational framework is not sufficient, it is expected that a wide range of tricks usually called "educational techniques" can be employed to drive home the point. The educator will point to "simple" tools, such as friendly punishment and kind criticism, special rewards, promises, encouragements, which might furnish an additional "incentive" to motivate desirable behavior. Crowned by the assurance of continued care and the outlook of "a chance in life," such a good "educational diet" can be expected to do wonders.

Well, it does. For thousands of children this is just what they need, and all they need. Given an educational framework such as just described and handled with the affection and wisdom implied, they can blossom into a full realization of their potentialities, in character as well as in intellect and performance. A good educational setting and a wise educational regime can work wonders—only, *not* with the *children who hate*. Why education and love "are not enough" ought to be painfully clear by now on the basis of the disturbances we have described in this book. In a nutshell: the main reason is that the so-called "simple" educational techniques usually referred to *are not so simple* as they are made out to be. To illustrate this for just a few of them: in order to enjoy a constructive and challenging activity program, a child must be capable of quite an amount of frustration tolerance, must be ready to get fun out of sublimated rather than primitive channels of drive satisfaction, must be ready for a considerable sacrifice of impulse expression of the moment in view of long range promise of future gain. In order to be "challenged" by fascinating life tasks or learning situations, a child must have some image of his own future, must be able to take the fear of failure without a breakdown, the victory over an opponent without an outburst of triumphant hate. In order to be motivated by friendly behavior on the side of adults and their institutions, a child must already have developed a real need for adult love and must be able to recognize adults as being loving even at times when they interfere in momentary fun. In order for punishment, criticism, reward or praise, promise or threat, to work at all, a child must at least be aware of his own guilt at the very moment when somebody else interferes in his life, and he must be able to differentiate between what he just got by luck and what he deserved. He also must be able to apply experiences from previous life situations to guide him in a moment of temptational challenge right now.

From our description of the egos of the children who hate and of some of their superego diseases it is clear that these children are not ready to benefit from a "good educational set-up" at all. They meet none of the prerequisites which even so "simple" a thing as a "good educational diet" presupposes as a condition for having effect. Exposed even to a good educational diet, these childen act like people invited to an elaborate feast at a time when disease prevents them from swallowing any food, or like people who have lost their sense of taste. Some of them, on top of that, are not only not able to make use of what is offered them, but their defenses are so well entrenched that even the kindest and best educational offering only gets their old pathology inflamed again.

In short, good education is *not* enough for the cure of the children who hate. Rather, the reverse comes closer to the truth: in order for a good educational diet to take hold of these children at all, their basic ego disturbances must be repaired first.

This is important to know. It ought to stop the educators from being so disappointed by those children who cannot digest what they have to offer, and from hating them on those grounds, and it ought to help the psychiatrist realize that it does not do to blame the educator or shove the problem off onto him. As far as the children who hate are concerned, we are all caught in the same web of clinical complexity.

## Below the Grip of the Psychiatric Interview

During the last two decades a new magical formula has become fashionable wherever people give advice to parents, teachers, and children's agencies. When confronted with a youngster about whom everybody is by now desperate, for many people and organizations already have tried their hand with no success, it is eagerly suggested that "a psychiatrist should see the child." It is quite flattering to psychiatry, by the way, that the educators themselves and even lay people have picked up the same chant. What started out like a propaganda slogan for a new scientific field has become an outcry for help by those in despair.

Psychiatry can no longer afford to rest on the laurels of public acclaim for its potentials. The children who hate certainly can remind us of the hard fact that they are not approachable through "straight psychiatry" either. Just because it is obvious that "education is not enough," it does not mean that the other medium is the answer for them, or at least not without severe modifications.

It is true that, over the last fifty years, there has been developed a most amazing "treatment medium" which has proved very capable of dealing with a vast number of disturbances which had been considered unapproachable before. We have in mind the *"psychiatric interview technique."* Originally derived from the techniques of child analysis, it has been well adapted to deal with a wide range of difficulties, especially those of the so-called "classical" neuroses, and a wide range of character disturbances to boot. It is true that we drop all pretenses of offering something "simple" when we talk about psychiatric interview techniques, and usually so much time, trained effort, and carefully designed treatment conditions are involved that opportunities for such treatment for the child population of this country are almost totally inaccessible and numerically inadequate. But, aside from the problem of availability of service, there is no doubt that there are a number of childhood afflictions which are by now known to be perfectly well treatable by this "psychiatric interview technique." The only trouble with it is that it, too, *does not suffice for the children who hate.* It is a wonderful tool, doing miracles for thousands of cases. The reasons why it is not the answer for the children who hate lie in the same direction as those for the insufficiency of a good educational setting as far as they are concerned.

For, this very "psychiatric interview technique," so well designed for all sorts of disturbances, also is tied to *certain minimum conditions* without which it cannot even begin to take hold. Unfortunately, our youngsters don't meet those conditions, and it is easy to see why.

Without branching off into too much theory at this moment, we might single out three of the main difficulties for mention: the problem of treatment rapport, the difficulty of communication channels, and the trouble connected with "action proximity." Even the play interview with considerably aggressive children demands a certain minimum of ego functioning as a condition, and the readiness of a child to relate at all must be given at least in low intensities for such interview work to take hold at all. With the children who hate, even these minimum conditions are usually not given. The volume of restlessness and aggression which they display transcends what any play interview set-up can cope with, the amount of excitement they produce forces the therapist into acts of interference long before anything like a "transference neurosis" can be developed at all, and the separation between the therapist's role and "the rest of their lives" offers their defenses an advantage which outweighs anything that we could muster in terms of strategic arrangements. The complaints of therapists who have worked with such children in "interview therapy" are unanimously emphatic about this point. During times of a "positive" relationship with such children, if it can be developed at all, they produce material, but there isn't the slightest carry-over into their "civilian life." Whenever they look for tools of resistance, they simply produce such problems on the scene of their lives that the therapist is powerless to cope with the aftermath. They either get themselves punished and pushed around by the personnel on the natural scene of their life or they finagle that personnel into feeding right into their pathology through the hypertrophically developed ego skills of manipulation described before. The therapist, then, either gets entangled in their warfare with the world around them, or he is put safely where he can do no harm: into the role of the "friend without influence." Any attempt to "handle" such defensive finagling of their life situations in the interview itself is made difficult by the ego defenses described above and by the strategic disadvantage inherent in the rapport conditions for the role of the therapist.[2]

Also, child psychiatrists themselves have urged that the possibility of using their techniques for treatment are tied to certain minimal conditions. For some of the more severe disturbances it has been claimed that success cannot be achieved unless great cooperation with the parents and the school can be secured, unless the frequency of interview contacts can be made high and dense. Sometimes it is even required that the parents go into treatment themselves. Without these minimum conditions, so the experts assure us, even a severe case of neurosis "should not be touched."

For the children we are talking about, these conditions are,

[2] For a fascinating description of an adaptation of child analytic techniques to a much younger child of similar type and background as the children described in this book see Editha Sterba, "An Ill-bred Child," *The Psychoanalytic Review*, XXXIII (1946), 341.

of course, unrealizable, and, besides, would not be sufficient. There usually are no parents who could or would take responsibility for them, and where they cooperate they do so only if somebody else takes those youngsters "off their hands." But even if this could be taken care of, our youngsters are much too mobile and neighborhood-skilled to be caught by a framework of adult control in open life. They are skilled in producing a never-ending chain of symbolic substitute figures in life situations whom they involve in their pathology and most of whom, like teachers, neighbors, policemen, and so forth, are far beyond the therapist's control. Besides, no normal institution for children, nor any normal foster home, could have the patience and wisdom of strategy which it would take to cooperate with the therapist even were it ready to want to do so. When these children are confined to a limiting and punitive institutional design, or to one without fully trained staff, their own ego defenses are given such a wonderful boost that it would be futile to try to compete in such unfavorable "terrain." As to the interview situation itself, their "evaporation rate for self-contributed links in the causal chain" is so great, their ability to deny and repress rapidly so efficient that an interview approach distant from the life scene doesn't stand much of a chance. If we add to this what we have seen in the chapter on "treatment shock," we can safely say that even where treatment begins to take hold, the spillover into the life scene of the child will be so great that no ordinary arrangements can be expected to take care of it. The youngsters will either become impossible to "live with" wherever they are, or they will play therapist and "real life personnel," including police and juvenile authorities, against each other in their masterly acrobatics of warfare with life, or they will use any life experience at will as new food for their delusional and persecutory interpretation of the world, thus fortifying themselves against the impact of interview-produced relationship as well as against insight at the same time.

It seems that the same statement must be made about the classical channels of psychiatric treatment as we had to make about the chance of getting hold of those children through good educational dieting: once you take children as severely disturbed as we described the children who hate to be, the "psychiatric interview technique" does not offer enough of a strategic chance. Rather the reverse is true: in order for "psychiatric interview techniques" of any style even to be usable on them, their ego first needs a considerable degree of repair in the areas where it cannot perform, and their hypertrophic defenses have to be reduced by a considerable amount to assure "treatability" to begin with.

It seems that there is no way out of the dilemma but the invention of a new design, which offers us opportunities of Strategy in a different dimension than either good education or thorough psychiatric treatment in themselves seem to grant. There is no simple way out, and even such a design will deal with innumerable hurdles and will have to find compromises between alternatives so far apart that they seem hard to bridge. Suggestions for such a design and a description of the details of a total strategy for ego support will be offered by the authors in their forthcoming publication, *Strategy Against Childhood Confusion: Approaching Treatment Through Everyday Life.*

# Index

(We wish to acknowledge the work of Mrs. Betty Kalichman in the preparation of this Index.)

# FREE PRESS PAPERBACKS

### A Series of Paperbound Books in the Social and Natural Sciences, Philosophy, and the Humanities

These books, chosen for their intellectual importance and editorial excellence, are printed on good quality book paper, in large and readable type, and are Smyth-sewn for enduring use. Free Press Paperbacks conform in every significant way to the high editorial and production standards maintained in the higher-priced, case-bound books published by The Free Press.

**Many of these books are available in their original cloth bindings.**
**A complete catalogue of all Free Press titles will be sent on request**